The Power of Images

For Mélanie
dolce città

The Power of Images
Siena, 1338

Patrick Boucheron

Translated by Andrew Brown

polity

First published in French as *Conjurer la peur. Essai sur la force politique des images. Sienne, 1338* © Éditions du Seuil, 2013

This English edition © Polity Press, 2018

This book is supported by the Institut français (Royaume-Uni) as part of the Burgess Programme.

This work received the French Voices Award for excellence in publication and translation. French Voices is a program created and funded by the French Embassy in the United States and FACE (French American Cultural Exchange).

Polity Press
65 Bridge Street
Cambridge CB2 1UR, UK

Polity Press
101 Station Landing
Suite 300
Medford, MA 02155, USA

ISBN-13: 978-1-5095-1289-8
ISBN-13: 978-1-5095-1290-4 (pb)

A catalogue record for this book is available from the British Library.

Names: Boucheron, Patrick, author. | Translation of: Boucheron, Patrick. Conjurer la peur.
Title: The power of images : Siena, 1338 / Patrick Boucheron.
Other titles: Conjurer la peur. English
Description: Medford, MA : Polity Press, 2018. | Includes bibliographical references and index.
Identifiers: LCCN 2017042160 (print) | LCCN 2017042620 (ebook) | ISBN 9781509512935 (Epub) | ISBN 9781509512898 (hardback) | ISBN 9781509512904 (pbk.)
Subjects: LCSH: Lorenzetti, Ambrogio, 1285-approximately 1348--Criticism and interpretation. | Palazzo pubblico (Siena, Italy) | Politics in art. | Mural painting and decoration, Gothic--Italy--Siena. | Mural painting and decoration, Italian--Italy--Siena--14th century. | Siena (Italy)--History--Rule of the Nine, 1287-1355.
Classification: LCC ND623.L75 (ebook) | LCC ND623.L75 B6813 2018 (print) | DDC 759.5--dc23
LC record available at https://lccn.loc.gov/2017042160

Typeset in 10.5 on 12pt Sabon by Servis Filmsetting Ltd, Stockport, Cheshire
Printed and bound in the UK by CPI (UK) Ltd, Croydon, CR0 4YY

For further information on Polity, visit our website:
politybooks.com

Contents

Foreword

Patrick J. Geary

For much of the twentieth century, as France transformed from a pre-dominantly agricultural to an industrial society, the centre of gravity in French mediaeval history was the countryside. From Marc Bloch's *French Rural History* (1931) through Georges Duby's classic study of the Mâconnais (1953), to Pierre Toubert's monumental study of medi-aeval Latium (1973), French scholars and the French reading public were obsessed with the deep structures and rhythms that defined a rural society disappearing before their eyes.[1] Patrick Boucheron, suc-cessor at the Collège de France of his mentor Toubert and Toubert's mentor Duby, is a historian of the city: He was formed in and around Paris, first at the venerable Lycée Henri IV, subsequently at the École normale supérieure Fontenay-Saint-Cloud (since transferred to Lyon), where he studied and later returned to teach, then at the University of Paris I Panthéon-Sorbonne, at which he taught before his election to Collège, where since 2016 he has held the chair of 'the history of powers in western Europe, thirteenth to sixteenth centuries'.

His love of Paris and his faith in its complex urban fabric, its people and its culture, are clear in his inaugural lecture at the Collège de France delivered shortly after the Bataclan theatre massacre in November 2015, where, quoting his great predecessor Jules Michelet, he affirmed that 'Paris represents the world'.[2] As a scholar, however, the cities to which he has devoted most of his life's work are those of northern Italy: Milan, first of all, the subject of his 1998 *The Power to Build: Urbanism and the Politics of Municipal Administration in Milan in the Fourteenth and Fifteenth Centuries*,[3] but more generally the urban spaces of late mediaeval Italy and their intellectual, political and artistic fecundity. Boucheron is a keen observer of the physical presence of the city: the importance of the built environment in the lives of city dwellers. However, as he emphasized in his inaugural lecture, 'these urban forms are nothing without the social energy that animates them, that enacts and transforms them'.[4]

Not surprisingly, then, he has been drawn, as have generations of Italian, German, British and American scholars of the Italian communes, to the *campo* of Sienna, to its Palazzo Pubblico, and within, to its Sala della Pace, on whose walls, in 1338, Ambrogio Lorenzetti painted the stunning triptych now known as 'the Fresco of Good Government', but which, as Boucheron points out, is not a fresco and, for centuries, was identified not with good government but rather with the contrasting images of war and peace.

In this rhetorically crafted and carefully constructed book, Boucheron both draws on and spars with the vast literature already dedicated to interpreting Lorenzetti's work, principally that of Rosa Maria Dessì and Quentin Skinner, in an attempt to approach these paintings with fresh eyes. Or, better, to reflect on the impossibility of approaching them, since, as he writes, today we cannot see them as they were meant to be seen, but only as vestiges. Not only is the image of war on the western wall badly damaged, not only are the images on the eastern and northern walls distorted by retouching and overpainting through the centuries, but the substantial changes in the building itself make it impossible to move through space to encounter them as one did in the fourteenth century. Thus, the role that Boucheron undertakes, that of the historian, is to guide the reader into an inaccessible and impossibly distant world, but one whose challenges and fears remain disturbingly actual in the twenty-first century.

For Boucheron, the fundamental misunderstanding of these powerful paintings is precisely to see in them an allegory of good and bad government, a visual representation of political ideology derived from Aristotle and filtered through his commentators across the centuries. Rather, Boucheron seeks to ground the paintings in the precise context of Siena in the third decade of the fourteenth century. The Sala della Pace was the chamber in which Siena's principal governing body, the Nine, met in deliberation. When the Nine commissioned Lorenzetti to depict 'war and peace', their concerns were not with a generalized theory of government but with the very concrete fear of civil strife and its ability to destroy the social fabric that bound together Siena's often fractious society. But even more, they feared the apparent alternative to civil strife: the overthrow of communal government by unitary lordship, the rise of the signoria, as was happening across northern Italy. The original title of Boucheron's book captures this exactly: *Conjurer la peur* – to ward off fear. The image of peace, which covers the eastern wall, shows peace not simply as the absence of war, but rather as the concrete effects of social justice: harmony, a harmony that can bind together all citizens. The western wall shows the results of war, but war in the mediaeval sense of *guerra*, that is, in the first instance, feud, factional conflict, which threatened, even more than external war, to destroy all that is good in the city. In between, on the north wall, separating war and peace, are the figures of the government of the city, the importance of peace, strength and prudence, magnanimity, temperance and justice, exercised by the commanding figure of the commune of Siena itself, the collective guarantor of peace and the defence against factionalism and, ultimately, the tyranny of one-man rule.

An English-reading public that has followed the development of Quentin Skinner's reflections on these paintings as well as those familiar with the work of Chiara Frugoni, Denis Romano and Rosa Maria Dessì, among many others, will recognize that Boucheron's detailed analysis of the paintings owes a great deal to the careful scholarship of his predecessors. The originality and significance of this book lies less in the novelty of its insights into the specific elements of the three wall paintings than in how he constructs his over-arching argument about the original context of the project and its possible meanings today.

Patrick Boucheron has a knack for making distant history resonate with contemporary issues and anxieties. Many of his projects, such as his collaborative *World History of France*,[5] are overtly political, aiming to undermine national chauvinist discourses. *The Power of Images*, too, is a political book. In an age when nations and regions in Europe, Asia, Africa and the Americas, threatened by the pressures of social, cultural and economic change, are once more looking not to mutual collaboration but to autocratic leaders as saviors, Boucheron asks us to stand in the Sala della Pace and contemplate the alternatives: harmony and tyranny, peace and war.

Notes

1   Marc Bloch, *French Rural History: An Essay on Its Basic Characteristics*, trans. Janet Sondheimer (Berkeley: University of California Press, 1966 [1931]); Georges Duby, *La société aux XIe et XIIe siècles dans la region mâconnaise* (Paris: Armand Colin, 1953); Pierre Toubert, *Les structures du Latium médiéval: le Latium méridional et la Sabine du IXe siècle à la fin du XIIe siècle*, 2 vols (Rome: École française de Rome, 1973).
2   Patrick Boucheron, 'Ce que peut l'histoire', available online at http://books.openedition.org/cdf/4507.

3   Patrick Boucheron, *Le pouvoir de bâtir. Urbanisme et politique édillitaire à Milan (XIVe–XVe siècles)* (Paris: École française de Rome, 1998).

4   Boucheron, 'Ce que peut l'histoire'.

5   Patrick Boucheron (ed.), *Histoire mondiale de la France* (Paris: Seuil, 2017).

Acknowledgements

I would have liked to be a browsing historian, following my nose down a winding path, moving with lighthearted curiosity from one set of documents to the next. Perhaps I might then have felt what Carlo Ginzburg calls the joy of the skier, who, venturing off-piste, feels the crunch of the fresh snow on a slope that he is the first to leave his tracks on and that he will never go up again. But I am rather 'obsidional' in character, besieged by obsessions more than manipulating ideas, and I keep busy digging the same tenacious furrow.

For over ten years now I have felt the gaze of Sienese painting resting on me and I have wearied many of my friends, colleagues and interlocutors with the questions it arouses in me. Since the long article I devoted to it in 2005, I have had many occasions to debate it, to have my arguments questioned, and to learn, in particular, how to think against myself. The reply that Quentin Skinner spontaneously gave me still strikes me as a model of elegance and probity, expressing what intellectual debate should be, and sometimes is.

Others too allowed me to pursue this theme, and it is a pleasure for me here to thank them for their help, their reading, their suggestions and their encouragement. They include: Étienne Anheim, Enrico Artifoni, Mario Ascheri, Enrico Castelnuovo, Romain Descendre, Rosa Maria Dessì, François Foronda, Jean-Philippe Genet, Stéphane Gioanni, Jean-Claude Maire Vigueur, Giuliano Milani, Jean-Claude Milner, Igor Mineo, Evelyn Prawidlo, Pierangelo Schiera, Sylvain Venayre, Andrea Zorzi. If you look closely, Léonie and Madeleine are also in the fresco. Can you find them?

On 7 August 2010, I delivered a lecture on this subject at the Banquet du Livre de Lagrasse, and it is to that very special time, and to all my friends in Corbières, that I owe something of the freedom of tone that this study drew from that occasion. If it has since become a book, it is thanks to the care taken over it by my French publisher, Éditions du Seuil, which I have great pleasure in thanking here, especially Olivier Bétourné, Hugues Jallon, Nathalie Beaux, Séverine Nikel and Raphaëlle Richard de Latour.

Finally, I cannot omit my son Mathieu, with whom I spent long hours putting together the 999 pieces (one of them is missing) from the jigsaw puzzle of the fresco. This book is also for him, *senza paura*.

Prologue

The site of an ancient urgency

You may not know its name, but you've already seen it. It's known as the 'Fresco of Good Government'. People haven't always called it this; and in any case, it's not really a fresco. Ambrogio Lorenzetti painted it in the Palazzo Pubblico of Siena in 1338, ten years before his life was suddenly cut short by the Black Death, as were the lives of perhaps half the population of a city that did not know it was already declining – though it had in fact already declined, irremediably. You've already seen this painting, as it has been displayed in detail for over a hundred and fifty years – like a piece of meat on a butcher's slab – as an illustration of all that is most flattering about our modernity. Here is Justice, there is Equity, and further on, Concord: feminine allegories with fine, high-sounding names. And here, too, in strident contrast with these, is the hideous maw of tyranny: the ugly grimace of a divided society, the soldiers raping women ... You've seen all this so many times: on the covers of books, for example, whenever unimaginative iconographers have to find some visible depiction of a rather vague abstraction, for a textbook on constitutional law, for example, or a treatise on ethics. But Lorenzetti's image also works very well for a book on agrarian history, city planning or urban sociology in the Middle Ages. His work swarms with a thousand singular details which for many people open an unexpected window on late mediaeval life.

So if you survey all the details of his work, you might feel a disagreeable sensation of déjà vu – the consequence of the omnipresence of advertising images. Are these images the icons of modernity? But if we say this, we are still falling prey to the tyranny of an impoverished language, for what we usually call an 'icon' in the modern sense is the complete *opposite* of religious imagery, marking as it does the loss of its aura. So it would be better to follow the great thinker of cinematographic imagery Serge Daney, and speak in terms of the *visual*. The visual replaces the image that you do not wish to see – and if you do not wish to see it, this is because it has become too similar to the world, a world that *we can longer see in the form of a painting*. The visual gives us something to look at, but it shows us nothing, because nothing escapes it: there is nothing outside its field; it provides no real experience, no otherness. To seek the image behind the visual is to try to allow this image to do its own work. It is an image in spite of everything, even if we try to force it to fade away. We need to allow it to make the most of its anachronistic qualities; we need to let it come to us (to each one of us) because it has come from very far away to gaze on *us*.

So do we need to embrace it in a single glance, abandoning any reassuring selection of mere details and instead surveying it as a whole? Perhaps we do need to accept its invitation to embark on what we sense will be a disquieting journey, as we will need to look on one side and then on the other, adjust our point of view, allow our gaze to roam over white walls where everything arrests and beguiles us, and where, too, the lines of a song painted in clearly legible letters cause us to linger: 'Turn your eyes to gaze, / you who rule, on the woman who is depicted here.'

But historians generally impose a method of descriptive neutrality on themselves: they describe before they interpret. This is a laudable effort, no doubt, but it is doomed to failure. To describe an image consists in putting it into words, and since these words have a history and a life of their own, since they think with and against us but most often behind our backs and without us, this apparently transparent operation is in fact an instrusive and a restrictive categorization that limits our reading. So no sooner has the first word been pronounced than it is already too late: you immediately hear the first cogs of the interpretive machine grinding away as it labours to reduce the meaning of images to texts already read, or texts we have just discovered for this occasion, when instead we ought to leave these images to come to us alone, in their own way and in their own time. But after all, we have to begin somewhere. So let's begin.

The paintings spread across three sides, the fourth (the south wall) being pierced by a window which comprises the sole source of light in the room.[1] This light first strikes the north wall with its parade of what we now call the allegories of good government. On the left sits a woman enthroned, holding a pair of scales with other characters gesturing around her; on the right, six women surround a great bearded old man sitting in state. These figures are all perched on a platform which places them on an intermediate level between the heaven of ideas (inspired by three theological virtues) and the ground of political action (where several different groups can be made out). This small wall comes between two lateral and completely different visions. On the east wall, twice as long, the effects of good government are displayed. The wall of the enclosure cuts the scene into two equal parts: first the happy city, where people work, dance and trade freely, then its countryside (the *contado*), where the land spreads out, arranged in harmony with the ordering of the city, as befits it. Opposite, on the west, the wall is not bipartite but tripartite, and on it we see, in a closer formation, the figures of bad government forming a court of vices presented as the monstrous double of the characters on the north wall. The effects of bad government on the city at war and on the dead land of the *contado* shape a landscape that is the complete opposite of that which adorns the east wall.

Ambrogio Lorenzetti's fresco presents, with calm determination, nothing less than a political programme as it spreads over three of the four walls of the Sala della Pace (Hall of Peace) where the Nine (i.e. the nine magistrates who governed the commune) used to gather. It is a programme of breathtaking boldness, since it proclaims what is or ought to be the slogan of any republic: if this government is good, it is neither because it is inspired by some divine light, nor because it is embodied by men of quality; it is not even because it can draw on a more solid legitimacy or more eloquent justifications than other governments; it is simply because it produces beneficial effects on each person, benefits that are concrete and tangible, here and now – effects that everyone can see and everyone can benefit from, benefits that are, as it were, immanent to the order of the city.

Such is the nature of this capacious and extended narrative, this frieze now known as the 'Fresco of Good Government'. But herein lies precisely the problem: by flattening it out this way, like a Trajan's column whose ribbon we fictitiously unroll as it spirals upwards to the heavens, books (and this book too, inevitably, just like all the other books the fresco has inspired) fail to convey the physical effect it produces. For though this painting has unleashed a flood of words and a continuous torrent of bibliography, before becoming a commonplace topic for art historians or an obligatory stopping-off point for political historians, it is first and foremost a place – quite simply a place. Siena, Palazzo Pubblico, Sala della Pace: here it is. The work is intangible, inseparable from the place where it was born, like the tanned skin of some ancient building, a kind of great cadaver. To feel surrounded by colours and framed by signs: Daniel Arasse has described the suffocating beauty of these places of painting. When you first go to see the fresco, it is never in fact for the first time: you've seen so many reproductions of it. That is why, with art, we never get to our meetings on time: we always arrive too late. What is so striking when we do arrive is the paradoxical smallness of the site: just seven metres long for the north wall, and twice as long for the others. It is an imposing work: the figures are placed well above eye level, yet they seem well within our reach – and each of them remains modest in size. It's like going back to a childhood home which has grown bigger in our memories. You look around and you say to yourself: 'But it's so small!'

This is the image I'm going to be talking about: not so much to trace its history, or decipher it patiently like one of those rebuses on which the iconographical approach is so keen, but to understand the power with which it is actualized. And to seek to grasp that stupefying persuasive force that lays hold of you and latches onto you, 'definitely', as the preacher Bernardino of Siena would say in the fifteenth century, overflowing the intense context of its realization to fly straight towards the present day. There are many reasons that make it so profoundly modern: here I'll mention just one. The walls of the Palazzo Pubblico of Siena are darkened by a threat weighing over the whole communal regime. The citizens of Siena are proud of their republic, but this republic is in danger. It is haunted by the ghost of the signoria which the painter depicts (to frighten himself, or to reassure himself?) as a horned monster emerging from the bowels of hell – or, rather, returning from a past that everyone had thought was over and done with. These days, it is surely obvious that democracy has been undermined and that there is no point – except as a way of calming our fears – in describing this menace as a return of murderous ideologies. But what label can we give to this surreptitious subversion of the public spirit which gnaws away at our certainties? When we cannot think how to respond, we are completely disarmed: the danger looms straight ahead. And Lorenzetti paints this, too: our paralysis in the face of an unnameable enemy, an indescribable peril, an adversary whose countenance we recognize but whose name we cannot utter.

1

'I thought of these images, painted for you'

'When I was away from Siena preaching on War and Peace, I thought of these images, painted for you; they were definitely a very fine invention.' It is 1425 and Bernardino of Siena is speaking. He is addressing a huge crowd; they cluster round like iron filings attracted by the preacher's feverish words. They have all flowed into the famous square, the *campo* of Siena. Romantic travellers (and the tourists of today, intoxicated by the thrill of the horse racing at the Palio) see it as erotic in its allure; they imagine it as a shell raising its scalloped edges to the city, which tenderly enfolds it. But this was not how it was viewed in the time of Bernardino. It was a basin, like the basin of a fountain, where people met to experience what it means to share a space, a portion of the city, and they moved around with gestures simple and clear as the limpid water which rises there. It was a basin that could contain a space like the *orchestra* of a Greek theatre: a fully controlled public space like that in Siena always mimes the monumentalized void of those theatres where the arguments on which the city was founded could be voiced.

And it was indeed a theatre – not just because the façade of the Palazzo Pubblico enclosing the square of the *campo* curves like a stage curtain swelling in the wind, leaving room for the invasive shadow of the Torre del Mangia to cast its shadow full length across it. It was a theatre, for those public sermons were great spectacles laid on by those mercenaries of the inspired word, worth their weight in gold, for whom the communes competed so fiercely.[1] Bernardino was one of those preachers, travelling from town to town, exhorting, threatening, correcting, scolding the people whose emotions they stirred, temporarily welding the hubbub of the public space into a chorus that sang in unison expressing a single desire.

Born in 1380 into the noble Sienese family of the Albizzeschi, Bernardino entered the Franciscan order in 1402. Here he learned the art of talking to ordinary people, drawing on all the tricks of a direct, physical, emotional rhetoric, disdaining neither facile effects nor theatrical gestures. Firstly in Umbria and Tuscany, and then in Lombardy and the region of Venice, his voice was heard, thunderous with menace, rousing the crowds. In Rome in particular, Bernardino caused disquiet: did he not risk neglecting the Trinity and the company of the saints by concentrating his teaching on the figure of Christ alone? In 1427, then again in 1431, Bernardino was placed under investigation. He was forced to retire to a monastery; he died in 1444 and was canonized six years later.

It was one year before his death that Sano di Pietro, the Sienese painter, depicted him standing in front of a large, orderly crowd, divided into two sections by a piece of cloth held across the square separating the two sexes. Such was the effect of his words: they enveloped, and they separated. From his pulpit, when he brandishes the IHS tablet bearing the name of Jesus with which the façade of the Palazzo Pubblico is also stamped, the preacher turns the entire city into a sounding board for the Church. There he stands, Bernardino, the shepherd of his flock, facing the *campo*. He speaks to arouse images in the minds of his audience. And frequently, as we are in Siena, he refers to the city's great painters – Duccio, Simone Martini, the Lorenzetti brothers, all those who, in the years before the Black Death, turned the Tuscan city into the capital of political art or, more precisely, the capital of the politicization of art. This is not because art flatteringly extolled or symbolized the virtues of power: it is because the way that it categorized things in civic terms meant that the creation of pictures was seen by all as an essentially political business. Thus Bernardino put those images into words and uttered the names of the famous artists, the pride of the city, who had painted them.[2] Not to interpret these images, but so that his speech could draw on the impression they had left (as he hoped) in the memories of his listeners. In all his listeners, or more precisely in each individual listener, he awoke a memory, just as we sometimes walk in the footsteps of some ancient trace; and in this way he reawoke the aura of the work of art: 'I thought of these images, painted for you.'

Two years later, on 15 August 1427, in a sermon on marital happiness and the hierarchy of the angels, Bernardino alluded to the Madonna attributed to Simone Martini and reworked in 1415 by Benedetto di Bindo. In September of that year, giving a sermon on the disciplined behaviour that young girls should adopt before marriage, he referred to another painting familiar to his Sienese audience: the Annunciation painted in 1333 by Simone Martini and his brother-in-law Lippo Memmi for the San Ansano altar in the Cathedral of Siena. We see him illustrating the reserve we must show if we are to protect ourselves from the temptations of the flesh, pointing dramatically to his right, indicating the grille on the window of the apartments of the Podestà. Later, on 25 September 1427, in a sermon that violently condemned sodomy, claiming that this vice was more widespread in Italy than elsewhere, Bernardino referred to the situation of Italy on the map of the world or *mappemonde* that Ambrogio Lorenzetti had painted in the hall of the Palazzo Pubblico. It still bears the same name today, the Sala del Mappamondo, and art historians ponder what that cosmogonic painting that made the immensity of the world so tangible must have looked like – but it can no longer be seen.

The people facing Bernardino, too, could not see the images that he projected in front of them in his words, penetrating through the façade of the Palazzo to which his back was turned. But they had seen those images, perhaps, or had heard about them; in any case they could imagine them. At least that is what the preacher supposed when he addressed his listeners in these words:

> This Peace is such a sweet thing that it brings sweetness to one's lips! And look at the word War, opposite! It is something so harsh, and brings such terrible savagery, that it makes the mouth bitter. Look! You have painted it up there, in your palace. Oh, painted Peace, what a joy it is to see it! Just as it is so sad to see War on the other side.[3]

This time it is Lorenzetti's fresco which Bernardino is discussing. He says 'in your palace' – this is the meaning of the expression *palazzo communale*. Following the Peace of Constance (1182), which conceded to them the political rights the emperor had failed to keep for himself, the cities of communal Italy had adopted, for their own use, the grave and solemn name of *palatium*, in which we can hear the subtext of sovereignty. The bishop laid claim to this sovereignty, but it was now the *comune* which wielded it; and *comune* was first and foremost an adjective referring to nothing other than the sharing of power. That is why it is essential to the very idea of the communal palazzo that one could have free access to it – or, more precisely, that it was claimed that everyone could have access to it freely. So with the paintings inside, it was *as if* they could be seen from the square. Bernardino played on this fiction of transparency (which is perhaps one of the essential fictions of the political realm); he is standing outside and saying: 'Look!' But what is there to see? Images that refer you to two words that confront each other: peace and war. The first (*pace*) can be uttered with a gentle expression; when you say the second word (*guerra*), your face twists in a grimace.

Thus, the important thing about Bernardino's sermon in 1427 is the way the preacher is asking his audience to 'look at' a public paint-ing they cannot see, but that they may remember, precisely because it is public. So he is not really evoking images so much as the imprint they had left in a memory that we may imagine was collective. And this imprint is first and foremost verbal, that is, corporal: painting makes words visible, and it is these words that Bernardino requests his audience to look at directly, and what there is to see is nothing other than the physical effect that one feels, personally, when utter-ing these words. The mouth twists and grimaces if it has to say the word 'war' (*guerra*); it is mild and gentle when 'peace' (*pace*) brushes against its lips. And this is what I wish to focus on here: the emotion of desire or suffering in speaking bodies.

But something else is happening. To make his audience remember what we call the 'Fresco of Good Government', Bernardino talked about happiness and sadness, peace and war – and not about govern-ment. Unless, of course, we take this word in the sense it had in those days, as the pastoral conception of power over people, an idea that was common in the Christian Middle Ages. *Regimen* was the art of guiding the behaviour of other people while governing one's own pas-sions; ruling rightly and conducting oneself rightly were one and the same thing, one and the same impulse, for the priest and for the king, who both had the task of leading their flocks to salvation.[4]

Two years after originally mobilizing this series of civic images in his campaign to lead the faithful along the right path of an ethics that was inseparably political and domestic, in 1425, Bernardino of Siena was already preaching on the *campo*. The thirtieth sermon in the Lent cycle developed the theme of Psalm 133: *Ecce quam bonum et quam jocundum habitare fratres in unum* ('Behold, how good and how pleasant it is for brethren to dwell together in unity!'). It was clearly a good day to talk about civic concord, and in this case, Bernardino presented his audience with Venice as a role model. He did so by first announcing his *divisio*: 'Firstly, concord. Secondly, the love of one's neighbour. Thirdly, the love between husband and wife.' And as he developed his first point, he described at length Lorenzetti's fresco:

> When I was away from Siena preaching on War and Peace, I thought of these images, painted for you; they were definitely a very fine invention.

When I turn to Peace, I see merchants coming and going. I see people dancing, repairing houses, working in the vineyards and on the land, sowing their seed, while others on horseback are heading out to bathe. I see girls going to a wedding, great flocks of sheep and many other things. And I also see a man who has been hanged so that holy justice will be maintained. And because of all this, everyone lives in holy peace and concord. Conversely, if I turn my gaze to look at the other side, I see neither traders nor dancers, but merely men killing other men; the houses are not being repaired but demolished and set on fire, the fields are no longer being worked; the vines are cut down, nobody is sowing the seed, nobody is going to bathe, and nobody can indulge in any pleasure – all I see is people leaving the city. Ah, women! Ah, men! The men are killed, the women raped, there is no flock other than the flock being dragged away as booty, men are killing each other, justice has been laid low, the scales in the balance have been broken, people are tied up in chains. And everything that is being done is done in a state of fear.[5]

Bernardino is not here describing an image, but the memory you retain of an image as you move away from it. Above all, it is really a *vision* that immediately twists the body – painfully, one imagines: when I turn one way, I see this, and when I turn the other way, I see that. This then that, peace and war, and nothing else. It is as if the room painted by Lorenzetti had only two walls, the two long walls which display what modern commentators call the 'effects' of good and bad government, with the emphasis always more on the former than on the latter, whereas it is obvious that Bernardino envisaged them as two equal parts of the same sensory experience.[6] And so this experience concerns peace and war; or, as we have said, words to utter but also figures to contemplate – here, justice 'tied up in chains' refers of course to its feminine allegory, which is indeed represented on the fresco. But both words and figures refer mainly to situations, that is, to configurations of historical time, which Bernardino essentially characterizes through their relationship with fear: the time of war is the time when everything happens under the constraint of a single feeling, that of terror; the time of peace is shown by the liberty of bodies in movement, coming and going, acting or remaining at rest, indulging in the freedom and joy of life, and always, as one of the inscriptions on the fresco proclaims, *senza paura* (without fear).

So we see them just as Bernardino saw them, people working and people dancing, those who stroll around and those who are hard at work, the merchants in the city and the peasants who have set off to trim the vines, the girl in all her finery ready for the wedding, trotting along so proudly. And we also see, because he forces us to see them, women being raped and houses on fire, the brutality of the soldiers and the waste land – everything which forms the dismaying spectacle on the other side. But there are also the things that strike Bernardino's imagination and that we can no longer see, at least not in the same way as he did. The little man hanging from the gibbet, held by the half-naked allegory of *Securitas*, certainly escapes the attention of many (even attentive) observers today as they gaze at Lorenzetti's 'very fine invention'. And yet, for the preacher, this is such a striking image that he sees it as opportune to refer to its memory in the minds of his flock; maybe this is because it is one of the keys to this work of art; and in any case we cannot trust our own impressions to measure the political force of images. And what about those men going to bathe on the one side while being prevented from doing so on the other? Where can Bernardino actually see them? Here, clearly, he is extrapolating. So the historian needs to draw on what he or she knows about the social importance of thermal baths in Sienese territory to understand the way in which those in the quattrocento whose eyes rested on Lorenzetti's fresco (and this was definitely true a century earlier, at the time it was painted) naturally extended the itineraries of the characters depicted, taking them to the Bagno di Petriolo or other bathing places that were familiar to them.[7] The image runs on, far away from us, suggesting what lies beyond the frame.

There is also, even more important, something which Bernardino does not talk about. Where are the allegorical figures on the little north wall that today's historians of ideas find so captivating? If we follow the preacher's words, we see neither the venerable old man proudly brandishing the insignia of sovereignty, nor the feminine figures creating a garland of virtues around him, and certainly nothing that constitutes the 'Fresco of Good Government' as the very image of our modernity. So it is not the principles that are important, but the effects – not good and bad government so much as peace and war. And that is why the hall which it honours with the dignity of these figures was called, and would be called until at least the nineteenth century, the Sala della Pace (Hall of Peace).[8] Admittedly, the universality of such a theme is likely to resist the political vicissitudes that risk making the fresco's partisan message seem anachronistic: what meaning could it have in the Italy of the quattrocento, when communal resistance to this version of seignorial authority seemed to be an old question, one that was now largely outmoded by the triumphant new order of the princes?

This, at least, is the interpretation of the image that Bernardino wanted to provide. Are we obliged to follow him? After all, this

Franciscan friar *forces* the meaning of the fresco's composition by coming between the work of art and us, subjugating it to the evocative power of his words; he imposes a clerical mediation, refers to 'holy peace', while nothing or almost nothing in the painting refers to God. We no longer need the preacher to trace the meaning of things – not even to 'be an effective educator' in the way so often advocated in the sickly infantilizing language of political communication these days. So we might be tempted to say: let's go and take a look, since the image is there, fragmented and available like a digital cloud; let's go and take a look, free and unhampered as we are. But hold on: we can see hardly anything. Between the image and us there hover shades that we need to disperse. These are the shades of all the gazes that have already rested on this image.

2

Nachleben:
the watchful shadows

In one fourteenth-century chronicle we read the following:

> And it was decided to paint Peace and War in the palace, with several
> wicked men who lived a long while ago and acted very badly, like-
> wise all those who had done good work for the Republic of Siena.
> Also painted were the four theological virtues with several symbols
> of prudence, effective management and astute understanding. And this
> programme for the said paintings was devised by Master Ambrogio
> Lorenzetti. And this painting is in the communal palace, at the top of
> the staircase, the first door on the left; and if you go there you can see
> it.[1]

Although this eye-witness account is anonymous, and known only
through belated seventeenth-century copies which may well contain a
few interpolations, the evidence in it is of great value: firstly because it
is the oldest one to have been preserved, and secondly because we can
already recognize in it several essential features of the work. As with
Bernardino of Siena, there is an insistence on the dichotomy between
peace and war, the work's visual accessibility (*e chi va el può vedere*,
'and if you go there you can see it'), and the fact that this accessibility
was the result of a political decision (*E fatto el palazzo si deliberò
di dipigniervi . . .*, 'And it was decided to paint [. . .] in the palace').
The authority of the name of Ambrogio Lorenzetti is firmly established here as well, since the responsibility for the overall programme
is ascribed to him (*E questo edifichamento di dette dipinture fecen
maestro Ambruogio Lorenzetti*, 'And this programme for the said
paintings was devised by Master Ambrogio Lorenzetti'). However,
unlike with the preacher, it is not an expert in meaning who makes
the images speak. The anonymous chronicler clearly recognizes three

theological virtues flitting on their wings through the blue of the sky, bathing the head of the impassive old man. They are Faith, Charity, and Hope, each identified by its Latin name or *titulus*: *Fides*, *Caritas*, *Spes*. But our author, a little intimidated by such a display of knowledge, probably adds the *Sapientia* that inspires justice at the other end of the small wall of allegories, thereby unusually creating four of them. Also, the muddle involved in this enumerative description with its extra element mainly reveals a symbolic bafflement in the face of the painting on the great walls, with its interweaving of the *segni di prudenza e d'asercizio et d'ingenio* (signs of prudence, experience and intelligence). Who are the wicked men who once caused so much harm to the commune? We can no longer recognize them.

The palace stands there, apparently intact. Work began on this great project in 1297, and it was mainly completed by 1311 – at least as far as the room for its nine magistrates was concerned. And indeed its façade is now probably much as Ambrogio Lorenzetti would have seen it when he crossed the square of the *campo* in 1338 on his way to paint his great composition in the Sala della Pace. An extra storey topping out the second gallery or triforate windows above the balustrade, the added monogram of Christ's name (the symbol of Bernardino of Siena), perhaps a second pinnacle turret on the central pier: there is nothing to disturb our visual impression. We cross the courtyard of the Podestà, climb the stairs, and there we are – 'if you go there you can see it', at least during opening hours and so long as you have paid the entrance charge to the Museo civico. However, the place creates a merely illusory sense of permanence, even if it affects a sovereign indifference to time. At the top of the staircase, the first door on the left? Well, not exactly: behind the pink shell of the building, its interior has been remodelled several times and archaeologists are somewhat at a loss when it comes to reconstituting the chronology of its different transformations.[2] This uncertainty has significant consequences for our understanding of how access was afforded to the little room where the Council of Nine would gather. It has not moved, of course. It is like a fossil – 'not merely a being that once lived', as Bachelard put it, but 'one that is still alive, asleep in its form'.[3] However, around it, everything has indeed moved. It is as if the delicate hues of the painting surrounding it had anchored it firmly to the heart of the building, a frail shell on which the changing rainbow colours of the waves are reflected.

So these days the visitor reaches Lorenzetti's fresco by crossing through the ebbs and flows of time that come between the fresco and us. And these modifications, of which the palace's interior architecture bears the trace, largely echo the painting. Lorenzetti's work was immediately reworked, copied and quoted. Every month in 1447, the *comune* of Siena paid the draper Jacquet d'Arras to produce 'four drapes depicting peace and war as in the Hall of Peace and War' (28 June 1447), and three months later, on 25 September, another payment order specified that the tapestry must show 'the good government of the prince, and peace and war'.[4] We do not know where this tapestry, now lost, was meant to hang. But it is the quotations and figurative echoes of the work, rather than direct copies of it, which structure the inner space of the palace. Iconographic themes very similar to those which Lorenzetti painted on the walls of the Sala della Pace can be found in the cycle of ancient heroes which Taddeo di Bartolo depicted in 1414 in the adjacent hall of the Anticappella (also called the Anteconsistorio or antechamber of the Consistory).[5] And when, in 1535, he composed the great allegorical painting in the Sala del Consistorio (Hall of the Consistory) extending behind the north wall of the Sala della Pace, the Mannerist painter Domenico Beccafumi completed this political itinerary in the last political cycle of the independent commune of Siena.[6]

By separating the Sala della Pace, where the Nine would meet, from the Sala del Consistorio by means of a great flight of stairs, modern changes to the palace have altered the route one takes; they force the visitor to go backwards in time from Domenico Beccafumi and Taddeo di Bartolo to Ambrogio Lorenzetti, thereby slowing down our access to the image, which can only be approached by crossing through the screen of reflections surrounding it like a halo. This is something which a book inevitably short-circuits: the slowness of one's approach and the confusion of the chronology. The reader should not imagine that he or she can dive headlong from the twenty-first to the fourteenth century: the gaze we bring to bear on an old image is inevitably constrained and contradicted by the shadow cast by all those who have preceded us, that phantasmal cloud of admirers who, absentmindedly or attentively, have gazed at it, described it, put it into words – and yet others who have ventured upon the task of copying it, reworking it, restoring it, extending it and ceaselessly transforming it, *ipso facto* enabling it to enjoy that particular form of survival which consists in nothing other than the twists and turns of its reminiscences, or what Aby Warburg called its *Nachleben* (afterlife).

So let's go and see it, even if we have to allow ourselves to be drawn along the supple and intense choreography of the memory's winding path. Does this means nothing to you? In that case just take a look at the heart of the happy city, where everyone is dancing. Let us follow the route again: we reach the Sala della Pace by zigzagging through places overflowing with paintings, those which extend Lorenzetti's fresco (Taddeo di Bartolo in the Anticappella, Beccafumi in the Consistory) and those which this fresco in turn extends (the *Maestà* of Simone Martini in the Sala del Mappamondo, of course, to which we will need to return: for the time being we will simply stare into the future which the image prophesies, and not the past which it shapes). But yet again, we have been going too quickly: without realizing it, we have passed into the Sala del Risorgimento, painted between 1886 and 1890 to exalt Italian unity. It was decided to locate it here, that is, in the old wing of the Podestà's rooms in the Palazzo Pubblico, just days after the death of Victor Emmanuel II (9 January 1878) in a city that was one of the first to declare its allegiance to him: now that it was freed from Florentine domination, Siena could celebrate the recovery of its independence at the same time as the achievement of Italian unity. So Luigi Mussini, who since 1873 had been in charge of restoring Lorenzetti's frescos, was commissioned to supervise the work on the painting. Heroic deeds and glorious battles splash their garish patriotic colours over the walls; the proud allegories of Italian concord as it was fêted in the poetry of Alessandro Manzoni took possession of the ceiling, while between the two, leaning out of their niches, famous men, from Dante to Garibaldi, stand proudly against a background of gold, displaying to our admiring eyes their acidulous hues as they strive to create a mediaeval effect.

For everything here – from the tension between realism and allegory that structured Lorenzetti's pictorial composition to the legends accompanying the *viri illustres* of Taddeo di Bartolo – extended and highlighted the ideal of mediaeval concord displayed in the Sala dei Nove (Hall of the Nine), decorated with the painting that people started only quite recently, in the late nineteenth century, to call 'the Fresco of Good Government'. Was it hoped thereby to bolster the future with a political hope that they feared might have been lost for ever? The mediaeval past stood there, fresh and available for use, open to everyone's gaze – yet it needed to be seen properly. And here was the clinching fact: before the nineteenth century, Lorenzetti's painting had remained in the state described by the anonymous Sienese chronicler and later on by Bernardino of Siena – a dramatic evocation of peace and war.[7] We need to be clear about this: it was not simply *perceived* like this, it *was* like this – and not otherwise. 'In the palace of Siena, he painted war and peace with his own hand,' as the sculptor Lorenzo Ghiberti admiringly noted in 1447 in his *Commentaries*,[8] while, a century later, Giorgio Vasari felt there was, in the war scenes of the painting, a historical representation of the battle of Sinalunga.[9] Here we find a constant feature of pre-Enlightenment interpretations: behind the figures painted by Lorenzetti, they systematically seek allusions to real people who can in theory be identified. For a long time, the allegories on the north wall, however captivating they may be for us, remained completely invisible; apart from the ambiguous allusion to 'the good government of the prince' in the commission (already mentioned) for the tapestry depicting it in 1447, we find no description of it before 1730. At that date, in a work devoted to deciphering the 'inscriptions, coats of arms and ancient monuments' of his city, the Sienese scholar Giovanni Antonio Pecci rather curiously identified the woman carrying the scales of justice as a personification of the city of Siena, whereas he saw 'on a majestic throne, Justice represented by an old man, with a white beard and with a crown on his head, holding in his right hand a sceptre and in his left a map of the world'.[10]

Where did he see such a map? Pecci's attributions are surprisingly precarious. However, they do oblige us to turn our gaze to the north wall, which was neglected in ancient descriptions, and thus to politicize the overall perception of the work. This is clearly the case with the abbé Luigi Lanzi, who severely criticized Pecci's interpretation. In his *Storia pittorica della Italia inferiore*, published in Florence in 1792, he envisages the fresco as 'a kind of poem imparting moral teaching', contrasting the vices of bad government with the 'qualities and effects' of virtuous power: 'Overall, this entire painting tends to train legislators and statesmen for the Republic impelled by no other sentiment [than] that of true virtue.'[11] Once it has been formulated, this republican interpretation seems so obvious that it ultimately cannot be distinguished from the work itself: nowadays, this is the only way we can see it, and this in turn implies that we reject former particular identifications that reduced the meaning of the figures to an outmoded past, and replace them with an allegorical reading that preserves intact the work's concrete and contemporary power.

This was the interpretation produced in the 1840s by Carlo and Gaetano Milanesi, scrupulous historians who collected the huge store of documents assembled in their *Documenti per la storia dell'arte senese* at the same time they were establishing a critical edition of Vasari's *Lives*. The first task they set themselves was to campaign against the old tendency to look for precise events behind the situations depicted (to see not war in general, but the battle of Sinalunga, as Vasari had already said, thereby establishing a long tradition) and real persons behind the painted figures. Thus the Milanesi brothers endeavoured to criticize the stubborn certainty of those commentators who claimed to 'recognize' the first of the councillors in the procession bringing the thread of concord to the noble personage enthroned in majesty as a portrait of one Toso Pichi, a Sienese notable whose existence is attested by fourteenth-century sources, but who subsequently enjoyed a posthumous life enshrined in folklore: according to legend, he fathered 148 children.[12] No, replied the Milanesis, the figures painted by Ambrogio Lorenzetti need to be read as allegories, and more particularly as Aristotelian allegories. For the first time, the great name is uttered – the name which still dominates scholarly debate. Aristotle and the Republic: the *Buon governo* has entered the age of modernity.

What happens if we enter the Sala della Pace through the Sala del Risorgimento, which itself opens onto the Sala del Consistorio and the Anteconsistorio? This obligatory route through the museum is ultimately a useful detour which, by forcing ever-shifting resemblances to confront one another in reflections and interweaving patterns, allows us finally to stand in front of the image – not facing the past, which has vanished for good, but looking into time as it speeds by in front of us.[13] It is not enough to say that the nineteenth century reinvented the Middle Ages, since only through that century can we gain access to the mediaeval past. There is more to it than that. Indeed, not only does the Sala del Risorgimento extend the Sala dei Nove and draw inspiration from it; it also projects itself fully into it by casting its shadow across it. This shadow turns it into an allegory. We can now understand how, as we stroll through it, and try as historians to understand it in a way that inevitably goes backwards through time, the Risorgimento comes before the *Buon governo*: it gives meaning to it, it invents it and brings it to life.

The risk of tracking down the ghosts of the *Nachleben* of vanished images is that we will fall prey to vertigo. Did Rosa Maria Dessì succumb to this vertigo when she wrote her great archaeological study of old interpretations of Lorenzetti's fresco, a study to which my present discussion owes so much? This might well be the case: she certainly has no hesitation in raising disquieting questions. In particular, she takes up the enthralling polemics aroused by the restorations of Lorenzetti's fresco carried out by Luigi Mussini at the end of the 1870s – this was, as you will remember, the same man who assumed responsibility for the programme to paint the Sala del Risorgimento. Giovanni Battista Cavalcaselle, a politician and art historian, forensically studied the pictorial material in the fresco of the Sala della Pace, trying, as his manuscripts preserved in Venice show, to trace the different mediaeval repaintings and the traces of successive restora-

tions. He severely criticized Mussini for carrying out an artist's restoration (and it was indeed painters of the Academy who were given
this task) rather than a historian's restoration, since he showed little
respect for the new, more scientific requirements. On different points,
Cavalcaselle caught him in the act: Mussini could be excessively inter-
ventionist, and he sometimes extrapolated unduly. How tempted was
Mussini to ensure that Lorenzetti's fresco would resemble its visual
echo in the Sala del Risorgimento?

To say that an image is transformed by the long history of the gazes
brought to bear on it, so that successive delicate layers, rather like
flaky pastry, have been deposited on its surface by this active vision,
is perhaps not simply a metaphor. Between 1355 and 1385, probably,
again in 1492, in 1518 and in 1521, perhaps in the 1830s, then in
1868–70, in 1873–80, as we have seen, and then again in 1951–2 and
finally in 1985, Lorenzetti's fresco was restored, retouched, repainted
– and even if the final restoration campaigns smoothed over these
successive interventions by creating the illusion of an innocent permanence, for a long time these interventions were reinterpretations,
transformations and reinventions.[14] When you read the old descriptions presenting the fresco as already in a state of disrepair, you can
only shudder. For Charles de Brosses, who visited Italy between 1739
and 1740, the palace was 'an old building with nothing to recommend
it or at least nothing interesting about it apart from a few paintings
older and uglier than it is'. A century later, another French traveller, Jean-Claude Fulchiron, found these paintings to be 'half-effaced'
and basically lacking in any interest (they 'depicted various episodes
in local history'). Only the painter Hippolyte Flandrin, a disciple of
Ingres, waxed more enthusiastic in a letter to his parents dated 1835:
'This hall, which used to be painted across its four walls, is unfor-
tunately quite ruined; but once you have seen such things, however
mutilated they may be, you can never forget them.'

Should this really alarm us? It is a sign of naïvety to think that,
in the Sala dei Nove, you can come face-to-face with a fourteenth-
century painting. It is as it is, as time has transformed it: it thus offers
itself to our gaze as a contemporary picture. It is a painting of our
time because here I am, standing in front of it, and I am alive. It is
an illusion to think that it will give us the truth about its past as it
really was. But it is also an exaggeration to think that it will conceal
that past from us for ever. At the conclusion of her work of scholarly
deconstruction, Dessì has her doubts. The old authors describe certain
details that we cannot discern, and yet they fail to see things that to
us are blindingly obvious. Does this mean that, following successive

restorations, 'pictorial matter has been lost for good',[15] or do we need to reconstitute the complex and devious scenario of the repaintings and pentimenti that have changed not only the meaning of the work but also the actual way it is put together?[16] Yet until the end of the eighteenth century, art lovers, scholars and travellers took no interest in the small north wall of the allegories. Are we to imagine that it was 'concealed' or 'covered by a tapestry'?[17] Not necessarily: sometimes, words can cover over, just as effectively as fabrics or repaintings, things that people do not wish to see, and most of the images that evade our vision are still in fact perfectly visible. It is perhaps impossible to look at things through trecento eyes; but we should probably make an effort to reconstitute both the social conditions of reception of the political image when it was painted and the processes whereby it again becomes real at the time when we see it. The *Nachleben* described by Aby Warburg is the history of a past that continues to survive – a 'ghost story for adults', as he wrote in his atlas of the intensity of memories known as *Mnemosyne*.[18] This past still prowls about, casting a dense magical cloud over the images, a cloud that we need to pass through if we are to reach what it protects: the 'untimely' in Nietzsche's sense – nothing other than the anachronistic feeling of urgency.

3

The Nine

On 26 February 1338: 10 florins (i.e. 31 *libri* and fifteen *soldi*); the same sum on 29 April, *pro parte pretti picture palatii*, and again on 30 June. Archived in the registers of Sienese accounts, mentions of payment are dispersed: a wage (*pretium* or *salarium*, both terms are found) for a painting (*pictura, dipentura*) made in the palace. *Pro salario picturarum* on 28 July, 2 florins, and another 10 florins on 24 September *per dipentura ch'a fatten el palazzo*. On 9 December, another 10 florins *pro parte de la dipentura che è fatta in casa de' Signori Nove*, and finally, on 18 February, 6 florins *per parte del suo salaro*.

Had Lorenzetti already finished? The structure of the accounts suggests as much. These payment orders addressed to Ambrogio Lorenzetti are preserved in the books of the Biccherna, the tax department of the commune of Siena, in the register of expenses (*Uscita dello scrittore*).[1] The painting in question is not named, but there can be no doubt that it is indeed the one painted by Lorenzetti in the Sala dei Nove (*in casa de' Signori Nove*) in 1338. In 1625, the Sienese Fabio Chigi (who became Pope under the name Alexander VII), surveying the inscriptions in the Palazzo Pubblico, saw it next to the painter's signature, in a place where we can no longer make out anything at all (except for a gap). So it must have been in 1338 that Lorenzetti decorated the hall where the Nine met: they made another two payments to him (for a total of 113 florins, in eight sums, the final balance being made on 29 May 1339, *per le dipenture que aveva fatto nel palaçço... per residuo del suo salario*).

So it took one year, from February 1338 to February 1339, to complete a work of whose commissioning we have no documentation. All that we can know is what is suggested in the dry litany of payments

minutely recorded by the Biccherna. Unless, of course, we concoct a
novel about the feverish desires of the commissioners, as did Pierre
Michon, in *Les Onze (The Eleven)*: 'Are you prepared to honour a
commission, citizen painter? Yes, he was, perhaps he was.' There were
only Nine of them in 1338, and yet we should really find some means
of expressing the feeling of urgency that took firm hold of them that
year as danger stirred and it seemed imperative to splash the walls
of the palace with images that would be cold and clear, precise and
extensive, reminding the populace of the meaning of the struggle they
were involved in.

What struggle was this? In 1338, the city of Siena had lived under
the government of the Nine for over fifty years. This regime, founded
in 1287, was well established and apparently respected, and would
last until 1355 – an exceptionally long period in the institutional
landscape of the early trecento, so prone to political instability. It
ensured that the city of Siena was a commune firmly rooted in an
Italy whose political map was being redrawn by dramatic changes
in territorial boundaries, transforming the old city states into the
capitals of regional states. From the time of the ancient episcopal
civitas occupying the highest of the hills on the site, the city developed
towards the north-west, extending along the *via francigena* leading to
Rome. And within the fold of the hills, between the upper city of the
bishop and the expansion of the suburbs, in the area which would
become the *campo*, was built the *curia consulum*, which, from the
1150s onwards, would be the meeting place for the representatives
of the secular power governing the commune. The latter developed as
an institution at the same time as the *contado* (city environs), which
it dominated to the south, from the river Ombrone to its confluence
with the Orcia. At that time the Sienese were Ghibellines, and supported the Emperor Frederick Barbarossa against their own Bishop
Rainieri and Pope Alexander III, even though he was a compatriot
of theirs. The main issue as far as they were concerned was to resist
Florence, their great rival to the north, which had assumed Tuscan
leadership of the pro-Church Guelph party.

On 4 September 1260, at Montaperti, Siena won a major victory
over its Florentine enemies, and this turned it into the *civitas
Virginis*, the city protected by the Virgin. Although this Ghibelline period in
Sienese political history was actually more complex and discontin-
uous than it may appear, it was a decisive time in the construction
of its civic identity, probably because it corresponded to the period
when the city was extending its territory into southern Tuscany,
far beyond the strict limits of its *contado*. But Siena could not long

contain Florence's expansion southwards. It was precisely to block this expansion (just after they had been routed at Colle di val d'Elsa in 1269) that the Sienese entered the Guelph alliance; the beginning of the government of the Nine, in 1287, was mainly a corollary of this shifting alliance. Florence, whose territorial state extended to just ten kilometres from the northern precincts of Siena, and now definitively included the cities of the val d'Arno and the val d'Elsa, acknowledged the extension of Sienese territory towards the Maremma, which provided it with access to the coast centred on the highly desirable port of Talamone.

This territory, then, which would reach its fullest extension in the fifteenth century (until the Treaty of Cateau-Cambrésis incorporated it into the Grand Duchy of Tuscany under the Medici family in 1559) already seemed, in 1338, to be firmly established; at the time when Ambrogio Lorenzetti was picking up his paintbrushes, Siena had just extended and consolidated its domain by capturing the cities of Massa Marittima (1335) and Grosseto (1336). But at the same time, in 1337, Florence began to absorb the territory of Arezzo, which was, together with the powerful maritime city of Pisa, the sole defender of the imperial cause against the Guelph alliance. Both economically and politically, Siena was now subordinate to Florence, which (with 100,000 inhabitants before the Black Death) had a population twice as large. However, the demographic importance of Siena was far from negligible: with between 45,000 and 50,000 inhabitants in the first half of the fourteenth century, it was surpassed by Milan, Venice, Genoa and Florence, but was clearly of the same size as Verona, Brescia, Cremona, Pisa, Bologna and Palermo – if we consider Italy alone, which was characterized by its exceptionally densely populated cities: outside Italy, it would be more apt to compare Siena with London or Paris. To the north of the cathedral, in the *tierzo* of Camollia (one of the three subdivisions extending out from the square of the *campo* as far as the city walls and beyond, thereby dividing the city from its *contado*), and particularly around the church of San Cristoforo, were massed the palaces of the rich bankers: first the Tolomei, the Bonsignori opposite, and further along the Salimbeni and the Malavolti. Although their wealth was still huge, it had already been eroded by their first bankruptcies (when the Bonsignori crashed in 1298, it shook the city's entire financial system), and, eclipsed by competition from Florence, their period of financial expansion was now behind them.

Siena declined economically as its townscape became more beautiful: this chronological coincidence has led certain historians to venture some bold hypotheses, even though their narrowly economistic approach now seems outdated – they suggested that the outlay on monuments was a form of setting in stone the wealth that could no longer be employed in really productive investments.[2] It is true that the fact that work stopped on the building of the Cathedral of Siena after 1348 still leaves us aghast when we realize that the contemporary Duomo lies within the transept of that ruined giant. But this contemporary impression, which might lead people to believe that Siena was vitrified by the Black Death and that what they walk around these days are the sumptuous remains of a long-vanished ambition, is misleading. For one thing, we are now rediscovering the significance of the architectural and urban developments that transformed Siena in the fifteenth century: Pope Pius II Piccolomini in the middle of the quattrocento, and later Pandolfo Petrucci, lord of Siena at the end of the century, were intent on magnifying the 'republican' splendour of the people's commune, following the antiquarian taste for classical forms that was current at the time.[3] Also, the thoroughly political passion which led the regime of the Nine to shape and embellish the city of Siena should not be understood as a mere mimicking of power: it was, in itself, political power in action, simultaneously the sign of power and its effectiveness, storing power in signs that were more forceful than mere force as they could thereby impose power's authority. Is this not exactly what Lorenzetti paints at the heart of his happy city in the Sala della Pace?

The Nine had already started to enlarge the cathedral and its baptistery in 1316 and to extend its precincts in 1323, but it was in 1338, at the heart of the civic space that so powerfully divided the city, on that square of the *campo* on which their palaces rose, that the Nine expressed their monumental message most eloquently. The Palazzo Pubblico, as we have said, was built mainly between 1297 and 1311, following an architectural model that definitely drew on the Palazzo Tolomei, at least in the arrangement of the façades and the rhythmic animation imparted to them by the horizontality of the cornices and the disposition of the windows.[4] In 1325, work was begun on the wing of the Podestà (on the left when you face the façade), and two years later the Nine also enlarged the prisons, which, as often in the civil architecture of communal Italy, were fully integrated into the body of the Palazzo Pubblico. It was probably also in 1327 that they began to pave the square of the *campo*, its nine brick sections spreading out like a shell, incisively separated by grey stones. This was an amazing piece of scene-setting: it monumentalized a civic space where statutory regulations normalized social customs. For while the public square was still a place for markets and trading, commerce in foodstuffs, seen as less worthy of urban decorum, was gradually shifted away from it. Once this operation had been completed, in 1334, it was followed by another and even more complex one: the Nine commissioned the engineer Jacopo di Vanni to bring a supply of running water to the fountain of Gaia, on the edge of the shell shape formed by the *campo*.

This technological feat, in a city where the provision of water required the installation and upkeep of an extraordinary network of subterranean channels in terracotta (the *bottini*),[5] was simultaneous with the refurbishment of the Palazzo Pubblico, which, just as the Nine were commissioning the frescos to decorate the Sala della Pace, now entered a decisive phase. In 1338, it was decided to build another assembly room for the Great Council (which had hitherto gathered in the Sala del Mappamondo), and this meant extending the building beyond the apartments of the Podestà. The same year saw the issuing of many payment orders concerning the construction of the Torre del Mangia. This major project would be completed in 1349, with the installation of the 'great bell of the commune' (finished eleven years later when a mechanical clock was installed). The tower then rose to a height of 87 metres, and its shadow weighed heavily on a city that had long bristled with patrician towers, even though the authorities there had been prone to decapitate displays of vertical arrogance ever since the thirteenth century.

It should by now be clear that Siena was proud of a triumphant urban splendour that imbued its political regime with a special degree of civic attachment. A broadened suffrage, political representativeness, a rapid rotation of responsibilities, the collegial nature of decisions, control of the exercise of power by verification of the accounts: the government of the Nine stubbornly defended the values and procedures of what, in the thirteenth century, had comprised the glory of communal institutions. Indeed, in 1338, the city was one of the most brilliant, most obstinate conservatories of these values and procedures, which everywhere else were being undermined. The 'Nine Lords', elected for two months after a complex process aimed to prevent any oligarchy from taking root, formed the executive of this regime. In the official records, these men were called the *Governatori e difenditori del Comune e del Popolo*. We should interpret this to mean that they defended the political balance of a compromise regime whose social base spread out from the *popolo* as a whole – all those who were not part of the old feudal aristocracy of the militia, forming an extended ruling class dominated by the bourgeoisie with its businessmen and its wealthy merchants. The fiscal details recorded by the

Tavoli delle possessioni from 1316 to 1320 give an idea of their fortunes: between those years, we find one hundred and twenty *Noveschi* (i.e. one hundred and twenty heads of households who had at least once been members of the magistracy of the *Nove*); among them, only three held no possessions in the *contado*.[6] They had real estate in the city which enabled them to impose their political presence, and investments in the countryside to underline this presence and convert their social power into more secure economic goods. This was the social world of the Nine that Lorenzetti depicted in his portrait of the happy city, on either side of the brick walls that shape these spaces rather than simply dividing them up.

This was, doubtless, a government of merchants, and the ruling class was certainly stable; and yet William Bowsky's prosopographic analyses of the identifiable *Noveschi* unambiguously demonstrate that this was still a socially open group. Ultimately, it was not all that far removed in its composition from the recommendations laid down in the city statutes of 1319–20, which stated that the Nine should be chosen 'from the merchants of the city of Siena or at least from the middling sort' (*de' Mercanti de la città di Siena o vero de la mezza gente*). In other words, the ideal of the common good was not, in the Siena ruled by the Nine, an empty slogan: it corresponded to a certain political experience which struck its contemporaries as exceptional in its durability, in an Italy that was being shaken by the march towards rule by lords or *signori*, in other words a process of *insignorimento* (take-over by lords) that was slowly corrupting it. Hence the need for that ruling class to take into account the demands of the 'small people', all those who, less fortunate but more numerous, and militarily organized, were exerting their political pressure – notably in matters of taxation, the judiciary and the town council, where the social stakes were the highest. As Machiavelli would put it later: good laws do not spring from a virtuous lawgiver, but from the contrast between the feelings of the great and those of the underprivileged, 'for states will never be ordered without danger'. The rule of the Nine was neither more virtuous nor more enlightened than any other: it was simply endangered. They attempted to preserve that rule, under pressure from their people, and commissioned the fresco not to exalt the wisdom of their power, but to depict civil dispute and the founding discord of political order.

Here, perhaps, is the proof: the Nine did not allow themselves to be depicted directly in the fresco they commissioned from Lorenzetti. However, we can clearly see – in the foreground of the north wall of the allegories of good government – the long train of the prudent men who rule the city. Here they are, in neat array, heading off in procession towards the throne on which the great bearded figure is seated. But just count them: there are twenty-four of them. Why twenty-four, and not nine? Historians have never come up with any really convincing answer for this oddity. Did the regime perhaps refuse to set itself up as an example, preferring to point to a recent past (before 1287) when Siena was governed by the college of the twenty-four who tried to establish a compromise between the nobles and the *popolo*? Or should we resort to some complicated calculations and deduce that these twenty-four men were the executives of the commune in 1338? This would mean, for example – as Nicolai Rubinstein suggests – seeing them as the twenty members of the Consistory (the *Nove* plus eleven magistrates of the *Ordini*) together with four recipients of taxes (*Esecutori delle Gabelle*).[7] Or perhaps we are barking up quite the wrong tree by thinking that the fresco alludes to Sienese institutions; maybe we should fall back on the twenty-four elders of the Apocalypse, or (but the two readings are not mutually exclusive) the *ventiquattro seniori* who walk along two by two in Canto XXIX of Dante's *Purgatorio*.[8] In any case, is not the poet of the *Divine Comedy* himself recognizable in the fourth row of the procession, in mauve robes, with his stern demeanour, his aquiline nose and his hollow cheeks? Some today indulge in day-dreams about this unnecessary hypothesis, though they have no evidence beyond a mere fleeting impression: it is as if they had depicted themselves in the two men who, behind the poet's back, are pointing at him as they turn aside to discuss him.

This move away from any explicit likeness is difficult to interpret, but it is found in several other places in Lorenzetti's fresco, which, through its dissimilarities, its gaps and its anachronisms, opens a window onto what is *not exactly* reality, but approaches it. Is the painting of the councillors realistic? The painter has scrupulously individualized them, through colour, the cut of their clothes, their features, ages and attitudes. In spite of the family resemblance that seems to hover over the group, each of them has his own face, and we feel – or at least those who looked at the fresco had the persistent feeling – that, behind those faces, there were men they could recognize. These were portraits, in other words – they resembled something: but what? A certain idea of the diversity of the individuals gathered together. Lorenzetti did not paint an indistinct mass, but a group that was in accord – or more precisely, as we shall see later on, a group held together by cords. A common impulse drives them, it is true – but look at how their gazes cross and the way their hands are sometimes aflutter: everything seems to bring out the variety of points of view. And yet there is one detail that strikes you as incongruous, one that long remained unnoticed, even though once you have spotted it, you will never forget it: the councillors are all the same height; they are all different but all equal, unlike the ignominious train of the condemned figures facing them.

The painter has depicted the instrument of this equity. Behind and to the right of the councillors sits the allegorical figure of Concord. She is a giantess, but she is on the same level as them: she represents, in short, virtue come down to earth. Her *titulus*, *Concordia*, is written on the symbolic attribute she holds on her knees. This is a plane, for planing wood. This is because the plane is the tool of *aequitas* that serves to make all things equal (*aequus*), level and smooth (*planus*).[9] In the context of 1338, the allusion is crystal clear: it is the tax system which 'planes' things smooth. As we know, one of the first demands of the *popolo* was that a fairer system of taxes should be brought in, based on an assessment of the wealth of each individual. This system rested on the declarations of taxpayers (*alliramento*) up until 1316, when it was decided to entrust *agrimensores* (professional 'measurers') with the task of drawing up a general inventory of holdings in the city and the *contado*, so that the aforementioned *Tavoli delle possessioni* could be established. But this fiscal inquisition needed to be constantly defended against the claims of the oligarchy, which was always out to increase the proportion of tax to expenditure (comprising the taxes that are now called 'indirect') – a less fair tax structure. And how can we fail to see that the twenty-four councillors, all equal in height, have been symbolically 'planed' by the civic instrument of a concord that has no compunction in levelling persons, wealth and values? If we find this difficult to admit today, this is because the abrasive force of liberal ideology (which acknowledges communal Italy as one of its glorious sources) has made 'levelling' into something negative. But the positive value of *aequitas* was endorsed by theorists of communal power such as Giovanni da Viterbo, who held that the magistrates of the city should be 'as much in love with equity as with justice'.[10]

This social carpentry has its pendant in the 'bad' part of the fresco. *Divisio* is a woman with her hair let down. Like the great figure on the throne, she wears a black and white dress – the colours of the commune. But her robe is made of two halves sewn together lengthwise, with the words *Si* and *No* written on them: symbolic complementarity has been transformed into a violent contradiction. Like *Concordia*, she holds a carpenter's tool, this time a saw, with which she is cutting into her own wrist. This is the discord of the factious, the complete opposite of the usual arguments between politicians: she divides, mutilates, separates. And out of the mass, what she extracts are not individualities, but frightened solitudes.

On the fresco they commissioned to decorate the hall in which they met, the Nine are not to be seen. But their emblem is there – nine virtues, nine dancers – both in the image and beyond it, in the city it presents. And above all on the square of the *campo* that they have built, its nine brick-paved segments opening like a fan – an echo chamber with its rhythm as insistent as a signature. We should probably hear this low murmur as the muffled expression of a certain disquiet. Throughout Italy, the spectre of the signoria was on the prowl and the *insignorimento* (take-over by *signori* or lords) of institutions was surreptitiously subverting the country's machinery. The signoria, which was defined both as the confiscation of power by a single person and as the extension of its scope beyond the city, presented itself as the political form in which the permanent conflict characterizing the communal system was transcended. In Lombardy, in Venice, the political space had already been completely reshaped by those territorial signorias which included the Visconti family in Milan, the Este family in Ferrara and the Della Scala family in Verona. In Tuscany, it was starting to raise its head: Lucca had fallen into the hands of Castruccio Castracani in 1316, as had Pisa; Florence had been on the verge of succumbing several times, as at Christmas 1325, when it yielded to the Duke of Calabria, Charles of Anjou. Siena attempted to put up a fight, but the political consensus of its *governo largo* (relatively democratic regime) was fissured by factional struggle and increasing social tensions. Even though the Tuscan commune was immune to the very widespread political exclusion of magnates that seriously affected many Italian communes, it attempted to keep the *schiette maggiori*, in other words the wealthiest and most powerful families, out of power.[11] Nonetheless, political tension was a permanent feature: there was the in-fighting between the Piccolomini in 1292, the Ghibelline plot of 1311, the civil war of 1318 and the Tolomei conspiracy of 1325. From April 1338 onwards, Pope Benedict XII launched judicial proceedings against the Bishop of Siena, Donosdeo de' Malavolti, who had been accused by the Piccolomini of embezzlement. This event was ignored by historians of Sienese political life until recently, but it cast a particular shadow across the immediate context of Lorenzetti's commission: it was probably an aggravated episode in the vengeful rivalry (the *faide*) between two of the most powerful families of Siena, but the actual shape assumed by the inquisitorial proceedings, and their consequences for the religious and civic life of a city whose bishop was temporarily prevented from acting, suggest the extent of the political crisis that gripped the ruling class.[12]

Thus, in 1338, ruling and defending the commune and the *popolo* was a real struggle for the Nine. And this struggle was also, indeed mainly, a question of words and images. That is why the years 1320–30 were characterized by an intense activity of political communication that we can without exaggeration call 'propagandistic'. True, not all political regimes have the same need to produce their own justifications: until the 1240s, the consular commune of Siena delivered political messages that were a matter more of celebration than of persuasion. It needed to create the illusion of unanimity, to mime *consensus*. The rule of the *popolo*, on the other hand, constantly had to provide evidence of its good will, and above all to highlight the concrete results of its actions. Even if it meant exhibiting the reality of *dissensus*, it was obliged to lay bare the realities of the political sphere. It needed to produce belief and obedience, as propaganda was *propaganda fides* (the propagating of the faith), and the *fides* or faith that it propagated was, in mediaeval culture, an inseparable mixture of faith and fidelity.[13]

However refined it might seem in its details, this political message came down to a few large-scale effects of meaning: in the republic of which the Nine dreamed, the ideal of a transparent norm converged with the language of civic glory, turning Siena into a second Rome. The Nine raised a statue of Aristotle in front of the Duomo; promoted the legend of the founding of the city by the sons of Remus, Senius and Aschius (depicted by Lorenzetti at the foot of the throne on which is seated the grand old man); endeavoured to compete with the University of Bologna by creating, in 1321, a new *Studium*; and referred at the head of their statutes in 1337 to Justinian's constitution *Deo auctore*. Were the city's rulers succumbing to what Mario Ascheri calls 'Sienese megalomania'?[14] In any case, this megalomania was also, perhaps mainly, expressed in several great communal commissions for public painting: Duccio's *Maestà* for the high altar in the Duomo (1308–11); Simone Martini's painting of the same subject for the Sala del Mappamondo (1315); the *Storie della Vergine*, since lost, by Simone Martini and the Lorenzetti brothers for the façade of the Ospidale Santa Maria della Scala (1335); and finally the commission for the Sala della Pace. Ambrogio Lorenzetti was the executor or producer of this ultimately paradoxical political ambition (which expressed, by means that might be thought immoderate, a normative idea of justice and moderation). But, more than this, he was also, in the full sense which his age now gave the word, its *artist*.

4

Ambrogio Lorenzetti, *famosissimo e singularissimo maestro*

AMBROSIUS LAURENTII DE SENIS HIC PINXIT UTRINQUE: the inscription, in fine gothic letters, fills the white ribbon that runs along the ground beneath the feet of the twenty-four councillors. It is spread out above our heads, and so we need to look up a bit in order to read it: Ambrogio Lorenzetti, of Siena, painted this, *utrinque*. 'On two sides', or, perhaps more precisely, 'on one side and the other' – in other words: Ambrogio Lorenzetti of Siena painted this and that. A strange detail, to which we will need to return. For the time being, we shall just note the solemn nature of the signature, and the fact that it is heightened by the use of Latin. In the word-saturated picture, Latin is reserved solely for the inscriptions which label the virtues and give the artist's name; the inscriptions in verse in the scrolls and the decorative borders commenting on the allegories are, by way of contrast, in the vernacular. Daniel Russo is doubtless correct in his suggestion that this mark of attribution needs to be seen as part of the long tradition of inscriptions that, from at least the twelfth century onwards, place 'the completed work of art and the humble mention of its maker under the eye of God', while emphasizing that 'if there is a signature in [Lorenzetti's] work, a constantly repeated signature, it is the number nine, which refers via the painter to the Nine magistrates who commissioned it and paid for the entire decoration'.[1] All the same, while this act of naming should be seen as akin to ancient and venerable forms of monumental inscription, and we should not overestimate the importance of the artist's signature (he had less *auctoritas* than those who commissioned the work), it is difficult not to see it as a claim being made by the *auctor*, less under the eye of God (which does not hang too heavily over the scene here) than under the gaze of human beings and their future.

The painter who signs his name in Latin embodies, for posterity, the model of the artist-philosopher. A hundred years after the completion of the Sienese fresco, Lorenzo Ghiberti described him in his *Commentaries* as a *famosissimo e singularissimo maestro* but also 'a very noble composer' (*nobilissimo compositore*) and also as a *huomo di grande ingegno* ('an extremely ingenious man'). Lorenzetti, he said, was an unrivalled draughtsman, 'much more gifted than the others', skilled in the art of composition. When he wrote these lines, Ghiberti had just finished the Gates of Paradise for the Baptistery of Florence (1425), a major composition of the Italian Renaissance which tried to adapt to the art of sculpting in bronze the investigations that painters had been conducting into the narrative structure of depicted scenes. From this point of view, Ghiberti deemed Lorenzetti to be a master. But his *ingegno* was not just an art of execution: *Fu nobilissimo disegnatore, fu molto perito nella teorica di detta arte.*[2] That is the main point: while Lorenzetti's work was studied and admired in the quattrocento for the skill of its perspectival construction, it was also considered to be an ingenious painting, and its author as one of those precursors who raised the condition of painters from the level of the mechanical arts, to which the tradition had confined them, to the level of the liberal arts, to which they belonged thanks to their mathematical treatment of space. Ghiberti's use of the term *teorica* is decisive: it is in becoming a theorist of his art that the painter achieves the dignity of the intellectual. This is the meaning of Ghiberti's *Commentarii*, the first theoretical treatise written by a painter. But as Richard Krautheimer has noted, Ghiberti does not use the term *teorica* except on very rare occasions: only the Ancients, Lorenzetti, and he himself can be called 'expert in the theory of this art' (*perito nella teorica detta arte*).[3]

We find a similar conclusion in Giorgio Vasari. A hundred years after Ghiberti, Vasari describes Lorenzetti as an artist and 'gentleman': he was 'an excellent master in painting', but also had

> given attention in his youth to letters [. . .] wherefore he was not only intimate with men of learning and of taste, but he was also employed, to his great honour and advantage, in the government of his Republic. The ways of Ambrogio were in all respects worthy of praise, and rather those of a gentleman and a philosopher than of a craftsman.[4]

Here too, it is easy to recognize in these lines the projection of a social ideal characteristic of Vasari and his time. But here too, the author of the *Lives* was not making it all up; he was recomposing fragments of accumulated memories that, in the second half of the sixteenth century, formed the available stock of reminiscences of Lorenzetti. He had 'given attention in his youth to letters' – this was indisputably true of the Sienese painter. On 9 June 1348, at the end of his life, he himself wrote, in his own hand, his will (*scritto su una carta di pecora per volgaro, scritto per mano di maestro Ambruogio,* as the document puts it).[5] The plague that would soon kill him was already causing such havoc in the city of Siena that, according to the text, it was no longer possible to find a single notary to transcribe under dictation the last will and testament of the dying. Conversely, in 1335, an account from the workshop of the Duomo recorded the payment made by the commune to a grammar teacher to translate a hagiographic text in Latin, meant to provide a source of inspiration for the *storie di San Savino* painted by Pietro Lorenzetti.[6] Unlike his older brother, Ambrogio had no need of those cultural mediators, as he had direct access to the written culture – both in Latin and in the vulgar tongue.

Of course, this does not mean that Ambrogio Lorenzetti was the fresco's sole designer. As we know, or can at least surmise, the verses of the inscriptions in the fresco and the 'song' in the decorative borders, to which we will shortly be returning, are the work of an experienced poet. This poet's identity is still unknown, as is that of the councillors who devised – according to what procedures? – the fresco's political programme. *Ambrosius Laurentii de Senis*: a single proper name, demonstrating the trust and esteem the political regime of the Nine granted to its artists, but also doubtless designating a collective identity, basically in line with communal ideology. If we wish, like Quentin Skinner, to draw the portrait of 'the artist as a political philosopher', and if we wish to do so without committing the usual anachronism of projecting the figures of Vasari's age back onto mediaeval realities, we need to accept that this will be a group portrait – or, more precisely, the portrait of a group and a time, a *situated* collective group.[7] Ambrogio Lorenzetti, a learned painter, certainly had the cultural means to interpret the iconographic programme proposed to him, however elaborately it had been worked up, and to adapt it more or less freely. We cannot say any more about the painter's political judgement – apart from noting that Vasari's remark that he had been employed 'in the government of his Republic' is partly confirmed by the sources, as we know that in 1347 Lorenzetti was elected to the Consiglio dei Paciari (one of the organs of the communal administration) and gave a speech in it on 2 November defending a proposal to reinforce the authority of the Captain of the People. The notary's minutes record the speech by *Magister Ambrosius Laurentii* and merely add that he gave the assembly the benefit of *sua sapientia verba* (*sic*: 'his wise words').[8] A speech in favour of the popular institutions of the city; and a speech that was deemed to be eloquent by the notary who recorded the deliberations that followed – these are tenuous signs, but they point in the same direction.

We cannot use this as evidence for reconstituting how big a role Lorenzetti played in the development (or interpretation) of the iconographical programme for the Sala della Pace: the state of the documentation available is not good enough. As we have seen, this documentation gives information solely about the payments made between the end of February 1338 and the end of May 1339, when he received 55 florins 'as the balance of his wages'. This sum, paid out once the work was completed – and, if necessary, once the conformity of the work to the instructions in the commission had been verified by experts – generally corresponded to the execution of the 'price made': that is, the payment of half the overall price of the work as fixed by contract. In Siena, the agreement was not always notarized; if so, in this case it has not been preserved. On reading the structure of the payments, we can surmise that provision had been made for an overall sum of 110 florins, half payable at the end, and the other in 10-florin advances every two months paid by the financial administration of the Biccherna from the time work began, so as to ensure its smooth running. For this price did not include merely the artist's 'wages': he had to use this sum to pay for pigments, material and perhaps also the wages of several aides and apprentices. The other non-standardized payments recorded (2 florins on 28 July 1338, 6 florins on 18 February 1339 – the latter amount probably marking the work's effective completion) doubtless corresponded to adjustments or regularizations for a labour whose overall cost (113 florins) will barely have exceeded the sum stipulated in the contract.[9]

Labour, building site, contract: on reading the bills of payment of the Biccherna of Siena, we start to gain an idea of Lorenzetti's social identity that is quite different from the sovereign image of the 'artist-gentleman' that Giorgio Vasari, the man who was at home in princely courts and acted as the impresario of Medici pomps, wanted to create of him. In the first half of the fourteenth century, the model of the building site was still the basis for social practices regulating the relations between those commissioning the work and the painter, who was not yet integrated into the official world. For, in this type of contact, 'it is labour for which one is paid, and not for the work of art itself': the latter had no price to speak of, except for the price of the time one had taken to fashion it.[10] Painting his *Maestà* for the cathedral, Duccio was initially paid 16 sous per day, before being paid per figure. The advances paid to Lorenzetti were in florins, the Florentine currency that, thanks to its stability, had become the international standard for commercial trade; this was already a privilege, as the statutes of 1337–9 specified that the commune should generally pay its wages (especially the wages it paid to its mercenaries) in Sienese lire. It has been calculated that Lorenzetti's different public commissions brought him in an annual salary of 280 lire. This was a tidy sum: in comparison, in 1333, a man working on the Palazzo Pubblico received 6 lire per month, and the treasurers of the Biccherna 100 lire per annum. But the total sum of 113 florins (some 357 lire) for the painting of the Sala della Pace can also be compared with other investments: the Nine spent almost as much (329 lire) on the candles for their chapel in 1338 alone, and, the following year, they paid 6,000 florins to Jacopo di Vanni for bringing water to the square of the *campo*.[11]

We still need to understand how Lorenzetti's 'great reputation' (as 'an excellent master in painting') was socially constructed: this was the third branch of the laurel wreath with which Vasari crowned the Sienese painter. The fresco in the Palazzo Pubblico formed the pinnacle of an artistic career that lasted thirty years, from 1319 (the date of the first Madonna to be attested: the *Madonna and Child* of Vico l'Abate, now in the Museo di Arte Sacra in San Casciano Val di Pisa) to his death in 1348. After a few commissions from Florence, this career was, from 1335, exclusively pursued in Siena, and increasingly depended on public commissions.[12] Even if historians probably exaggerate its importance (because it is public sources that predominate in the documents and in the historiography that draws on them), it was public commissions that structured the market of fame. Duccio, Simone Martini, Pietro and Ambrogio Lorenzetti: Vasari's litany of the great names in Sienese painting corresponds to the succession of hegemonic positions on the market of public commissions. It was this which regulated the circulation of artists between the construction sites of the commune, the cathedral, the Ospedale Santa Maria della Scala and, to a lesser degree, the great churches of the Mendicant Orders. It presupposed the organization of painting workshops in which the names of the masters appeared as 'brands' that disguised the collective dimension of artistic labour. Not until the 1330s did there appear a first generation of second-rank painters whose names have been preserved: the brothers Lippo and Andrea Vanni, Niccolò di Ser Sozzo, Bartolomeo Bulgarini, and so on.

If we set aside his prolific production of Madonnas, though this was a decisive factor in the construction of his renown as a learned painter and the development of his subtle art of arranging figures in space, Lorenzetti mainly owes his fame as a 'political' painter to his great narrative cycles painted as frescos. Even here, we need to ensure we are using the words correctly: we are giving the label 'fresco' to the painting with which Lorenzetti decorated the Sala della Pace in the Palazzo Pubblico of Siena, since the common usage of the term now covers every kind of mural painting. But his work here is, technically speaking, not a fresco: Lorenzetti actually painted it *a tempera*: that is, by soaking a dry wall (*a secco*) with an emulsion binder such as egg yolk. Painting *a fresco*, on the other hand, consists in applying pigments 'in the fresh' of the coating before it has time to dry. This technique, which requires more rapid execution, generally ensures a greater degree of stability for the pictorial matter – and this is why, when Lorenzetti's work was repainted in 1492, as it had quickly deteriorated, it was done so *a buon fresco*.[13]

In 1335, Ambrogio and his brother Pietro painted the frescos (now vanished) in Ospedale Santa Maria della Scala. This was a first stage in his gaining a public commission, since the *fabbrica* of the Ospedale Maggiore di Siena had, since 1309, been taken over by the communal administration, following the model of the 'works of the cathedral', which, in communal Italy, were civic building sites integrated into the council management of the authorities. The same could be said of the great church of San Francesco which Ambrogio decorated with his *Storie di santi e martiri francescani* (stories of Franciscan saints and martyrs) in 1336–7. After this date, he occupied the place left vacant by Simone Martini's departure for Avignon, even if his workshop was less economically important. In any case, he could gain more frequent access to the heart of the communal state by taking over responsibility for the iconographic programmes laid down by the civil authorities. According to the chronicler Agnolo di Tura del Grasso, in 1337 he painted frescos of *Storie romane* (Roman stories) on the outer wall of the communal palace, not far from the newly rebuilt prisons.[14] Then came the commission for the Sala della Pace, this time inside the communal palace – a palace which, in some ways, he would never leave until his death in 1348. In 1340, Lorenzetti was given a public commission to decorate the loggia of the palace with a *Madonna in Maestà con le quattro virtù cardinali* (Madonna in majesty with the four cardinal virtues), and in 1345 he painted a map of the world which Ghiberti described as 'a cosmography, depicting the whole of the inhabited world'; this work has since been lost, but it still gives its name to one of the halls of the Palazzo Pubblico. There were Virgins in majesty but also, perhaps, there was a realistic representation of castles and fortified villages in the same Sala del Mappamondo – not to mention Lorenzetti's *biccherne*, painted wooden tablets serving as a cover for the registers of the financial administration: the series of these, produced continuously since 1258, is one of the great Sienese expressions of the relation between art and administration,[15] and Ambrogio had now turned himself into a full member of the tradition of civic art in Siena. And it was also for the Palazzo Pubblico that Brother Francesco de San Galgano, the *camerlengo* (chamberlain) of the administration of the tax department at the Biccherna, commissioned him to paint his 1344 *Annunciation*, now in the Pinacoteca of Siena; the highly subtle perspectival construction of this work, with its single vanishing point, was still being studied and admired in the quattrocento.

Because the exact moment depicted in the *Annunciation* designates the sudden, stupefying irruption of divine infinity into the mortal finitude of Mary's womb, and thus of the incommensurable into the measurable, it is also a place where painters can experiment with the mathematical treatment of space. Daniel Arasse has demonstrated this with brio, while incidentally criticizing the famous hypothesis of Erwin Panofsky, who saw Ambrogio's *Annunciation* as the prototype of modern artificial perspective in which painters arrange all the vanishing traces so that they head towards a single horizon, something which the narrowing of the tiling on the floor away from the spectator makes clearly visible.[16] These days, it is more commonly held that it is in his brother Pietro's work that we find, from the strictly technical point of view, the most promising advances in centralized, unifocal perspectival construction – especially in the *Nativity of the Virgin* (1335–42), which he painted for the San Savino altar in the Duomo of Siena.[17]

Pietro the illiterate, the one who needed others to read out the legends that he was to depict in painting, and not the *doctus pictor* (learned painter) Ambrogio: we will need to bear this in mind when we patiently scrutinize the details in the paintings of the Sala della Pace, trying to reconstitute the political messages they skilfully communicate. For painting is at its most eloquent when it draws on its own methods, and not when it attempts to devise images for a discourse that has been fabricated elsewhere, in the implacable ordering of texts. Hence this detail, noticed by Arasse: take a look at the gold ring hanging from the Virgin's ear. Ever since the Fourth Lateran Council (1215), ear-rings were one of the distinguishing marks imposed on Jewish women in Italian cities. And Mary was definitely Jewish at the time she received the message of the Angel Gabriel: when she went to present her child in the Temple, she was respecting the Law of Moses. With a few brush-strokes, taking from the golden background of his composition just enough to heighten the Virgin's lobe with a luxuriously defamatory sign, Lorenzetti painted the tipping point between Law and Grace.[18] It is in this sense, too, that the 'trusted painter of the Nine' can be described as learned painter, and these two virtues – political fidelity and cultural mastery – converge in the notion of a civic art of which the historiographical tradition has made the fresco known as 'Good Government' an unsurpassable horizon.

The *Annunciation* was Ambrogio Lorenzetti's final painting. With him died, on 6 April 1348, the last survivor of a whole generation of painters and scholars exterminated by the Black Death. In Siena, the plague was so brutal and devastating that it cut a great swathe through the pyramid of the ages, which for a long time thereafter would remain, like a gaping inconsolable absence.[19] In any event, the Black Death drew a definite line under one chapter in artistic history – one that we still admire nowadays, with the particular kind of nostalgia that superb disasters inspire in our modernity. Of Duccio's six sons, three became painters, as were the brothers and brothers-in-law of Simone Martini. It is thought that Pietro Lorenzetti was childless, but we know for certain that his brother Ambrogio had neither disciples nor heirs. No member of his family survived – his testament bequeaths all his belongings to the Confraternity of the Virgin of the city's hospital. This was the final curtain: Siena would never again be the glorious home of avant-garde painting. The avant-garde moved away – to Florence, of course, where the great epic of the Renaissance, as Vasari would label it for us, continued. The poet Mario Luzi imagines the journey of Simone Martini, who, as death was lurking, and wishing to see for one last time the *Maestà* with which he had honoured his homeland, left Avignon to return to Siena. Luzi describes the temptations of Florence: 'She draws him into her skein, / but he is uncertain / whether to brave her labyrinth / or to keep on the bank, without crossing the bridge.'[20] This temptation came from the great metropolis, where the adventure was continuing. Meanwhile, in Siena, over-faithful painters would wear away their talents repeating, in all the routine of their admiration, the glorious themes of their ingenious predecessors, even though by the start of the fourteenth century they had been overtaken by the audacities of Alberti. But how lovely they were still, those themes, so full of sweetness and consolation that it was worth trying to pretend that the line of descent had not been broken.

5

On each side:
allegory, realism, resemblances

Are they the same women whom Lorenzetti painted on each side of the walls? Take this one, leaning out of her window over the shop selling breeches. On the square, people are dancing to the sound of a tambourine; she's sticking her nose out, doubtless curious to see what's happening – nothing more. Her frail presence, plumb with the building's austere grey façade, which cuts exactly through the median axis of the cityscape, adds a vibrant touch of colour, and we say to ourselves: that's all it is, life itself; life as you can peacefully live it in a well-ordered city where everyone is getting on with their own business. The young woman to the left of the venerable personage enthroned on the platform of the north wall might seem to resemble this first woman, with the same straight nose, the same unruffled face, and the same blonde plaits. But the arms of this stately woman are laden with treasure; her figure is surrounded by symbols; she is wearing a crown; and over her head are handsome letters in gold telling us solemnly what she is: *Magnanimitas*. So we think: this woman resembles the first one but she is not of the same kind, for it is not her own life that maintains her in being – she represents an idea that transcends her and outlives her. On the one side, we have yet one more reality effect among many others, added to the noisy swarming scene of urban life; on the other side, an allegory, whose milky-white flesh is nothing other than the incarnation of a great unchanging principle identified once and for all.

Lorenzetti painted *utrinque*, as his signature proudly announces: 'on each side' rather than 'on both sides'. For, in the Sala della Pace, there are three sides: three walls that contrast two different orders of reality, war and peace. And each order is figured in two equally different ways: they give their names to the intangible principles on which that order is founded, and they make visible the concrete situations which that order entails. And this is why, during the relatively recent time (a hundred and fifty years at most) in which we have ceased to try to recognize more or less cryptic allusions to real people everywhere in the fresco, we have spoken of the 'allegories of good and bad government', on the one hand, and the 'painting of their effects', on the other. Let us add one more detail to this range of dichotomies: whether good or bad, these effects are displayed both in the city and in its *contado*, on each side of the walls separating them. We have already said all this, and described the effect of the dissymmetry that parcels these binary oppositions out across three walls. The principles of tyrannical government, its effects on the city at war and on its devastated hinterland can be taken in at a single glance, along the whole west wall, while the allegory of the virtues of good government is organized and displayed on the north wall, and the painting of the peaceful city and its tranquil countryside can be seen on the east wall. Thus the specific word used in Lorenzetti's signature, *utrinque*, can now be understood in a different way: Lorenzetti, the skilful painter, has succeeded in reconciling two figurative orders that are in complete contrast with one another. On the one hand he has painted allegories and, on the other, realistic scenes. And in both cases he has been an innovator.

The use of political allegory comprised the most striking innovation in the pictorial programme of Siena. At the end of the thirteenth century, the celebration of the virtues of communal government still took its models mainly from Scripture: this was true – though we could give many other examples – of the Sala dei Notai in the Palazzo dei Priori in Perugia (1297), where Moses appears as the embodiment of the good ruler, defying Pharaoh.[1] The political effectiveness of an image such as this rested on a cultural competence which art historians still deem, rightly or wrongly, to have been very widespread in mediaeval societies: it consisted in identifying the major figures in religious history by their distinguishing iconographical features. In this particular scenario, the political message was an added extra: it was less a way of borrowing, misappropriating or commandeering a certain sense than of creating a twofold reading. A few discreet clues, or indeed the localization of the image, alert the attentive spectator (that anonymous and docile hero of iconographic analysis) to read it more carefully, asking, for example, what on earth Moses is doing in the communal palazzo. The spectator thus spontaneously adds to the common and unexceptional meaning of the religious image a second, properly political level of reading – a surplus of meaning.[2] There is nothing of this kind in the Palazzo Pubblico in Siena: the most famous part of the composition (the most famous because it is the one most commonly discussed these days) displays feminine allegories, their arms heavily laden with symbolic objects – here, a woman with an hourglass; there, another woman holding her spear – that have an existence neither in real life nor in spiritual life. There is nothing to be recognized here; everything is to be imagined.

This was the nature of political allegory. It established a direct connection between an image and its meaning – a connection that bypassed the codes of identification of the religious image. It was semantically primary but historically secondary. For it presupposed, if it was to be understood, a familiarity with political ideas (especially those in the Aristotelian and Thomist traditions), and an intellectual openness to abstraction that could spread only when it was fostered by a general cultural movement – and Lorenzetti's fresco constituted an essential stage in this process. Nicolai Rubinstein's path-breaking article from 1958 on the 'political ideas' – a misleadingly anodyne expression – at work in Lorenzetti's oeuvre focuses on precisely this point in the argument.[3] The conclusive studies of Maria Monica Donato have also contributed to this line of thought, by tackling in serial form the whole field of political painting in communal and post-communal Italy.[4] These studies clearly show that Florence and Giotto were the inspiration behind the monumental and narrative allegory used by Lorenzetti in Siena. In the 1320s, Giotto painted a fresco on the walls of the palazzo of the Podestà of Florence 'representing [the commune] as sitting in the form of Judge [*in forma di giudice*], sceptre in hand [. . .] accompanying it with four Virtues'.[5] This later reference in Vasari enables us merely to form some idea of that work, now lost, which was also alluded to in two sonnets by Antonio Pucci. These sonnets discuss a composition that drew a contrast between, on the one hand, an image of the commune as *rubata* – that is, stripped and assailed by characters who had come along and torn its clothes (an obvious allusion to the struggles between factions fighting over the allocation of public resources) – and, on the other hand, a depiction of the commune triumphing over the *rubatori* described by Vasari (who noted that the whole scene was designed to 'frighten the people').[6]

The idea of drawing this contrast between two modes of government by using allegory to describe their political properties and their concrete effects was essayed by Giotto in the Scrovegni Chapel in Padua (c. 1305). The monochromatic depictions of *Iustitia* and *Iniustitia* comprised a persuasive prototype for Lorenzetti's fresco.

Justice was shown as a woman wearing a crown, enthroned in a gothic setting, holding in her hands the two pans of the scales, over a peaceful frieze with scenes of people dancing and working the fields. Injustice was seen as masculine, embodied by a man in arms, entrenched in a ruined fortress partly hidden within a dark forest, overlooking scenes of war and desolation.[7] This Giottesque model of 'the ideologization of the commune' spread quickly through Tuscan political art: it is also found in the frescos painted by Taddeo Gaddi for the tribunal of the Mercanzia Vecchia in Florence as well as those in the Audience Chamber of the Palazzo dell'Arte della Lana, where the commune is depicted as having the features of Brutus (drawing upon a Roman allusion that was also very frequently employed in Siena). But the most remarkable use of this allegorical model came when it was hijacked for the propaganda purposes of the signoria, in the Cathedral of Arezzo, as bas-reliefs on the mausoleum of the bishop and lord of Arezzo, Guido Tarlati, sculpted between 1329 and 1332 by Agostino di Giovanni and Agnolo di Ventura, both from Siena. Here we see the figure of an elderly bearded nobleman, enthroned in majesty, embodying the commune. But while a first panel, with the title *Il comune pelato* (the commune stripped), shows him stripped of his finery by an angry mob, the second depicts him restored to his dignity and his authority, acknowledged by loyal supporters and prisoners kneeling before the *comune in signoria* (the commune as lord).[8] Thus, the Giottesque model can support a discourse legitimizing the way that the commune has been placed under the lord's supervision. This is considered to be, not a betrayal, but on the contrary an implementation and guarantee of its political virtues – a highly significant fact to which we will need to return. At all events, it demonstrates the fundamentally reversible character of all political allegory.

It is a 'well-established prejudice' for our modern age that 'any work of importance must be a beginning, if not an origin', as Hubert Damisch rightly points out.[9] These days, we are surrounded by political allegories whose meaning has stabilized, and that are easy to use: for example, the figure of Marianne, representing the French Republic on postage stamps, can be immediately recognized by anyone. Her profile may vary with successive stylizations, and given a new and updated look, but she is always the same woman, she 'looks like' someone or something (even if we are not quite sure who, or what); she can be recognized without hesitation from a few distinguishing features that are quite difficult to enumerate, but that are sufficiently familiar to us that we can employ them, unconsciously, as criteria of identity. There is nothing of this kind in the Palazzo Pubblico of Siena:

here, the allegorical identification is invented in real time, and life-size – thus, any identities we may seek cannot be immediate and certain, but are tremulous, wavering and hesitant. Are we right to assign the same inaugural character to the way Lorenzetti uses realistic figuration, and to marvel at the way he 'photographs' the city of his time, as it *really* was? 'Realism', of course, is one of the trickiest words in art history, fraught with many ambiguities – as is the term 'naturalism'. The issue here is nothing other than the illusionism of the mimetic image that increases its legibility – and it is important to note that its origins also lay in the Giottesque revolution with its narrativizing of images, something Lorenzetti attempted, with dazzling success, in the nave of the upper church in the basilica of Saint Francis of Assisi.[10] Once we consider the illusionism of mimetic resemblance as one symbolic code among others, it contrasts with and is linked to allegory as another, complementary form of pictorial persuasion – rather in the same way that portraits and coats of arms were closely related at the end of the Middle Ages, displaying as if in a mirror 'the natural face and the heraldic face' of one and the same subject.[11]

For, at that time, even though artists demonstrated what Jean Wirth cautiously calls 'a sustained interest in the accidental aspect of the visible',[12] the mimetic illusion of resemblance could never, in itself, be the subject of the painting. Of course, the ambivalence of modernity would always have us think otherwise, lulling us into acceptance of the soothing artifice of an immediate contemporaneity, showing us, in Lorenzetti, our own hesitant emotions in the face of the world's sonorous certainty. How can we escape this when we see those great walls with their interweaving of countless little stories, obliging our eyes to rest at times on a few mute details – the curve of a tile, the interpolation of a cypress, the dark commas of the vines – that seem to proclaim nothing other than a staunch endorsement of the sheer objectivity of things? In the Pinacoteca of Siena, there are two small tablets, one representing a city by the sea (identified by some as the port of Talamone), and the other showing a castle on a lake. They were long attributed to Lorenzetti, and might date from 1338–9, in which case they would be contemporary with the fresco in the Palazzo Pubblico. They contain no human figures, tell no story – they seem to be nothing more than an invitation to day-dream, maybe in the small, delicately rimmed boat resembling two closed lips. J.-B. Pontalis finds this boat alluring: 'Every time a woman attracts him, he sees in his mind's eye Lorenzetti's little boat. It is empty; he will be the only passenger in it.'[13] The art historian Enzo Carli preferred to see it as the first European example of a 'pure landscape'.[14] But this interpretation has been disputed, as have the dating and the attribution to the painter of the Nine: a painstaking study of the wooden fibres on the edges of the tablets apparently reveals that they have been broken off in modern times, and what seems to be a newly autonomous land-scape, without any other subject, might just be the effect of a much later cutting, making it the 'detail' of another, lost work of art.[15]

So what are we doing when we hunt down traces of the real in the portrait of the city supposedly painted 'after nature' by Lorenzetti if not 'detailing' its representation? The risk then is that we will dismember its meaning just as surely as did art lovers who in bygone days heedlessly cut up paintings so as to detach the fragments that they felt were really worthy of interest. So the most effective way of proceeding is to try to relate what we take to be 'realistic' representations to historically attested practices. Let us have another look at the example of the castles and fortified towns. Several of these, all different, can be discerned on the east wall, polarizing the well-ordered territory of the peaceful countryside; and it is tempting to recognize behind each of these highly individualized silhouettes the real places of the strategic constitution of Sienese space: we know that this was, after all, the main issue of the 1330s. Now, the Nine wished this territorial policy to be accompanied by a systematic endeavour to grasp the area figuratively, so they commissioned from their painters what the historian Uta Feldges has very aptly called 'topographic portraits'.[16] The commune sent the painters out to survey the very places of the *terra* that had been acquired or conquered, so that they could draw them after nature. Thus, we still have the receipts of the payment made to Simone Martini to paint the castles of Montemassi and Sassoforte (May 1330), then Arcidosso and Castel del Piano (December 1331), all of them situated in the commune's zone of territorial expansion, towards Maremma and Mount Amiata.[17]

So in this case it was a sort of professional obligation on the painter to produce a figurative image after nature; this is what he was paid for by the commune, and 'realism' here needs to be connected with a precise political use of the painted image. This use was first documented in 1314, even if the deliberation attesting to it already set it within a certain tradition: 'The *castello* [of Giuncarico] is to be painted in the palace of the commune of Siena, where the council is gathered, and where are painted the other *castelli* acquired by the commune of Siena, and this painting is never to be removed, scratched or injured.'[18] This deliberation by the great council of the commune of Siena dates from 30 March 1314; the surrender of the castle that it seeks to incorporate into an eternal memory was finalized on the

day before. It is clear that this painting was not just a representation, and went beyond the function usually ascribed to it (such as to
exalt, legitimate or communicate something). It was indeed part of an
'administrative structure', namely the registering of documents and
the creation of a memory for the commune. The representation after
nature of the castle of Giuncarico entered into the communal palace,
that store of accumulated images and memories, just as its name was
written in the registers of the commune that formed its documentary
space – and just as it was made physically part of the territory of the
state of Siena.

The representation entered the communal palace once and for all
– at least in theory. But the history of the commune's territorial expansion is a faltering and uneven one, and what the 1314 deliberations
present as a definitive and immutable inscription was very soon erased
by time. The same applied to the defamatory paintings: these only
rarely survived an immediate context of production that exhausted
their meaning and relegated it to the past. Of all those 'castles painted
in the palace', the only one to have come down to us intact is that
in the upper part of the west wall of the Hall of the Great Council
(known as the map hall or Sala del Mappamondo), where, in the
background of the very famous equestrian figure of Guidoriccio da
Fogliano, some people claim to recognize the castle of Montemassi, in
Maremma, captured by the Sienese on 28 August 1328. But what is
depicted here is less a 'topographical portrait' than the picture story
of a city being besieged, and the narrative aspect of this scene makes
it unsuited to the strictly documentary use that seems to have presided
over the figurative policies of the Nine.[19] The same may be true of the
mysterious tablets that were attributed to Lorenzetti, and the way
he depicted castles and fortified towns on the fresco in the Sala della
Pace may also be interpreted as a discreet but indirect allusion to this
practice, one in which the older artist, his master Simone Martini,
had distinguished himself. Yet again, the Sala della Pace appears as
the echo chamber of the Sala del Mappamondo, just as the magistracy of the Nine (who sat in the Sala della Pace) was nothing but
the political emanation of the great council (which sat in the Sala
del Mappamondo). Here, in sovereign splendour, is enthroned the
Maestà, and here we doubtless find the assembled topographical portraits of the castles conquered; and this authorizes Lorenzetti to paint
utrinque, in political allegories and figurative 'realism'.

On each side: there we are again – in fact, there is no escaping it.
When the modern spectator distinguishes between what seems allegorical and what seems realist, he or she is drawing on a hermeneutic

category that imposes on the image a cut-and-dried straitjacket that limits the way it can be interpreted. So historians of political ideas will be invited to decipher the allegories on the north wall in the same way that we raise our eyes to the heaven of abstraction, while specialists in social history will be asked to scrutinize the depiction of works and days, down on the ground level of a daily life whose savour it is their task to resurrect. The former will explain the figures by texts, the latter by facts – and in both cases they will prevent the images from exercising their full power, convinced as they are that the true meaning of these images lies outside themselves. Thus the apparent duplicity of the work reinforces a 'disciplinary dichotomy' which in the final analysis considerably reduces its scope, since the political meaning of the latter resides solely in a visible, tangible and effective circulation between the principles of government and its effects.[20]

How are we to overcome this division between the different roles? First, no doubt, by noting that mimetic illusion and allegory are not necessarily separated so strictly on the walls of the Sala della Pace. What is happening at the feet of the woman with pellucid skin (she has been seen as the embodiment of magnanimity) seated on the platform of virtues? Look, and you will see, separated from her by soldiers in arms, wearing helmets and brandishing their spears, two knights in armour, kneeling under the throne of the great personage, and offering her a miniature castle as a sign of homage. This scene is the secularized counterpart to the traditional scene of a church dedication in which a prince offers the saint enthroned in majesty a model of the church he is dedicating to him; it forcefully points to the sacred dimension of this act of political submission. This was the territorial submission of the feudal subjects of the Sienese state to the sovereign rule of the city – and in this case the castle echoes the 'topographical portraits' of the *castelli* in the Sala del Mappamondo. But it is also, more ideologically, the political submission of the *milites* (soldiers) bearing various social values (courtly culture, connoted here by the demeanour of the figures, the style of their hair, their neat beards, and so on) and laying their offering at the feet of the commune, the force of law and the Common Good. This offering is a tower (basically, the building may also represent one of those towers belonging to the nobility with which Italian cities still bristled) – a symbol of their power over the city. Just behind them, the condemned men, tied with a rope, one of them sentenced to death (his eyes are bound by a black cloth), are led in triumph to the centre of the fresco by men in arms. The latter form two distinct groups: first, the communal militia proper, brandishing spears and shields in the air (their shields bear the lion rampant, the emblem of the *popolo*); and second, behind them, in the background, the men of the *contado* recruited by the Nine in 1302 to maintain the peace. What the image suggests is the complex relations of alliance and domination between the city and the *contado*, the split between the militia and the *popolo* in political society, the social and cultural antagonism whose conflicts are mediated by the law, and the division between legitimate force and untamed violence. We could suggest many additional historical interpretations for this scene alone; it is clearly more than the allegorical representation of political abstractions, but also shows the concrete conditions of the exercise of power.

If allegory is not an escape from reality, the opposite is also true: the apparently 'realistic' representation of the effects of good government comes with a powerful allegorical element. We can perceive this only if we manage to extricate ourselves from the traps for our vision laid (like a hunter's snares) by Lorenzetti in many parts of his fresco – traps that are the effects of the real. And since we have just been reconsidering the allegory of *Magnanimitas*, which is not so ethereal as might be imagined, let us also take a fresh look at the young woman filled with curiosity who rather resembles her as she leans out of her window. She has been called a splash of colour intended to bring out the rhythm of the rather severe bays that divide up the sombre façades of the palaces. And indeed, almost every opening gives us a glimpse of some incongruous detail that produces diversity or dissymmetry, reminding us that architecture is simply a welcoming envelope for the human propensity to occupy places. To the young girl's right, a pot plant sits on the window-sill. Further on, there is a bird in a hanging cage. Are these maybe an allusion to some malicious little anecdotes about the young girl, shut in and watching the bride trotting away, crowned and perched on a handsome white horse? There is no *titulus* here: the bride is a bride, in all her singularity, and not the embodiment of some general idea. But are we sure that this wedding procession is there just to tell a story – that it may not yield some allegorical reading?

It is clear that the relationship between Lorenzetti's fresco and the real – that is, the space represented and the time narrated – is not in the least mimetic. In other words, the great walls of the Sala dei Nove present us with visions of the city (*visioni*) rather than a view out over the city (*veduta*). This can easily be confirmed by two simple but telling details. In the urban panorama spread out across the east wall of the Sala della Pace, the two most clearly identifiable architectural elements are the silhouette of the Duomo undergoing rebuilding and its campanile at the far left of the composition, and the Porta Romana topped by the sculptural group of the she-wolf suckling the Sienese twins on the far right. But, as specialists have often noted, these two buildings are not *entirely* alike: significant differences, which would obviously not have escaped the eyes of the Sienese of that time, have slipped between the urban signified and the pictorial signifier. In the case of the campanile, the bays are not consistent with the building as it could be seen in 1338; the same is true of the city gate, which in Lorenzetti's fresco comes with an opening whose arch resembles nothing that was known to exist in Siena in the fourteenth century.

This distortion in the order of representation is a huge problem for art historians who would like to see the Sala della Pace paintings as a realistic portrait of the city of Siena observed from the top of the Torre del Mangia. Recent investigations, to which we will need to return in more detail, also suggest that Lorenzetti composed his urban panorama in an incredibly complex manner, combining at least six distinct points of view onto the real city of Siena, producing an artificial and discordant landscape that undermines any 'natural' vision of the city.[21] In addition, Max Seidel has drawn a persuasive comparison between the architectural elements painted by Lorenzetti and various archaeological data: clearly, the painter included several direct allusions to the structure of his city's buildings – especially the system of openings, windows, bays and porches, but also balconies, awnings and porticoes, always depicted very accurately and *in detail*.[22] However, this accuracy is lacking in the gate and the campanile – the two monuments that protected the city. So we cannot explain this oddity as the result of some clumsiness, or as some nebulous 'artistic licence': it is evident that, when he wanted to, Lorenzetti was perfectly able to compose a 'topographical portrait' from nature. But this is something he did not want to do in the Sala della Pace, where he combines effects of the real with dissimilarities from the city's most celebrated emblems. Hence Hans Belting's crucial suggestion that the painter was here developing a twofold language, or at least a two-stage discourse: his work 'was intended first to describe an ideal city and then to make sure that this ideal city was the city of Siena'.[23] The city was not intended to be immediately recognizable, even if this meant diluting a moral and political message that was not limited to a local context but aimed to be continuously reaffirmed, so as to gain a universal value. Between the ideal city and Siena, then, the relationship established was one not of identification but of comparison: the effects of good government contributed to building the ideal city, and the city of Siena, as it was really, here and now, could be seen *as like* this ideal city.

This function of the accurate detail combined with a certain difference in narration fully justifies our use of the literary category of 'the reality effect', whose meaning depends entirely on the kind of description at work.[24] From this point of view, Lorenzetti was much closer to the rhetoric of comparison developed by Petrarch than to the imitation of the painters; indeed, it was in contrasting his own activity with mimesis that the poet defines what an effect of resemblance might be for him, in a passage from his *Familiar Letters*:

> [T]he similarity should not be like that of a portrait to the man it is portraying, for in this case the more similar it is to its model the more the artist is praised [. . .], but like that of a son to a father. In this case, even though there may often be a great dissimilarity of individual features, yet there is a sort of shadow, what painters now call *aria*, which one specially sees in face and eyes, and this causes a similarity that reminds us of the father as soon as we see the son, even though every feature may be different if we resort to measuring; something hidden there has this effect [. . .]. So too we writers should see that, though something may be similar to the model, yet many things should be dissimilar.[25]

6

Esto visibile parlare:
the walls speak to us

A shadowy, passing resemblance, some mysterious *je-ne-sais-quoi*. It is like the son's face, which reminds us of his father's. This is how Petrarch describes poetic mimesis, which does not claim to reproduce nature but creates an intelligible reality in which, for one similarity, there are many dissimilarities. Before Petrarch, Dante had confronted the shades.[1] He travelled with them into the afterlife. He realized that, like the image, the shade is an imitation of the body: its trace reminds us that a body was once there, and the shade is, as it were, the signature of a solid body. But shades cast no shadow, and the souls that Dante meets in the *Purgatorio* are amazed to see his solidity: 'Tell us: how do you make yourself a wall / to shield the sun, as if you had not yet / entered within the trammels of death's net?'[2] That is why the poet wants to be a painter of shade, imitating the 'similar bodies' or 'bodies fit for that' (*simili corpi*) that God alone can fashion when he produces images. One example is the Angel of the Annunciation, on the cornice of Mount Purgatory, 'carved in a gesture of pure gentleness, / he did not seem an image keeping silence. In truth, one might have said he spoke the "*Ave*".' The walls speak to us. And who but the Everlasting can produce this 'discourse visible' (*visibile parlare*)? 'The one who sees no thing that's new to Him / produced this form of discourse visible – / so new to us, so fresh since not found here.'[3]

If we make painting into a visible language, then, we are claiming the poetic power that belongs to God alone. But here lies the paradox: there is not a single cleric to be seen in the well-governed city painted by Ambrogio Lorenzetti. True, we can recognize the cathedral, but it is more of a 'dissimilar' detail, quite off-centre. It is placed some way from the middle of the happy city, hidden away in the corner of the east wall. The city at peace seems to be empty of God – and this flies in the face of all verisimilitude, especially if we are expecting to find the 'realistic' representation of a mediaeval city here. But its painted image is saturated with words. Various *tituli* label the allegories, inscriptions run along the walls, and escutcheons are placed there to describe the story as it unfolds, while scrolls in the sky set forth edifying lines of poetry exhorting us to provide the correct interpretation of the lesson we are being given. Everywhere there are painted letters, singing and encouraging us, commenting and leading us. They summon us, they guide us, they instruct us to 'Turn your eyes' and 'Look'. Writing has invaded the painting and imposed its reign on it: the reign of the readability of a *visibile parlare*.[4]

This visible language is 'new to us, so fresh since not found here'. So where *does* it come from? In the Palazzo Pubblico of Siena, we can give a simple answer to this question: the writing comes from the room next door, from the vast Sala del Mappamondo to which the Sala della Pace in some ways acts as a mere echo chamber. Here, in all her sovereign majesty, is enthroned the great Virgin painted in 1315 by Simone Martini, and in her gentle and stern presence she dictates whatever effect may be produced by the masculine, secular counterpart to her depicted by Lorenzetti in the features of the venerable old man. The *Maestà* is the 'sovereign, patron and advocate' of the commune, and every aspect of her speaks of the transfer of the sacred word into the political space of the government of men.[5] As noted above, ever since its victory over the Florentines at the Battle of Montaperti in 1260, Siena had prided itself on being the *civitas Virginis*, the city protected by the Virgin Mary. The representation of her in majesty was a major theme in Sienese painting. A payment made on 12 August 1289 to a painter by the name of Mino tells us that there was already one fresco of this type in the Hall of the Great Council.[6] However, Simone Martini's masterpiece points back to a more recent and more illustrious precedent: he takes up the iconographical theme developed by his master Duccio in the 'Virgin in Majesty' (*Maestà*) that the government of the Nine had commissioned from him in 1308 for the high altar of the cathedral. What was the *Maestà*? Less an image associated with worship than the 'a gift which the town offered in order to ask the Madonna for protection'.[7] This is why the commune had turned the ceremony of carrying the huge retable from the artist's workshop to the Duomo into a civic ritual: this was on 9 June 1311, and the archives of Siena noted even the payments made for the 'trumpets, chalumeau (pipe) and castanets' that set the tempo for the steps of the population that, according to the chronicle of Agnolo di Tura del Grasso, thronged there to accompany the protective image of the triumphant Virgin.[8] Four years later, in 1315, this wave of civic and religious fervour extended its political scope even further: the *Maestà* commissioned by the Nine from Simone Martini to decorate the Hall of the Great Council took direct possession of the Palazzo Pubblico.

This political take-over was all the more spectacular since we know that the Nine were at the very same time ordering Martini to extend the decoration of the palace halls, adding secular images such as the figurative representation of the castles seized in the local territory. This is the context in which we need to read the two stanzas that run under the steps on which the heavenly court surrounding the Virgin in Majesty is assembled. These stanzas comprise the earliest known example in European art of a 'poetry in painting' written in the vernacular. It is the Virgin who speaks, accepting the offering of the 'angelical little flowers, roses and lilies, / with which the heavenly meadow is adorned'. However, not everybody turns out to be worthy of this identification between the city that she protects and the paradise that she promises: 'But I sometimes see that certain people, proud of their status, / despise me and abuse my city.' These enemies are not invisible: there they are, among us, easily discernible: 'Let everyone turns his gaze to those whom my words condemn.' As she lambasts the wicked, the Virgin exhorts the citizens to defend the commune's virtues against them: 'But if the powerful should molest the weak, / crushing them with their contempt or their violence, / your prayers are not for them / nor for those who abuse my city.'[9]

From the metrical point of view, these Dantesque tercets are inspired by the cantos of the *Divine Comedy* and show how quickly Dante's work had started to become known throughout Tuscany, even though the *Paradiso* had not yet been published and would be so only in 1322. The historian Furio Brugnolo suggests that these words in the painting were written by the lawyer and poet Cino da Pistoia, who was a friend of Dante's in Florence and then came to teach in the university at Siena: Cino's political and poetic activities demonstrate the 'cross-breeding between different kinds of knowledge' characteristic of his generation.[10] It is also more than likely that these inscriptions date not from 1315 but from 1321, the year in which Simone Martini himself embarked on the restoration of his fresco. The political climate had become more tense, so it may have been deemed necessary to boost the work's moral and political impact, making the warning to the powerful more explicit. Is it the same vigorous exhortation that resounds in the Sala della Pace painted by Lorenzetti? There is one evident clue that allows us to gauge its echo. On the knees of the Virgin in Majesty painted by Simone Martini, the infant Jesus holds a scroll in his left hand. On it is written the first verse of the *Wisdom of Solomon*: *Diligite iustitiam qui iudicatis terram* ('Love justice, you who judge the earth').[11]

The very same verse is found in the Sala della Pace, in a halo of golden letters around the great allegory of Justice to the left of the composition on the north wall. As for one of the most famous verses in the 'song' that runs along halfway up the wall depicting the effects of good government, it can be interpreted as a poetic variant, in the vernacular, of those biblical words: *Volgiete gli occhi a rimirar costei, vo' che reggiete che qui figurata* ('Turn your eyes to gaze, / you who rule, on the woman who is depicted here' – words that are based on the beginning of one of Dante's sonnets (*Rime*, LIX): *Volgete li occhi a veder chi mi tira* ('Turn your eyes to see who is drawing me along').[12] They are echoed in turn by the imperative phrasing of the lines of verse that instruct magistrates to gaze admiringly on the Roman heroes painted in 1414 by Taddeo di Bartolo in the adjacent hall of the Anticappella: *Specchiatevi in costor voi che reggete / Se volete a regniare mille e mille anni / Seguite il ben comune et non v'inganni* ('Reflect on their examples, you who rule, / if you wish to reign for thousands and thousands of years / follow the common good, without fraud').[13]

The effect of this quotation, echoed from one hall to the next, is clearly decisive. The civic injunction can be heard as the translation of a religious admonition into the political sphere. We should probably not exaggerate the degree of novelty involved here: the use of the first verse of the *Wisdom of Solomon* to alert the powerful to the fact that they need to love justice was a commonplace in the political discourse of communal Italy.[14] Its trace can be followed in the political literature of the *ars dictaminis*, which, as I shall be showing in more detail later, offers rhetorical models for the use of the professionals of persuasion, namely the magistrates of the Italian communes (one example is Giovanni da Viterbo, another the *Oculus pastoralis*), and also of the preachers (from Pietro Cantore's *Sermon to the Judges* to the sermons of the Dominican Remigio de' Girolami in Florence in 1295). In all these cases, the mandatory *thema* expressed 'a sacred legitimation of juridical *potestas* and, at the same time, the promise of a government of peace and concord'.[15] Much more audaciously innovative, on the other hand, was the effect of the translation as such: the biblical verse brandished by the Virgin in Majesty in the Sala del Mappamondo illumines the allegory of Justice on the north wall of the Sala della Pace, but it is still written in Latin. In the inscription exalting 'the benefits that stem from it' (i.e. Justice), however, it is boldly transformed into Tuscan: by being set out in the vernacular, it is politicized.

It was indeed at just this time that *volgarizzamento* – translation into the vernacular – was being adopted as an innovative political move, one that was fully backed by the government of the Nine. In 1309–10, they commissioned the notary Ranieri di Ghezzo Gangalandi to translate the city statutes.[16] What does their preamble state? 'That the said statute is to be left on the Biccherna and stay affixed to it, so that the poor and others who are ignorant of Latin and all who wish may consult it and copy it if they so desire.' And, further down, rubric 134 of the same statute notes that it must be written 'in the vernacular, in large clear letters, well-shaped and legible, on good parchment'.[17] One could hardly wish for a clearer expression of the political and indeed specifically republican ideal that exalts the legibility of the norm and openly displays it to society. The new statutes of 1337, which would remain in force until the middle of the sixteenth century, were also translated into the vernacular by the notary Ser Mino di Feo, just as Lorenzetti was painting his fresco in the communal palace. Bram Kempers suggests a little simplistically that the fresco is a translation of the city's statutes into a suggestive pictorial form.[18] This may be true, but in any case it is worth remembering that the paintings in the Sala della Pace are part of a cultural context marked by the need, widespread among the communes in the period of the *regimi di popolo* (popular regimes), to broadcast a politically self-justifying message to the greatest number of people. The paintings here were probably restating in their own way one of the ambitions of Christian pastoral teaching: ten years later, in the Palace of the Popes in Avignon, the cycles of painting coordinated by Matteo Giovannetti, an artist who had certainly been connected to the Lorenzetti brothers, show a similar effort to create *propaganda* in the sense of propagating a political belief.[19] According to the *Vita* of Pope Clement VI, he wanted there to be written, 'under each of these images or figures [. . .] their words or their writings upon the above-mentioned things or others of the same kind, in large legible letters'.[20]

Legibility: that is the keyword. By intruding into the painting, the *visibile parlare* imposes the hermeneutics proper to scripturality, which had hitherto lain outside the figurative order. Between the *titulus* and the allegory there is an organic bond: the former serves to explain the latter, following a rhetoric of designation and unveiling whose subtler typography can be described.[21] The painted letters break free from their scrolls and spread out right across the three walls of the fresco in a 'politically committed song' of sixty-two lines of verse, entailing an overall interpretation of the pictorial composition: as a result, our perception of the image is modified, suggesting that a painting can be read in the same way that a text is interpreted. But this metaphor, in which images are 'read', creates as many problems as it solves, since it over-extends the notion of textuality to the figurative order. The latter may indeed stimulate and arouse discourse, but it is forever eluding the apparently omnipotent sway of this same discourse.[22] One of the most acute points made in Louis Marin's semiotic studies was the trenchant way in which he resolved this ambiguity. We cannot deduce the 'precise readability' from the immediate and sovereign visibility of so-called representational works of art, since while the text calls out for a 'knowing and knowledgeable gaze', the image is content with a 'respectful and admiring gaze'. 'Yet the two gazes have different and perhaps even contrary conditions and intentions.'[23]

In Lorenzetti's work, the words are in the painting. They are there so that the painting can speak to everyone, in a direct and accessible way, head-on. This fact needs to be considered in itself, in its raw dimension as a political commitment. But how are we actually to interpret these painted writings? It would clearly be absurd just to ignore them. And yet this is exactly what many historians of political ideas do; they are always ready to reduce the meaning of images to the texts which they tamely illustrate, and yet these same historians prefer to exhume the writings that they suppose are the work's 'sources' (obscure or unrecognized, if possible) rather than to read the writings that the work exhibits directly, the *visibile parlare* that is there right under their noses. Even Quentin Skinner, in his impressive political reading of Lorenzetti's painting, probably did not make the most of these texts: he basically focused on analysing a single line of verse that he deemed to be crucial (*un ben commun per lor signor si fanno*), concentrating on the meaning of a single word (*per*) and producing a philological reading of it that left the specialists unconvinced.[24] He thereby underestimated the overall meaning of the great principles of semantic opposition that a structural analysis of the painted writings would suggest. All the same, no one should think that such an analysis will itself provide us with the key to the enigma. This would be to fall prey to the opposite error. For the 'political song' declaimed in several places of the fresco does not account for the subtle and discreet polyphony hummed by the images. It sets the tone, no doubt, with which each individual voice needs to harmonize. But it does not in the least collapse the uncertainty inherent in the images, but merely guides the gaze that takes them all in, helping it along with a few lines of meaning stable enough to sustain one's understanding but still aquiver with the tremulous ambiguity proper to poetic utterance.

So it is the poetic that we need to discuss: the poetic as a set of places, rhythms and voices. Places: let us begin by localizing the points at which painted writings are inscribed within Sienese painting. To begin with there are the *tituli*, naming the allegories and giving them a cut-and-dried meaning. Hence the procession of solemn abstractions, the imposing train of Latin words which, with their golden letters, forge a clear explanatory link in which image and word are equated: *Pax, Fortitudo, Prudentia, Magnanimitas, Temperantia, Iustitia*, and so on. Its negative reflection is found on the west wall, where the insolent, perverse counter-values of tyranny are enthroned: *Avaritia, Superbia, Vanagloria*, and so on. The latter also float in golden letters on the deep and uncertain blue of the heaven of ideas, while others are inscribed more tenaciously in the space of representation: engraved at the top of the crenelated wall of the citadel of tyranny, they label those evil councillors, *Crudelitas, Proditio, Fraus, Furor* and *Divisio*, or on the platform of the tyrannical monster they designate the *Iustitia* which that monster is violating – and the last letter of the word is hidden by the sorrowing face of its allegory, in an illusionistic effect that dramatizes the mutilation involved. Perhaps not enough attention has been paid to the subtle interplay of decentring and conceal-ment with which the painted letters highlight the flatness of the space of representation or emancipate themselves from it. *Concordia* is thus the only *titulus* on the north wall whose brilliance and height do not outshine the figures to whom it refers to. Engraved on the wood of the plane which the allegory is holding firmly on its knees, it is as if the word had just landed in the world of men and women.

Perhaps, too, it has lost not only the gold of its letters but also the severe solemnity of Latin – we cannot, after all, be certain that *Concordia* is Latin rather than Italian. The *visibile parlare* of Lorenzetti's fresco takes full advantage of the diglossia proper to mediaeval culture: the *tituli* are set out in Latin, the language of sacred authority in which the verse from the *Wisdom of Solomon* is written: *Diligite iustitiam qui iudicatis terram* ('Love justice, you who judge the earth'). Elsewhere, the learned vernacular of Italian poetry is always deployed. Only the artist's signature, as we have seen, escapes this linguistic division – and this merely reinforces the bold self-assurance of his proper name. The contrast this creates is all the more striking as the signature is displayed in a strategic spot in the fresco, the broad white ribbon that on three sides underlines the lower level of the painted scenes, separating them from the decorative frieze beneath, where the medals are set. More precisely, the signature interrupts the long inscription running almost the full length of the west and east walls,[25] so that anyone who wants to take them in all at once has to sweep across all of the figures depicted. Indeed, this is what the poem explicitly instructs us to do, in the imperative mode: 'Turn your eyes to gaze, / you who rule, on the woman who is depicted here' (A2).

This sliding, panoramic mode of reading contrasts with the more staccato way in which the escutcheons which confront each other two by two force one's gaze to amble along from one allegory to the next. The first two escutcheons concern the allegories of the principles of good and bad government, thus contrasting the left side of the north wall (A1) with the right side of the west wall (B1). The first escutcheon, positioned between the two medallions that allegorize grammar and dialectic below the procession of the twenty-four councillors roped together, takes seven lines to hymn the civic benefits of Justice, 'this sacred virtue' (A1). The second, to the right of a bust depicting Nero's suicide, also refers to the figure of a Justice in shackles above it: 'Wherever justice is bound in chains, / nobody can ever be in harmony with the common good' (B1). Symmetries in sound and echoes of meaning here reinforce the visual correspondences. They foster a balanced reading of a work of art that is perceived in the violence of the antitheses which Bernardino of Siena used as his main tool for persuasion. This is also the case with the striking contrast between the two figures of which the preacher reminded his audience in 1425: *Timor* (on the left of the west wall) and *Securitas* (in the centre of the east wall), both holding a scroll in the shape of an unrolled parchment waving in the wind which, in five lines, describes the social effects of fear (B3) and the victory over fear (A3).

These are the different places in which the *visibile parlare* is located in the painting. They are echoed in the metrical contrasts minutely described by Furio Brugnolo. The first part of the two inscriptions running under the eastern wall (A2) and the western wall (B2) is composed of two quatrains of hendecasyllables (lines of eleven feet each characteristic of the Italian poetry of the trecento, with the tonic stress falling on the tenth syllable) set out in an ABBC rhyming pattern, with the third stanza having two shorter feet (heptasyllables, i.e. seven feet), following the pattern cDdEE. In spite of the gaps in the inscription running under the 'bad' side, it is easy to surmise the wealth of phonetic echoes (e.g. in the fifth line *da lei / di lei*) which turn the lines of verse into alternating replies. This is also true of the two scrolls of *Timor* and *Securitas* built on the metrical pattern ABbCC with five-line stanzas (*pentastico*) characteristic of painting showing evil figures.

So *senza paura* (A3, line 1) corresponds to *senza dubbio di morte* (B3, line 4) – for if the inhabitants of the city at peace can make their way 'without fear', in the city in thrall to tyranny 'no one passes without fearing death'. As for the poetic construction of the two escutcheons on justice (A1 and B1), it seems even more refined: it consists of two stanzas ABbC, and ends with a third that halts on a line of seven feet (*settenario*) following the pattern CDdEE. According to the specialists, this is one of the first examples of imitation of Dante's well-known song on the *Petrosa* (*Così nel mio parlar voglio esser aspro*).[26] Its asymmetrical stanza structure creates a subtle set of correspondences right from the first line: *Questa santa virtù, <u>la dove</u> regge* (A1) / <u>*Là dove*</u> *sta legata la iustitia* (B1). Then, in line 5, *lo qual, per governor* (A1) / *la qual per adempir* (B1), and in lines 9 and 11, *per questo[...] per questo* (A1) / *questa [...] questa* (B1). But the rhymes and assonances serve merely to contrast, two by two, the inscriptions painted *utrinque*, 'on each side', of Lorenzetti's work; it also means they can be linked up in a complex network of meanings that cannot be entirely reduced to the interplay of symmetrical contrasts. Thus the *la dove regge* (A1, line 1) of the escutcheon on the principles of good government refers to the *vo'che reggiete* of the inscription describing its effects (A2, line 2), just as *gli occhi rivolti* (A1, line 6) refers to *Volgiete gli occhi* (A2, line 1).[27]

We could make the process as complex as we wish. First, we might note that certain palaeographic nuances (perceptible if not altogether obvious) have led to the suggestion that the work was composed in two phases. Second, we could point to the fact that the recent restorations have found letters repainted and superimposed: here again, this could indicate certain reworkings later than 1338 – this is undeniable, as we shall see, in the case of the problematic *titulus* around the head of the venerable personage on the north wall in which we now read *C.S.C.C.V.* Modifying the painted inscriptions of a work of art is one of the simplest and most immediate ways of giving it a real political scope – as was already probably the case for Simone Martini's *Maestà*. The first re-transcription of the painted writings in the Sala della Pace in the Palazzo Pubblico of Siena goes back to the second half of the fifteenth century: this is a manuscript now held in the Biblioteca Marciana in Venice. Its text does not give the two scrolls of *Timor* and *Securitas*, while it does mention two stanzas that are not now visible.[28] There is still some uncertainty here, but not enough to paralyse all analysis: the painted work that we can investigate today is nothing but a vestige from the past – an object that time has handed down while wearing it away, transforming it and reinventing it. A palimpsest, no doubt – how could it be otherwise?

As the reader will have realized, the fact remains that the walls speak to us, even as their voices fade. While I needed here to evoke the places, the metrical patterns and the voices of painted poetry, what are we to say of the elusive author? While the painter's name is exhibited in an imposing manner, that of the poet who composed the sixty-two lines accompanying it has vanished for ever. One thing is almost certain: it cannot have been Lorenzetti himself, but must have been an able versifier, a fine connoisseur of Dante's poetic innovations. Based on some philologically rather fragile comparisons, these lines were long attributed to Cecco di Meo degli Ugurgieri, who wrote a commentary on Dante's *Divine Comedy*.[29] The latest view, defended by historian Maria Monica Donato, seems to rest on more solid hypotheses, especially from the metrical point of view: she has suggested the name of the Sienese poet Bindo di Cione del Frate, whose political song *Così nel mio parlar* also shows the influence of Dante's versification.[30] His *Canzone di Roma* later depicted an allegorized Rome coming to him in a dream, 'ancient, solemn and virtuous', bewailing her captivity and ordering the poet to ask Charles IV of Luxembourg for an Italian king to rule over Italy.[31]

Donato is an eminent specialist in the Italian political painting of the later Middle Ages. She does not, however, make a completely convincing case for her idea that these lines of verse 'suggest the order of reading' for the images painted by Lorenzetti.[32] Because the red initial of the Q in *Questa santa virtù* has one stroke that descends further, are we supposed to think that the escutcheon on the north wall presents the opening of the narrative set out on the three walls of the Sala della Pace? But the escutcheon facing it on the 'bad' side of the fresco, under the allegories of the court of vices, also has a red initial, whose shape (the L of *Là dove sta legata*) completely rules out such an effect. As for the inscription running under the effects of bad government, its first lines are missing. Shades are still on the prowl here; they include the tetchy and obstinate shade of the memory of Dante. This shade silhouettes the contrasts in the painted poetry of the *visibile parlare* that guides our gaze without forcing it, accompanies it without imposing on it. The poetry is in the painting: it sheds light on everything and explains nothing. True, writing cannot free itself from the tyranny of linearity, as it inevitably has to follow a certain successive order; but here, writing is set out in such a way, with so many echoes and displacements, that it cannot impose a single trajectory. There is no order of reading as it is a matter neither of order nor of reading; what counts is the simultaneous presence of temporalities all crumpled up in one single place of images. So it is high time we entered it at ground level, remembering the vertigo of Borges in his story 'The Aleph': 'What my eyes saw was *simultaneous*; what I shall write is *successive*, because language is successive.'[33] Language, the language that Dante vanquished, tracking down in his *Divine Comedy* what he called the 'perfumed panther'. And since we need an order once we have decided to turn the pages of a book and not just allow our gaze to wander round a closed room, here is one such order that will guide us from now on: through Hell first, then Purgatory, and finally Paradise.

7

Guernica in the lands of Siena

You have left the door behind you. Not the door that opened under the little north wall, and was reserved for the Nine, from the staircase that led directly to their apartments. You are not one of those people who, for two months at a time, are the reluctant guests of this palace, obliged to remain enclosed in the heady company of the allegories exhorting them to act well. You are there to see, just to see, the Nine sitting under their painted doubles, or to see those scenes that, according to Bernardino of Siena, stay in everyone's memory. So you have followed the itinerary laid out by the anonymous author of the fourteenth-century *Cronaca senese*: 'in the communal palace, at the top of the staircase, the first door on the left; and if you go there you can see it'.[1] Now we know: the successive refurbishings of the palace have modified the itineraries and we can no longer trust the entrances taken by today's visitors to understand the different ways people used to gain access.[2] The door leading from the Hall of the Great Council with the *Maestà* was put there in the fifteenth century, probably at the same time as the two others, also framed by a matt grey stone that impinges on the white ribbon along which the writings are arranged. The original entrances are now walled up: they are simple openings outlined by the white ribbon and its red border. The first door is higher up; to the left of the north wall, it is the door of the rulers. The second, to the right of the wall, is the door of the ruled.

You have passed through the door and there you are straightaway, surrounded by paintings, facing the 'bad' side of things. What can you see? Next to nothing: it is all murky, indistinct, as if chewed up to produce a dull and dirty ochre. On closer inspection, it is the neutral hue that modern restorers use to isolate missing sections in the pictorial matter – the very colour of the absent painting. But look again:

little by little your eyes grow accustomed to this turbid mixture and start to make out shapes, outlines, contrasts. In the distance rise metal-blue hills topped by ghostly fortresses, in a reddening sky. But what is that pallid troop plunging down on the left? Men in arms, some on horseback and others on foot: a pale *mesnie* or household visible only thanks to its milky outlines. This phantom army is approaching a broad, winding river that cuts through a sterile plain; just a few thin little trees stand out on it. This is a dead land. It no longer brings forth anything but these suffocating, empty, fearful wastes. Only death creates a landscape. Just look across the river: there is a village on fire. Soldiers are leaving it, heading over the bridge having committed their crime. And further on, there are yet more: a horseman with a long red cloak astride a black charger, two infantrymen with light, short jackets, armed with pikes and shields, all leaving the town through a tall crenelated gate.

Ruined houses, closed doors, deserted streets: a town at war. The only activity visible is one of destruction. We can make out various silhouettes in the upper part of a palace; part of the balcony has lost its balustrade and the debris lies scattered over the ground. The figures are wielding great pickaxes: they are demolishing the building. Further off, bare bricks, broken-down stretches of wall, smashed windows: not a ruin, but the process of ruin, the slow disintegration of things that follows on after their paralysed torpor. All the shops are closed, apart from the armourer's. The armed troop is pouring through the streets, like a river overflowing its banks. The soldiers prowl round, menacing, looking for something to do. Here is a *sbirro* (officer of the law) with a strange black-and-white costume, laying his hand on a citizen who is turning round: probably he has him by the scruff of the neck, unless he has just slapped him. In any case, his other hand is resting on the pommel of his dagger, ready to unsheathe it. Other figures are writhing and twisting in the gymnastics of assault. Their tense, hunched bodies contrast alarmingly with the placid expression on their faces, which register no emotion, behind the barrier of a half-smile.

But there is one woman showing fear and crying aloud: two men have seized her, a soldier in a short tunic and an elegantly dressed man who looks imposing in his white merchant's cloak. She is wearing a fine red dress and, on her head, a crown; she looks as if she is dressed for a wedding. Is she betrothed to the man lying at her feet? Behind her, Lorenzetti has painted two curious characters from whom historians have long preferred to avert their gaze. But look: they have gone up to one another and are fondling each other; the older one is pointing at the younger man's genitalia. This scene of homosexual seduction is a reference to the condemnation of sodomy by the communal governments: at the time, this activity was being denounced all the more aggressively as the vice *contra naturam* (against nature) was associated with anxieties over depopulation.³ And this is what is being depicted here: the city at war is deserted and sterile. On the opposite wall, indeed, there is a lady who physically resembles the one who is being assaulted: she is blonde, wears a crown, is dressed in scarlet and rides triumphantly at the head of her wedding procession. For clearly, if we turn round to look at the opposite wall, we will see the dismaying contrast, in the town as in the *contado*: neither sowing nor reaping, neither a well-populated countryside nor cheerful activity: 'I see neither traders nor dancers, but merely men killing other men; the houses are not being repaired but demolished and set on fire', as we have already seen Bernardino of Siena exclaiming. For the bad city is defined solely by what it lacks. '[A]ll I see is people leaving the city,' the preacher continues, and then adds: 'And everything that is being done is done in a state of fear.'⁴

It is this fear whose face has been depicted by the painter. You have only to look up and there it is, level with the city gate, floating in its ragged black clothes, brandishing its long dark sword: *Timor*. Its hair in disarray, its complexion muddy, its features drawn, it is as skinny as a ghost and has the staring mask of death. We cannot fail to see a comparison here with the reaper in the *Trionfo della Morte* that Buonamico Buffalmacco painted at the same time (between 1336 and 1341) in the Camposanto of Pisa.⁵ We truly are in hell. But this is a political hell, for it casts the shadow of the justice of the afterlife onto this earth.⁶ This is the meaning of the warning to be read in the scroll of *Timor*. It expresses the fear of danger – 'thus by this path / no one passes without fearing death' – revealing in contrast how crucial the issue of territorial control was for communal regimes (and this was probably the case right from the earliest signs of the urban self-governing political movement in the twelfth century). Ensuring the security of circulation, extending the space in which transactions could be guaranteed beyond the city walls: this was the first effect of a good communal government. What is being played out here is nothing less than the very idea of the common good, and that is why *Timor* exhorts us, first and foremost, to respect civic values: 'Because all seek their own good alone, here / justice is in thrall to tyranny.' What should we fear if not ourselves, the way we have forgotten the principles of civil life on which is based the very possibility of a shared existence? What else can we fear but our own anger?

War – yes, quite likely, but not the war waged by an aggressor from the outside, coming along to overturn the established order: rather, the war of all against all, bringing savagery to the very heart of the city. As a historian, one might put it this way: the inextricable interweaving of the alliances and divisions that form the tangled skein of intrigues proper to communal Italy engenders such an intense level of conflict that, in this case, all wars are civil wars. But one could also say, taking refuge in a more Platonic terminology, that what we have here is not war but sedition, *stasis* rather than *polemos*. For the Greeks, *stasis* was the turmoil in the divided city state that produced disunity and civil war. It was a movement, but it was also, in philosophical language, the immobilization of the flux of existence, which was thus frozen. It brings 'the bond of division' into the heart of the city, and raises conflict in it as if erecting a stele.[7] Nicole Loraux has shown how Greek taxonomy comprised a very precarious shelter for those who sought to take refuge in it from the wickedness of the world. Admittedly, Platonizing is often a kind of euphemistic activity – and euphemism is an essentially Greek word. In Aeschylus, the Erinyes of blood and vengeance that Athena has managed to keep at bay from the city become 'the Kindly Ones' and proclaim: 'May the insatiable sedition (*stasis*) of evil never rumble within this city,' but also: 'May [the citizens] give each other grounds for joy in a thought of shared amity, and may they hate with a single mind.'[8] In the depths of these Greek words, uttered in an attempt to appease and lower tensions, we can still hear the throb of tumult.

One of the most effective ways of euphemizing war is to look the other way and decide, quite simply, not to see it. The scenes I have in mind cover a third of the surface painted by Lorenzetti. But it is not going too far to claim that most of those who have analysed this work more or less ignore this. It is true that the poor preservation of the pictorial matter discourages aesthetic judgement – so much so that it seems no longer to be worthy of attention for the history of art. From this angle, the Google Art Project, which has started to collect high-definition images of the reassuring beauty of the world, has adopted the radical, high-resolution procedure of simply leaving out the 'bad' parts of the fresco, thereby producing the digital artefact of a one-sidedly optimistic vision of the government of men and women. The historians of the Sienese fresco do not simply wish away the 'bad' parts, but even they are more interested in political ideas than artistic forms; they condescend to considering the west wall only as the tarnished and misshapen reflection of the wall opposite, like the visions of hell on the typanums of cathedrals: according to Jean-Claude

Bonne, the disorder depicted here is simply 'the tragic inversion and/ or the grotesque mirror of the heavenly order'.[9]

This is probably one of the consequences of the kind of idealist reading prevalent in specialists of political doctrines, hypnotized by the little north wall of allegories distributing its effects on each side – again, rather like the Christ of gothic porticos, trenchantly dividing the saved from the damned. It always follows the same order: the main principles, then their beneficial effects, and then, in a hellish annex, their negative effects – which are nothing other than the reverse of the 'good' effects. In terms of political philosophy, however, a realistic vision of the operations of power forces us to start with the realization of its concrete effects: good government is defined less by the virtuous principles that inspire it than by the positive consequences to which it leads. As Machiavelli would put it, this is the *verità effetuale della cosa* (the practical truth of the affair): the truth of the political is uttered on the basis of its real, objective effects.[10] So how did these *cose d'Italia* present themselves at the time Lorenzetti was painting? In terms, this time, of political history, we are forced to reply: they were more akin to the way the artist depicted them on the west wall. Indeed, we might describe the other wall – even though it is so often seen as a realist painting of the life that was led in a peaceful city in those far-away mediaeval days – as nothing but a mirror that, as it were, shows the realities portrayed opposite, only the right way up.

After all, war was the permanent horizon of the political life of Italian city states from the thirteenth to the fourteenth centuries. For the past twenty years, the historiography of life in the communes has sobered up and lost its irreducible idealistic optimism, a product of the genealogical fervour with which, for so long, it sought the origins of our public liberties in the mediaeval past. If we wished to draw just one lesson from this, it would be easy to state it in these terms: there is a continual re-evaluation of the culture of hatred in the way that societies are organized.[11] As they were reconsidering the decisive role of the militia in urban elites and the crucial place of knightly culture in their value system, historians were also recognizing the key word in communal political systems. This word was *odium*. We need to remember that these societies, so imbued as they were with the practices of writing, were both profoundly judicial in nature and at the same time intensely violent. True, this was a *regulated* violence: aristocratic vengeance, for example, was one of the ordinary ways of settling conflicts. But it often took the less ritualistic form of unbridled violence. We need to understand, for example, the care with which Lorenzetti placed, in each of his scenes, horsemen and infantrymen side by side. This marked an essential distinction in the waging of war. Jean-Claude Maire Vigueur has shown that the *cavalcata* (or *speditio*) was a limited, regulated form of conflict, reserved to the militia. But this is not important here: rather, those who fight on horseback (the *milites*) and those who fight on foot (the *pedites*) – following a fundamental distinction in communal Italy, both for the way the military was organized and for political life – are here united. They form the communal militia, namely the set of the commune's military forces (including both the city and the *contado*) that was known as the *exercitus*. 'In addition, the more people it brings together, the more the communal *exercitus* seems to be a machine whose aim is to destroy and crush rather than to fight.'[12] Its many troops lived off the land, destroyed the harvests, pillaged and burned. There was an Italian trecento word to express this, a word that expressed less the brutality of the event and more the banality of a common practice: *guasto*.

So that is exactly what Lorenzetti painted on this side, without exaggeration or undue insistence: *guasto*. An army pouring down and devastating the land, systematically indulging in arson, pillage and rape, and ruining (*guastare*) the territory. War seen face to face, not in the paroxysm of some sudden catastrophe, but as a regular, routine activity, almost a seasonal event. War as Siena waged or suffered it several times in the first third of the fourteenth century, especially to defend its land against its Tuscan rivals, especially in Maremma. A war of annihilation – on a reduced scale, no doubt, but a war of annihilation all the same. And there was another way of euphemizing it: by reducing it to something exceptional and localized in a battle that can be given a name. This is true with Giorgio Vasari: in the first edition of his *Lives* (1550), where he praises Lorenzetti for being the first in modern painting to have 'counterfeited in the travailing of the figures the turmoil of the air and the fury of the rain and of the wind'[13] (but was this not also true of the flames licking the village?), he also writes: 'In a large hall of the Palazzo della Signoria in Siena he painted War, Peace and the events of the latter.'[14] This is all he said. And yet he was on the right track: not good and bad government but, and in this order, '*la Guerra, la Pace e gli accidenti di quelle*'. Then, in the 1568 edition, Vasari had second thoughts and specified, wrongly, that he was referring to '*la Guerra d'Asinalunga e la pace appresso*' ('the War of Asinalunga, and after it the Peace and its events'). The Battle of Sinalunga, in the Val di Chiana, took place in 1363; it is commemorated in the Sala del Mappamondo in the communal palace by a fresco painted by Lippo Vanni in 1372, and Vasari was confusing this with Lorenzetti's work. This was also probably because, as a historical painter, depicting great battles in the paunched bellies of princely palaces, Vasari could not imagine anyone painting war without seeking to shelter it behind the authority of a name. And the names of battles also had a fetish value.

He was not the only one to do so. There are many historians who have homed in on the contextual facts behind Lorenzetti's allegory. Does the width of the river allude to the plains of the Po where Siena had so many enemies? Attempts have also been made to recognize different symbolic and architectural elements referring to Siena's great political and territorial rival, Pisa, the Ghibelline city. In the 1330s, the struggle for control of the Maremma – in particular the strategic defensive site of Massa Maritima – led the two cities into a merciless war. Siena finally conquered Massa Maritima in 1335, but only after an exhausting and bloody campaign, a dirty war in which the Pisans made several incursions into the *contado* of Siena.[15] The image of a territory ravaged by the *guasto* of an enemy *exercitus* did not serve merely to draw a contrast with the appealing panorama of a city at peace; far from it: it was probably meant to remind the Sienese of the painful ordeals of their recent past. Unless it was sending out an even more ambiguous message, as Rosa Maria Dessì has recently suggested.[16] In 1338, another Ghibelline city, Grosseto, surrendered to Siena. The act of surrender, written in the vernacular, granted Siena *imperium* over Grosseto; it was signed on 17 March and read in public on 13 April in the palace – just as Lorenzetti was engaged on the painting of his fresco. Might he have been asked to add some allusion to the ravages of war that the arms of Siena had just inflicted on the *contado* of the recently subjected city? This may seem a somewhat surprising suggestion as it reverses the roles. But in any case it cannot diminish the meaning of an image which is not limited to the past by its contextual interpretation. The city at war is not just Pisa or Grosseto, any more than the happy city is Siena, even though it may resemble it. The memory of political events does not exhaust the sense of the work, and does not transmit any single unambiguous message. It acts as an echo, and adds to the rumble of nameless wars its own particular stridency, the vibration of time itself.

So there are not just several discourses at work here, but several interwoven narratives, each with its own temporality, sometimes as brief and sudden as the event, sometimes as broad and slow as memory. So we need to hear all of them, including the symbolic narrative presented by the quatrefoil medallions framing the composition, whose frieze forms the lower and upper borders of the three walls of the Sala della Pace. Some of these medallions have been worn away, or destroyed by the later doors pierced in the north and east walls, but they, too, have been completely neglected by interpreters of the work. And yet their function is to alert our gaze by suggesting a second interpretation of the scenes depicted, thereby reinforcing or highlighting them. This is the case with the pontifical insignia set over the happy city, while the medallions of the emperors Nero, Gaeta and Antiochis dominate the city at war; and the same applies to the way the seasons and the divinities are set out: winter is on the west wall and summer on the east, while Mars is on the west wall and Venus on the east. This emphasizes the symbolic contrast between the two walls.[17] Does this mean they form what Jack Greenstein calls the 'symbolic synopsis' of a relation between Peace and War on the one side and the configuration of the planets and seasons on the other?[18] By resorting to astral symbolism, Lorenzetti was indeed borrowing the common language of communal iconography, as used to such great effect by Giotto in his decoration of the wide vault of the Palazzo della Ragione in Padua between 1306 and 1312.[19] Compared with the unfathomable complexity of this model, Lorenzetti's use of astrology was very limited: the celestial signs can express the vicissitudes of history and maybe even announce them, but the fact remains that it is people – people in society – who make this history, insofar as they are political animals.

This is why it is ultimately to these people that the exhortation expressed in the painted writings is addressed. War, in truth a hideous matter, here displays its real face: the maw of tyranny. 'Let lordship be taken over her [i.e. tyranny] / and let each man busy his spirit and his intelligence / with always subjecting everyone to justice, / to forestall such black damage / and strike down tyrants.' We stand in front of the 'bad' part of Lorenzetti's fresco as if confronting our fears – and rather than allowing ourselves to be overwhelmed by panic, the only way out is to find the right words to label them with. This is the meaning of the political iconology of Carlo Ginzburg: in Picasso's painting *Guernica* he seeks the violent conjunction between the old and the contemporary, as in the celebrated frontispiece to Hobbes's *Leviathan*, depicting the nightmare of that cold monster the State devouring individuals.[20] Hobbes said of himself: 'Fear and I were born twins.' To translate Thucydides describing the *anomia* that followed the arrival of the plague in Athens in 429 BC – 'no one was held back by fear of god or by human laws' – the philosopher used the word 'awe', suggesting both 'awful' (inspiring fear) and 'awesome' (inspiring respect). This was his way of expressing the essentially political nature of fear – not the *Timor Dei* of politicians but the fear signified by the Latin word *vereor*, which could be translated as both 'I fear' and 'I revere'. Terror or reverence? That is the point we have reached. That is why we need to advance further, approaching the tyrant and his court of vices, and even venturing into the monster's maw, for here alone can be seen the yawning gap that constitutes the very gap of the political.

8

The seductions of tyranny (what the image conceals)

How could anyone love him? He is fat, pale and grotesque. He stinks like a goat. He is trying to look mean, but if you look more closely at his wan mask, as round as the moon, you will see how his scowling eyes, his fangs and his horns are all separate, disjointed. You do not really feel you need to be frightened of him. As children would say: *you can't scare me!* If you look away from the suffocating scenes of devastation, of *guasto*, and focus instead on the little theatre of the court of vices on either side of them, you will escape the grip of *vereor*, and feel neither terror nor reverence. Allegories perched on a platform, lined up as if on parade in front of the crenelated wall of a citadel – everything is where it should be; everything is labelled; everything is already in its reassuring place. So this was what it was all about – nothing more than *Tyramnides*, tyranny. This was, of course, the key word which Greek and Roman philosophy bequeathed to Italian political thought. Aristotle had drawn a distinction between the tyranny of usurpation and the tyranny of exercise, defining tyrannical power as the monstrous obverse of a proper rule, the corruption of authority that became domination and thereby separated from all legitimacy. Thomas Aquinas, followed by Gilles of Rome, saw tyranny as the decadent form of all degenerate power: even the people can behave in a tyrannical way.[1] The fact remains that in the communal Italy of the years after 1310, the accusation of tyranny became an obsessive theme in political invective. This accusation was mainly levelled at the emperor and his allies the Ghibelline aristocrats, but it continued to target a growing number of people. In his celebrated *Tractatus de Regimine civitatis*, the legal thinker Bartolo da Sassoferrato defined the tyrant as the man who abandons the defence of the common good and concentrates on his own private interests.[2]

Drawing on authors of Antiquity (from Xenophon to Seneca), works on ethics from the first third of the trecento sharpened this definition, describing the tyrant as a slave to his own passions, incapable of submitting to the law of a reason freed from desire and instead wallowing in the hubris of greed, cruelty and lust.

Lorenzetti's representation of tyranny relies on these three types of source (philosophical, juridical and ethical),[3] but it mainly highlights the tyrant as a prince of vice, a figure of ungovernable passions. Cruel and lustful, the wicked king of this infernal Babylon stands over both the goat – an obvious symbol of unbridled sexuality, here acting as the maleficent double of the nursing she-wolf depicted on the other side – and the figure of justice in chains. He clearly embodies the twofold negation associated with tyranny, 'as both the inversion of the common good and as the destruction of justice'.[4] His repulsive bestiality is reminiscent of the masks worn in the plays of Seneca, masks that the poet Albertino Mussato used in the production of his *Ecerinis*, the first evidence of a renaissance of political tragedy in Europe. This was in 1315, in Padua, just as Giotto was painting his astrological scenes in the communal palace – the Palazzo della Ragione, where *ragione* refers to both reason and justice, here merged into the civic ideal of the *regimi di popolo*. But these regimes were then under threat from the aristocrats, and, as a humanist, Mussato decided to stage their political ascendency as a way of combating the power of the master of Verona, Cangrande della Scala. But he used a historical detour to achieve this end: *Ecerinis* is the tragedy of the return of Ezzelino da Romano, a bloody autocrat allied to Emperor Frederick II, whose terrifying and unpredictable power had spread panic through the Veneto in the mid-thirteenth century.[5]

In the very first scene, Ezzelino's mother Adeleita confesses to him the secret of his birth: he is not the son of his father, but sprang from a monstrous beast who had emerged from the smoky bowels of the earth to possess her. Here, tragedy takes the form defined by Dante, who was drawing on an erroneous etymology that saw it as the song (*oda*) of the goat (*tragos*). Ezzelino is thrilled by his dark origin. 'Speak, mother,' he says: 'I delight to hear of all that is grand and savage,' for this supernatural descent is the sign that he can revel in excessive wickedness: 'We shall be judges worthy of the paternal tribunal if through our acts we lay claim to our father's kingdom: wars, deaths, ruins, perfidies, tricks, the perdition of the entire human race, that is what he loves.' And, logically enough, the Chorus has the last word, telling the spectators: 'As much as you can, be warned by this and learn this unshakeable law.'[6]

The fecund belly and the foul beast: it is impossible these days not to hear Mussato's warning as an echo of the universal struggle against barbarity, an 'unshakeable law'. Indeed, the poet (the first who was crowned as a poet in a public ceremony, before Petrarch, in the same year of 1315) was constantly playing on this concordance of different time-frames, if only with the aim of organizing annual public readings of the *Ecerinis* in Padua, between 1315 and 1318. This was Mussato's way of forging a link back to the political origins of Greek tragedy, a song of freedom that can only be sung when we are anxious we might lose it. In the monster painted by Lorenzetti, there is something of this power of persuasion – with the obvious bestiality of the creature being enough to keep at bay what appears as absolute evil in the exercise of power. Hence the very explicit character of the composition, which, unlike other allegories in the fresco, is pretty unambiguous. '[T]hus it is that tyranny takes the upper hand,' as the lines in the escutcheon state: 'for it [i.e. tyranny], in order to accomplish its misdeeds, / accords both in thought and deed / with the corrupt nature / of the vices that accompany it.'

The first of these vices is labelled in the *titulus* as *Superbia*. This beautiful young woman stands her ground, her face delicately enframed by blonde tresses, her rich scarlet robes indicative of her haughtiness. Her right hand rests on the pommel of her sword, and she represents the potential use of force – which, in ancient philosophy, is the potential for being and not being. Instead of lashing out, she merely keeps her sword sheathed, hanging over our heads. This is the precise image of sovereign power: the state of emergency that does not need to act in order to be realized, but simply needs to convince everyone of its Aristotelian *energeia*, deprived of any real effectiveness. As Giorgio Agamben says, '[A]n act is sovereign when it realizes itself by simply taking away its own potentiality not to be, letting itself be, giving itself to itself.'[7] That is why *Superbia* is left in suspense, like the keystone of the maleficent construction, or rather like the scourge of a pair of scales held in a state of suspense. And that is why she holds the yoke, one side of which inclines towards the head of the horned monster she stands over: for she is the very figure of dominance.

Superbia is the pride of the system of seven deadly sins drawn up by the Church Fathers and given its final form in the scholastic theology of the thirteenth century. Pride is the original vice which unleashes all the others. One day, Lucifer turned away from the common good in the belief that his own merits were self-sufficient – the exact theological definition of pride, the 'beginning of sin' as Sirach 10:13 puts it. Hence his ruin. However, the primacy of pride in the genealogy of evil does not derive from theological considerations alone: *Superbia* is the feudal sin *par excellence* and easily lends itself to any political reading, especially in a communal Italy that more than anything fears the *grandiglia* of the powerful, that brutal arrogance which, in the legislative systems of the *regimi di popolo*, justified the exclusion of magnates.[8] In mediaeval classifications, pride was often associated with vainglory. Both of them stem from the vanity of the desire for excellence. So here we see *Vanagloria*, a lovely woman admiring her fine features in a little mirror. She is so passionately absorbed that she does not seem to realize that the branch she is holding (the branch of eloquence) has shrivelled up. She is entirely caught up in contemplating herself; she is silence or volubility, and in any case she is a disorder of efficacious language – another obsession of the value systems in the communes, where to govern well meant to speak well.

'Oh, what vainglorying in human powers! / How short a time the green lasts on the height / unless some cruder, darker age succeeds.' These lines from Dante come immediately before the ambiguous and endlessly discussed praise that the poet bestows on the painting of his time: 'Once, as a painter, Cimabue thought / he took the prize. Now "Giotto" is on all lips / and Cimabue's fame is quite eclipsed.'[9] The fact that Giotto – who most likely painted an allegory of vainglory in the palace of the Lord of Milan, Azzone Visconti, in 1335–6[10] – was included in the *Divine Comedy* in his own lifetime seems to have made a great impression on his contemporaries. Vainglory did, it is worth noting, have a close link with the illusionist powers of painting, and more broadly with the comedy of appearances – a feminine comedy, inevitably. That is why this flirtatious figure here leads us to mention the sumptuary laws of the trecento, another legislative obsession of communal Italy. The arrogant luxury and insolent beauty of women threw preachers into a rage: they saw it as an act of violence against the order of the city. So the meddlesome regulations aimed at curbing these displays were connected with the laws against magnates, from the ordinances of Bologna in 1288 to the statutes of the Captain of the People in Florence in 1322 forbidding anyone to dress *more magnatum* (in the manner of the magnates).[11]

Completing the vicious trio of tyranny is an ashen, wrinkled figure who definitely inspires less envy. This is Avarice, shrivelled by her own exclusive passion for money. She is shouldering the harpoon of the money-grubber, and in her clawed hand she is gripping a press squeezing two pouches. Between the sterile *Avaritia* who inspires tyranny and the lustful goat that tyranny dominates, *Tyramnides* appears as a disgustingly ambiguous figure, an unbridled libidinal economy that endlessly cranks its self-destructive pleasure organ. As the Middle Ages drew to a close, pride, the origin of all the vices, and avarice, the source of all evils, competed as to which would be the deadliest of the seven deadly sins, at a time when feudal arrogance and bourgeois greed comprised two socially symmetrical dangers. If the ternary structure of *Superbia*, *Avaritia* and *Vanagloria* painted by Lorenzetti may refer to the three concupiscences discussed by Peter the Lombard in the twelfth century,[12] this structure clearly made no claim to conform to some theological pattern, but rather adapted the pastoral theme of the deadly sins to the most concrete and burning of political issues in the social life of Italian cities: the control of violence, the distribution of wealth, the regulation of the use of language and the economy of appearances.

On either side of the horned monster enthroned with all the sovereign attributes of the empire of evil, holding a strange chalice that may be a diabolical parody of the cup used at the Last Supper, we see the wicked councillors of tyranny. There are six of them, three on each side, allegories of evil whose reassuring counterparts are on the opposite side of the fresco. In this arrangement, lined up on the platform, they compose a political discourse every bit as explicit as that of the allegories of vice looking down at them. *Crudelitas* is cruelty, a nasty dishevelled shrew strangling a newborn baby while gripping a poisonous snake. Her back is turned to *Proditio* or Betrayal, on whose knees is another symbol of innocence, a lamb – but just look at its hindparts, transformed into a scorpion's tail. Another bestial detail helps us identify Fraud (*Fraus*). It is easy to miss it the first time we look. Dressed in her blue robe with its elegant folds and geometrical patterns, she holds a stick or a ruler (a standard measure for length?), and she would almost inspire confidence – were it not for her giveaway hairy paw and her clawed foot protruding from under her dress. With *Furor*, the bestial features reach a climax: we see a centaur, with a man's torso topped by a boar's head; it is carrying a dagger and in its other hand it clutches a stone that it is preparing to throw. Then comes *Divisio*: a woman split in half whose robe, in the black and white of the colours of the commune of Siena, comprises two strips cut lengthwise, so that the contradiction she expresses (*Si* and *No*) can be resolved only by the mutilation she imposes on herself. This social division leads inevitably to its consequences: armed war, whose helmeted allegory, brandishing a sword behind her head, bears her name on her black shield – not the *bellum* of classical Latin, but the harsh rough neologism of *Guerra*. She is ready to strike, pausing, perhaps,

like *Superbia* – time has been arrested and is held in suspense. She is
the war that is still to come.

Cruelty, betrayal and fraud exacerbate the violence of social relations, and this fury entails a division that cannot fail to lead to war:
it is thus a political scenario that is suggested by the six allegories
painted by Lorenzetti. This chain of moral causes and social effects
gives a narrative form to the anguish of Italian urban society subject
to the cruelty of social violence, the betrayal of political fidelity and
the collapse of relations of trust that guarantee the security of trade.
It expresses the reign of *odium*, that aggravated state of conflict that
historiography traditionally designates by the name of 'factional
struggles'. Indeed, behind these grand and rather vague principles,
we can doubtless glimpse the concrete situations and burning issues
of communal life. Quentin Skinner's analysis helps us to politicize
the attention we pay to these allegories, as when he compares the
iconography of *Furor* with an announcement of the statutory regulations of the commune of Siena (the *Breves* of 1250) concerning
'*fures*, malefactors, and those who throw stones at houses or the civic
buildings of Siena'.[13] Wild behaviour, lack of civility, the ruining of
public facilities? It may seem rather trivial: far from it. For one of
the ideological issues at stake in the defence of the common good
consisted, for communal regimes, in communicating the idea that the
'houses or the civic buildings' of the city were protected by the sacred
character of the laws mentioned by the defenders of the civic ideal.
Or, in other words, the benevolent shadow of the sacred that was cast
by religious buildings that were sometimes the responsibility of the
commune extended across the whole set of municipal building sites
that it was creating.[14] The Dantesque centaur depicted in the court of
vices was thus like the madmen denounced in the statutes of Siena in
1250: by throwing stones at buildings, it ruined the urban order at the
same time as it insulted its sacred character.

Can we go further and identify more precisely the regime or political situation that was being so harshly criticized? In this case, the
notion of political and religious sacredness may put us on the right
track. It was doubtless difficult for a trecento eye to miss the signs
of party allegiance that saturate this 'bad' part of Lorenzetti's fresco.
The crenelated wall, and above all the double gate of the city in thrall
to hatred (as opposed to the single arch of the peaceful city), quite
unambiguously connote the imperial sovereignty of Ancient Rome.
The supporters of the Ghibelline alliance symbolically appropriated
the historical lexicon of the Roman *imperium*. The architectural sign
here acts directly as a visual signal – or, as we would say these days,

as a logo or pictogram.[15] And if the spectator (probably always less attentive than iconologists might imagine) still failed to notice this, he or she might finally be alerted by the medallions set out on either side of the two long walls of the Sala della Pace: the happy city is protected by the symbols of Venus, fertile seasons and the Church, while the city at war is dominated by the effigies of Mars, winter and the emperors.

Guelphs on one side, Ghibellines on the other. Yes, doubtless – even if this bipartisan division needs to be seen for what it is: an always quite flexible way of formulating the widespread factional conflicts that tore political societies apart. Admittedly, the Guelph alliance, bringing together certain interests of the Papal Church, the Angevins of Naples and the Tuscan merchant oligarchies in the face of the Ghibelline lords and their imperial protector, did not have the compact homogeneity of one power bloc opposing another, as was claimed by a liberal Cold War historiography fascinated by the 'Florentine way of life'. It overlapped with the aspirations of the elite sector of the *popolo*, while the militia probably had a 'spontaneous sympathy' for the set of traditions, cultural reference points and lifestyle known as 'Ghibellinism'.[16] Nothing more was involved, even if in 1311 the descent of Emperor Henry VII into Italy gave a more concrete and immediately practical content to the idea of an alliance with the imperial powers. But even here, the situation of Siena was more ambiguous than has long been thought: recent historiography is forever re-evaluating the Ghibelline component of its political identity, forged at the time of its glorious struggle against Florence. True, Florence's rise to power had, since 1270, forced Siena to adopt a strategic Guelphism. But this change in alliance, motivated by a realistic grasp of the power relations that the government of the Nine fully endorsed, cannot be seen as any intangible and unremitting support for a particular camp, alliance or body of doctrine.[17]

The fact remains that Ghibellinism was closely linked with the advent of the urban signorias, historically favoured (with countless qualifications, as one might suppose) by the domination of the militia and the political interplay of the emperor's supporters in communal Italy. In 1338, not many cities failed to succumb to the brutal or creeping domination of their institutions by the lords: Genoa, Florence, Siena, Lucca, to some extent Bologna and Perugia – not to mention the specific case of Venice. But none of them managed completely to escape the experience of *insignorimento*: that is, at the very least, the (perhaps brief) establishment of a lord's personal power over the city.[18] In Siena, the Ghibelline Provenzano Salvani had set himself up as the *dominus* after the great victory over the Florentines

at Montaperti in 1260 and until his death at the Battle of Colle di
Val d'Elsa in 1269. He exercised a personal, albeit relatively infor-
mal, power that rested on the *parte ghibellina*, the Ghibelline party,
controlling the Council of the Twenty-Four.[19] We can note in passing
that this memory could not have struck Lorenzetti (or those who
commissioned his work from him) as so problematic as to prevent
him from depicting twenty-four councillors on the north wall of the
allegories, in place of the Nine that might have been expected there.
As the reader may remember, this arithmetical oddity has not yet been
given a convincing historical explanation[20] – it floats over the fresco
like the shadow of some remorse.

Like the contrast between Guelphism and Ghibellinism, the distinction between *comune* and signoria can no longer be viewed as a
binary antagonism. On this point, too, the historians of communal
Italy have for a decade been engaged in a significant de-dramatization,
simplifying categories, laying bare the real practices of government
behind the institutional labels – especially when it comes to justice,
municipal feeling and social politics.[21] By 1974, the great Italian historian Giovanni Tabacco had already sensed the existence of these
signorial and yet perfectly communal experiences.[22] If we focus on
the concrete exercise of power, it soon becomes apparent that the shift
to a signoria is not a form of regime change but a reshaping of communal institutions, which the *dominus* now controls and deforms,
even as he asserts himself as an ardent defender of the civic virtues on
which it is based. This is clearly evident from the layout of the cities
of the time: some lords, such as Castruccio Castracani in Lucca in the
1320s, destroyed the monumental order of the city so as to impose on
it the brutal and traumatic stigma of a citadel, hijacking public space
by devitalizing the urban centre and depriving it of its political function.[23] But what usually happened was that the architectural policy
of the lords in the fourteenth century consisted in occupying the sites
of communal power, protecting and embellishing them, recycling the
traces of a past that they claimed to be extending into the present with
their desire for *buon governo*.[24] The warnings given to the Paduans
by the play *Ecerinis* did not stop the Da Carrara family from taking
power in 1318, dominating the city until 1405, the year when it was
incorporated into the state of Venice. Throughout this long period,
Padua was the target not of the *fures* destroying the houses, but of a
constant policy of urban embellishment that efficiently and insolently
demonstrated the good government of the signoria.

That was the real danger that the political painting commissioned
by the Nine was meant to ward off; that was the true meaning of the

sense of urgency that possessed them. It was not the risk of tyranny or the ravages of war that prowled through the streets of Siena, but the seduction of the signoria. The threat was not the terrifying mask of the tyrant with his sharp fangs, but the gentle smile of the victor as displayed on the funerary effigy of Cangrande I della Scala, who died in 1329, dominating his city of Verona with the calm confidence of a man who knows he will never be forgotten. In the letter that Dante wrote in 1316 to dedicate to him the *Comedy* that was not yet called 'divine', the poet justified something that several of his friends might have viewed as a volte-face. Here he was, the exile from Florence, enamoured of the civic ideals of *libertas*, responding to the sirens of a lord's court by placing himself under the protection of the master of Verona, Cangrande della Scala, such a dubious personage that his very name told everyone what he really was: a dog of war. But what did people actually say about him? According to Dante, his renown 'brings some to hope in their prosperity, casts down others in fear of destruction'. These days, we would say: the signoria is a topic for debate, leading to the exchange of contradictory opinions on which the very legitimacy of the political order is based, and this comprises the most valuable part of the communal legacy. However, the poet does not deign to enter the arena, but affects a thoroughly aristocratic pose: in the face of this ever-active lord, exaggerated praise strikes him as just as excessive as indignant protest seems futile. So he will merely follow his own inclinations. 'For us, however, to whom it is given to know the best that is in us, it is not proper to follow the tracks of the herd, but rather we ought to confront their errors. For, being lacking in intellect and reason, though endowed as it were by divine freedom, they are restricted by no custom.'[25]

There are, in fact, probably two tragic senses of politics. One is expressed by Albertino Mussato in the *Ecerinis*, and is combative and desperate: he sees the dwelling erected by Ezzelino da Romano as an offence against God, a formidable citadel whose pride scars the heavens. Dante's response can perhaps be read in his *Paradise*, where he in turn evokes the topography of terror: 'a hill starts up – though not to any height – / from which there once came down a burning brand / who ravaged all the countryside around'.[26] A single root for good and evil, the common origin of every kind of power: that, assuredly, is a form of lucid disenchantment that undermines any belief in binary oppositions. In 1311, Dante had attended the imperial coronation of Emperor Henry VII in Milan. So had Albertino Mussato, and there were many Italian intellectuals who thought that this champion of the Ghibelline cause, allied to his representatives setting up

signorias everywhere, might be able to free communal Italy from the
permanent state of conflict exhausting the country's resources in a
war of all against all, imposing himself as what another Paduan, the
humanist Marsilius of Padua, called the *Defensor Pacis* ('defender of
the peace').

The signoria managed to convince an increasingly large swathe of
political society that it came bearing peace and not war. This happened in Verona, and also in Milan, where Giotto himself painted a
fresco of the good government of the Visconti; in Arezzo, where the
funerary monument of the bishop and lord Tarlati affirmed that the
comune in signoria would be sustained;[27] and even in the rival city of
Pisa, where the lord Fazio della Gherardesca founded a university in
1338 so as to display what a chronicler of the time called his 'great
goodness'.[28] We can understand the intense effort that the commune
of Siena put into political communication only if we realize how
effective signorial propaganda was, and how uncertain the outcome
of this war of images would be.[29] While in 1338 there was an urgent
and imperious need in Siena to persuade the signoria to wage war, this
was because an increasing number of citizens thought that war might
lead to peace. An armed peace, admittedly, but peace all the same. In
the 1380s, the Florentine chronicler Marchionne di Coppo Stefani
very clearly expressed the pacifying function of the signorialization of
communal institutions: as he put it, 'it is better to make peace together
and not have discord than to have a tyrant after discord, and then
peace' (*è meglio pacificarsi insieme e non avere discordia, che tiranno
dopo discordia e poi la pace*).[30] That was the real political choice: the
people's peace or the prince's peace.

Florence is a very clear example of this. Most of its signorial experiences (from the peace of Cardinal Latino in 1280 until the peace
treaties and truces imposed by the representatives of the Angevin
kings in 1317, and then again under the signoria of Duke Charles of
Calabria in June 1326) were linked to efforts to impose peace. As for
the signoria of the Duke of Athens, Gautier de Brienne, in 1342–3, it
left the Florentines with fewer bad memories than the chroniclers and
the defamatory depictions that comprise official memory would have
us believe. The city archives still hold the registers in which, between
September 1342 and March 1343, 266 peace treaties were recorded,
sworn at the behest of the lord.[31] Christiane Klapisch-Zuber has
examined the files of these 'ducal peaces', showing how much this systematic attempt to reconcile the parties in a civil peace was an essential part of the signorial affirmation of the Duke of Athens: this was
how he managed to gain recognition for what a chronicler astutely

called 'the powers of a lord, and the power to shed blood and make peace and war as he saw fit in the city of Florence'.[32]

So this is what the image conceals. The signoria was not the opposite of the commune. It was one of its potential developments, the pursuit of its history by other means. To many people, the authority of a single man no longer aroused fear: it struck them as an acceptable variation on communal institutions, so long as it remained only temporary. And this was precisely what made it seem so alarming to those who truly loved civic liberty. For what they were powerless to prevent was the way the discourse of peace was being hijacked by the lords. If these lords were to be believed, they alone could ensure tranquillity, bringing to an end the exhausting conflicts that were so endemic in ordinary communal life. So what was the solution? Not to lose heart, to mobilize again, to take back the stolen words one by one. To say: signoria is empire, empire is tyranny, tyranny is war. To say this all the more forcefully as this was a truth that could no longer be taken for granted – and perhaps people were already starting to doubt it. But to say it in the full knowledge that the words of the political are eroded and weakened the more often they are uttered, and that there will soon be no point in waxing indignant and denouncing power by brandishing great categories the way one sets flags fluttering in the wind. *Tyranny, yes – so what? Why not, after all, if tyranny can make itself look attractive*. Time is pressing. We need to emerge from the Minotaur's labyrinth before his jaws close on us. Find the thread. Look, there it is, at the feet of the captive woman.

9

Concord with its cords

So we just need to follow the cord. It binds the lovely captive who lies under the platform of the tribunal formed by the court of vices. A *titulus* provides it with a name: it is Justice who has been bound. So Justice is the first victim of tyranny. Vanquished, shamed, tearful, she is completely covered by an immaculate robe as tight-fitting as a shroud, though its fine folds seem to quiver like a white flame consuming her – unless they are the rippling of the wave in which she is drowning. A few people have come to witness her humiliation; but they are mere dwarfish figures before her fallen grandeur. The painting is in a very poor state of repair, and all we can make out are occasional faint outlines, giving us just a glimpse of their small stature and malign appearance. But the personage in blue holding Justice on a leash can be seen clearly – and when we see that image today, we cannot fail to think that we have seen others like it, others that we would rather not have seen at all, but which we *did* see nonetheless: the images of those prisoners being held on a leash. 'A scene that now forms part of the records of our age,' as the poet Dominique Fourcade puts it,[1] a scene that really leaves us aghast insofar as it provokes an event of language – this is what, now, holds *us* on a leash.

In his other hand, the henchman is holding the tasselled end of one of the three red ropes attached to a golden disc. The two others twist loosely along the ground, undone, next to the pan of the scales. If we turn our gaze to look at the other side, to the small wall on the north, we will be able to identify it: this is the scale of a balance held by the sovereign figure of Justice, a grand allegory dressed in her scarlet robe with its sumptuous gold embroidery encrusted with precious stones. So we have now gone to the other side, round the corner of the wall. Here we again come across the cord, but not the same cord.

From the two scales of the balance that Justice holds in equilibrium, hanging from the flail brandished by *Sapientia*, proceed two threads which are being grasped by *Concordia*, the figure holding the plane on her knees. Everything here is perfectly neat, straight, tight. These two threads weave a single cord, which the egalitarian procession of the magistrates, levelled, as the reader will remember, by the plane of equity, brings to the great personage enthroned like a judge in the middle of the platform of the virtues, and knots to his wrist. It is not the same cord, as this one does not bind but loosens. It is what the mediaeval theorists called the *vinculum concordiae*, that which binds individuals in a society of their own free will and holds them together. This 'bond of security', as Cicero put it – his words were quoted by St Augustine in *The City of God* – is the best and lightest bond for ensuring a safe life in society.[2] So it brings together free citizens, able to live in solidarity with one another: or, more simply, in *concord*.

Thus, to pass from one wall to the next, thereby escaping the empire of tyranny, we simply need to follow the cord. But we could equally well follow another thread, that of the painted writings extending over the three sides of the composition. So let us unravel the skein of the *visibile parlare* where we had left it, under the 'bad' allegories of the west wall. 'Wherever justice is bound in chains, / nobody can ever be in harmony with the common good.' As for tyranny, it 'accords both in thought and deed' with the vices that accompany it. This strident interplay of assonances (*s'acorda / a dritta corda / discorda*) is echoed in the painting itself, where certain figures acquire a more intense presence if we utter the name of the objects they represent. With the cord, it is as if Lorenzetti were managing to get words to rhyme with images, the *Concordia* which holds the cord becoming *con cordia*. The historian should probably be wary of this poetic inclination, and remember, with Furio Brugnolo, that *accord*, in the Italian of the trecento, had not yet acquired the sense of musical harmony that Chiara Frugoni saw as one of the keys to the composition as a whole.[3]

What matters is not playing with words but remembering, just as an example, that the expression *a dritta corda* can have very precise and concrete meanings in the records of the practice of communal government. This is true of urban statutes: there were so many of them from the thirteenth century onwards that laid down norms for the arrangement of the networks of highways and the schedule for upkeep of buildings, often giving officers specialized in the municipal defence of the common good to check that private dwellings did not protrude onto public spaces with awnings, balconies or other corbellings, and therefore required that façades be aligned *ad cordam*. This was just the expression used in the statutes of Siena of 1262, while the records of the officers charged with the task of ensuring that these alignments were respected (the *Viarii*) specified in the last decade of the trecento that the strict limit of public space was to be drawn from one house to the next, *a dritta corda*.[4] The twenty-four councillors holding the cord embody, in their very stature, the urban ideal of a city measured out by cords.

But there is more: if we follow the thread of the writings, the loosened meaning of a work that initially strikes us with the brutality of its dichotomies can be 'accorded' more flexibly. War and peace, as Bernardino of Siena put it: yes, doubtless, but in one and the same great image. The commune and tyranny: this is the message that the allegories continually hammer out – true enough, but this is a contrast that Lorenzetti does not so much depict as point to. As we have seen, the persuasive force of his painting lies precisely in the way it divides things into two sharply separate categories when everything in the lived history of the political regimes of the trecento contributed to blunting their edge. The painted writings, for example, exhort the citizens – both governors and governed – to face up to things and by themselves draw the great division between divergent political options whose boundaries were blurred by temporal confusion. The long inscription running under the west wall does not describe the misdeeds of tyranny but incites everyone to resist them: 'Let lordship be taken over her [i.e. tyranny] / and let each man busy his spirit and his intelligence / with always subjecting everyone to justice' (and it is worth noting in passing that the word for 'lordship', '*signoria*', here refers to nothing other than power, in a neutral sense, as was usual in the political lexicon of the day). As for the inscription that runs under the east wall, it does not exalt the benefits of the commune but also enjoins those who govern it to action: 'Turn your eyes to gaze, / you who rule, on the woman who is depicted here.'

And who *is* depicted here? Justice, of course. 'Gaze at all the benefits that stem from her,' exhorts the long wall of 'effects' on the east. The wall of the 'principles', on the north, explains in philosophical terms her capacity to create accord by drawing on the vocabulary of the *regimen* (*Vo' che reggiete*: you who rule) and by contrasting it with the image of Justice bound (*sta legata la iustitia*) of the escutcheon opposite: 'This sacred virtue, wherever she rules, / leads to unity the multitude of souls, / and these, gathered to this aim, / make the common good their lord.' Ubiquitous in the painted writings, she is also mirrored in the image. And there she is, enthroned in majesty on the left of the composition; but there she is again, sitting to the right of the bench of the virtues, with no possible ambiguity since she is surmounted by her *titulus: Iustitia.* The way the figure seems to be clumsily repeated here, like a stammer, has troubled several commentators.[5] It is clearly here to alert our gaze, which simply needs to seek reassurance from a few basic iconographical principles. For example, one principle involves seeing the stature of the characters arranged hierarchically not in order of their distance from us (since they are allegories) but in terms of their symbolic rank in the order of representation. The venerable bearded old man at the centre of the composition, endowed with the attributes of sovereignty, stands out over everyone else by his tallness, but Justice on her throne of glory follows him in order of size. Then come the virtues, slightly smaller than Justice, with six framing the old man and the seventh, Concord, being less a virtue than a social ideal. The latter is situated at a lower level, flush with the common earth that is trodden by men – councillors, prisoners, soldiers – while dominating them with her height. As for the theological virtues (one over the head of Justice, three over the old personage), while they are clearly of the same stature as the humans, their supernatural consistency – fleeting phantoms floating in the heaven of ideas, lacking the feet that would enable them to land on the soil of earthly life – obviously sets them apart from this hierarchy of height.

So this hierarchy needs to be combined with another classificatory principle which is also vertical since it draws a contrast, from top to bottom, between the blue in which the downy wings of the virtues are spread and the earth which welcomes the political actions of civil life. And, in an intermediate position, we find the platform of the allegories representing the principles of the good government of men and women. The principles, but the practices too. True, the great personage is dominated by the crowned virtues which their *tituli* designate respectively as *Fides, Caritas* and *Spes* (Faith, Charity and Hope). But he in turn dominates the six feminine allegories sitting with him. In other words, these values do not transcend government as so many great principles that need to be applied piously, but emanate from it as its very own qualities. So what we find here is the primacy of political practice, essential for an understanding of what comprises the innovative power of Lorenzetti's painting, even if those who refuse to see it as anything other than the expression of ideas and doctrines always thereby render it insipid. Now if the painter depicted justice twice over, this is because justice is both a practice of government and one of the principles on which it is based. But Lorenzetti represented the actual practice of justice higher up, both in a more beautiful form, and as more sovereign than justice as an ideal of government. This is *Iustitia magna*, in contrast to *Iustitia in abstracto* sitting demurely on the bench of virtues, but without the instrument of her practical activity, namely her scales. So we need to begin with her, since she triggers the unfolding of the political narrative that Lorenzetti, through and beyond the apparent hieratic aura of these solemn figures, is bringing to life before our very eyes.

Between 1304 and 1306, in the Scrovegni Chapel (also known as the Arena Chapel) in Padua, Giotto painted the allegories of the seven virtues, of which justice comprises the clearest figurative model for Lorenzetti's version.[6] She sits enthroned in majesty, wearing her virginal veil, the mantle of the Mother of Mercy and the closed crown of the Queen of Heaven. In the palm of her right hand she holds a small winged figure who is rewarding one of the elect – probably an artisan behind his bench (a goldsmith?), sharing in the increase of wealth – and in the other hand a gaoler just about to strike a prisoner.[7] But Giotto painted this in grisaille, like a statue in a fictitious niche framed with the volutes of gothic architecture.[8] This *trompe-l'oeil* principle enables him to keep these painted abstractions at bay, thus suggesting, by pretending to give them the permanence of marble, that they really represent basic principles insofar as they are made part of the very foundations of the figurative order. Lorenzetti used this procedure for the medallions framing the fresco – the seasons, divinities and signs of the zodiac, the insignia of power and the symbols of knowledge on which the very possibility of representation is founded – but not for the allegories within it. Quite the opposite: it is as if the painter were imparting to those statues a breath of life that makes them stir and quiver in their bright hues.

The great folds in the ancient robes produce the effect of majestic sails, and the taut ropes strung from the beam of the balance like guy-ropes on a mast: to our surprise, we find ourselves gazing at this sumptuous composition as if it were a dream vision of a great vessel at anchor. *Sapientia* is its principle, in the Aristotelian sense of the term: the fixed point from which hangs the chain of causes and effects. She has a concentrated stare as, wrapped in her ermine mantle, holding a book, she brandishes in her right hand the end of the scales. The knowledge contained within this scarlet volume confers considerable dignity on the person holding it: it is the law, which inspires the right decisions. And it is a verse from the Wisdom of Solomon – as we have seen, the same words displayed by the divine child on the knees of Simone Martini's Virgin in Majesty (*Diligite iustitiam qui iudicatis terram*, 'Love justice, you who judge the earth') – which illumines the crowned blonde head of the allegory with its finely drawn features, at once so gentle and so stern. Of course, we must constantly compare it with the *Maestà* in the hall next door in the Palazzo Pubblico of Siena if we are to gauge the stupefying boldness of its secularized echo here in the Sala della Pace.

So we have a verse from scripture whose silken roundedness curves on both sides of the mast of the scales and is extended along the wings of the two angels busying themselves over its two plates. To the right of Justice (our left), a red angel is about to decapitate with a sweep of its sword an unfortunate figure with his head lowered, having dropped his own dagger on the ground, while another, on his knees, turns his back to us, holding the palm of glory: he too is bowing his head to receive his crown from the angel's other hand. To the left of Justice, the white angel is also leaning down towards two people who have each placed one knee on the ground; the scene seems more difficult to interpret. Two *tituli*, now difficult to make out, do, however, enable us to identify it: over the red angel was written the word *Distributiva*, and over the white angel, *Comutativa*. This learned distinction stemmed from the *Nicomachean Ethics* of Aristotle (V, 5), probably via the *Summa Theologiae* of Thomas Aquinas. Actually, Aristotelian terminology, in Robert Grosseteste's interpretation, draws a contrast between distributive and corrective justice – the notion of commutative justice stems more from the Thomist scholastic tradition.[9] To simplify some extremely complex debates, we might put it this way: commutative justice simply regulates exchanges between equals while distributive justice makes up for inequalities by rewarding good conduct with honours and punishing bad behaviour. The red angel hands out rewards and punishments while the white angel guarantees the fairness of a transaction. Is the latter angel acquiescing in an exchange proposed to him by the two persons dressed as wealthy merchants, of two spears for a bale of fabric?[10] We can also hypothesize that the objects here changing hands are measuring standards (length for the rod, capacity for the cylinder) – an allusion to a crucial problem for the urban governments of communal Italy, which, from at least the thirteenth century, set out to guarantee the security of exchanges by imposing a stable system of weights and measures.[11]

Balancing the scales: Justice manages this without any apparent effort, simply by slightly correcting their tilt with the delicate pressure of her thumbs. But she is probably being helped by the firm gesture of Concord, who, at her feet, counterbalances this admirable composition. Concord and the plane of equity – the *aequitas* which Aquinas describes as 'the quality which enables us to moderate the letter of the law', and which Cicero says, in the *Duties*, constitutes (together with concord) one of the two foundations of civil peace.[12] The slight pressure from the thumb of justice, then, is the act of will which alone can bring about equity in social terms. Here, Mario Sbriccoli has recognized the triad *Ratio–Iustitia–Aequitas* of the first allegories of justice, going back to the twelfth century.[13] However, we here find ourselves being brought back yet again to the doctrines of political philosophy when everything suggests that it is practices of government that are being highlighted. Maria Monica Donato is no doubt right to say that justice is the main theme of the fresco decorating the Sala della Pace,[14] but what matters here is the exercise of justice and not the abstract principles that inspire or legitimate it. Follow the thread: it leads from *Sapientia* to *Concordia*. Justice is doubtless a learned practice, inspired by Roman law, but it is completely focused on one goal: concord and equity – in other words, civil peace. This is what Lorenzetti is proclaiming, with the means proper to painting, in the dazzling array of his colourful figures: there can be no stable government without social justice – insofar as the latter does not merely rest content with guaranteeing exchanges between equals, but endeavours to smooth out any inequalities. So we might say, in the final analysis, to accord all of this with the name of the Sala della Pace and, no doubt, with the name of the fresco itself ('Peace and War'): Lorenzetti paints the pacification of a society by the exercise of justice.

This justice, as we have seen, required fiscal equity at a time when, in Siena as in all the other cities of communal Italy, political debate was focused on the fundamental issue of the extent to which an assessment of fortunes played a part in calculating a proportional tax. It also required a whole set of urban statutes and regulations concerning the equality and security of exchanges, as well as municipal arrangements and the management of public facilities, turning the city, in its material forms, into the space of the norm. This ideal of transparency, expressed in the fiscal investigation into the assessment of fortunes as well as in the desire that a well-regulated city form a structured urban arrangement, also involved penal justice. For the legal systems of Italian cities had, since the second half of the thirteenth century, undergone a decisive transformation, here again driven by the widening of the social basis of communal regimes to include the *popolo*, who made it into one of its main political demands. In plain and simple terms, this meant the development of the investigative procedure in relation to the accusatory procedure. The latter was a mode of conflict resolution by conciliation and arbitration between two plaintiffs, while the former rested on a sovereign act through which the judicial authority decided that a misdemeanour has been committed when a threat to public order had been posed, and tried, through inquiry into and comparison between contradicting evidence, not just to re-establish peace, but also to construct the truth. In the reality of social practices, this new procedure accommodated itself to a compromise form of justice and did not radically undermine the judicial pluralism of communal societies, in other words the ability, when resolving con-flicts, to resort to the judicial forms of mediation as well as the extra-judicial forms of more or less ritualized vengeance.[15] The fact remains that this ideologically entailed 'the advent of the penal': that is, the reconfiguration of the legal act in the sphere of the common good, by which justice became both public and punitive.[16]

This demand for a severe and spectacular justice, which attacked the very bodies of the condemned to inscribe the mark of their pun-ishment on them, was one of the most constant demands made by *regimi di popolo*. It found vigorous expression in the image that so impressed Bernardino of Siena on the east wall of the 'effects': the allegory of *Securitas*, floating in the heavenly blue of the Tuscan sky right above the pink walls of the happy city, and holding a scaffold in which we can see a hanged man, blindfolded. And yet she is a charm-ing figure, this lithe blonde lady with her round breasts, wearing next to nothing: art historians remind us that she is the first female nude in Western painting to bear a positive symbolic value.[17] Yes, doubt-less, much more than the *Timor* opposite – and yet, like her nasty counterpart, she carries death in her hands. Is there an incongruous clash here? No: this death is the legitimate death that the wicked must face. So this *Securitas* must be both desirable and pitiless. In this way, fear will be overcome: *Senza paura*, as its scroll promises. Without fear, people will be able to travel along the roads. '[A]s long as this commune / remains under the signoria of this lady / for she has taken all power from the guilty.'

And here they are, the guilty, led in triumph to the great personage enthroned on the north wall. One of them also has his eyes hidden behind a black veil – meaning that he has been sentenced to death. Under close escort they move along to the feet of the allegory of justice, the other figure, sitting at the end of the bench of virtues, holding the sword in her right hand and the crown in her left. As we have said, she represents distributive justice, but as a value and not as an exercise. So she has no scales and, haughty in her fine green doublet, remains indifferent to the sinister procession of punishments that unfolds down below, framed by two armed knights on horse-back. But all the same, on her knees lies the head of a decapitated man. This line of condemned men, forced to make a spectacle of their humiliation in a sort of communal perp walk, is going in the opposite direction to the procession of councillors. For the cord that hampers them is not one of those bonds which set one free. As the inscription running under the west wall warned: '[A]nd may anyone who seeks to trouble her be, for all his reward, / sent away and undone, / he and all those who follow him.' These are the men who, henceforth, will not be able to travel freely along the roads – they are the ones who, henceforth, will know fear.

A dritta corda: if you pull the cord tight, you can see clearly unfolding before you a political narrative that aims completely at the goal of a pacifying justice. Or, in other terms, of a peace in justice, since it is this demand for concord which, in concrete terms, can contrast this civil peace with the signorial peace on which the new masters of the Italian cities pride themselves, and which the painting here reduces to its tyrannical origins. In this way, the sonorous echo of words in the *visibile parlare* of the escutcheons and inscriptions enables us to extend this cord *utrinque*, on each side of the little wall of allegories. The cord links the *Timor* of the west wall to the *Securitas* of the east wall, passes through a justice shackled, humiliated and abandoned at the foot of the platform of vices; it is continued and lifted by the allegorical arrangement of the north wall, and heads off again towards the long wall of the beneficial effects. It makes it possible to connect hell to paradise via the purgatory of concepts and ideal principles. But it obviously converges on that venerable and enigmatic great personage. So is *he* the judge?

10

With the common good as lord

In 1958, Nicolai Rubinstein published an article called 'Political Ideas in Sienese Art' in the prestigious *Journal of the Warburg and Courtauld Institutes*. Rubinstein, a German-Jewish historian who had fled the persecution of the 1930s and gone to London, where he focused on the clientelism of the Medici and the way they imposed their rule on Florence behind the mask of their party, was already venturing beyond the strict limits of his own speciality. Nonetheless, this was the first overall study of the political iconography deployed by Ambrogio Lorenzetti across the three walls of the fresco – even if Rubinstein did concentrate, as did so many others after him, on the little wall of the allegories. His article opened the floodgates to a spate of exegeses which have since continued to swell bibliographies, with scholars bringing up all the heavy artillery of their erudition and analytical subtlety to investigate the textual sources of a work whose wealth seems inexhaustible.

This is because the idea put forward by Rubinstein was so simple and powerful that it could not fail to arouse a desire to complicate matters a little. For him, the fresco of the Palazzo Pubblico in Siena needed to be readable as the visual summation of Aristotle's political philosophy, as it had been transmitted, adapted and, so to speak, baptized by Thomas Aquinas in the thirteenth century. It thus illustrated the Aristotelian-Thomist worldview that historians now recognize as the doctrinal base on which stands the entire political philosophy of the *regimen*, the mediaeval government. The proof of the frescos' erudite origin lay in this question: where else, if not in the *Summa Theologiae* of Aquinas, could be found the (entirely theoretical) distinction between commutative and distributive justice? Now the keystone of this system of thought was the Aristotelian concept of the

common good, in its Thomist reformulation as the 'basis and criterion
of good government'.[1] Therefore, the majestic old man who dominates the virtues on the north wall in such sovereign fashion cannot
be anything but an allegorical personification of the common good,
and Lorenzetti has placed him at the centre of a composition that,
perhaps for the first time in the West, displays, with clarity and rigour,
a system of thought that represents a first stage in the growth of an
autonomous political culture.

This was the overall interpretation that, in 1986, was criticized by
Quentin Skinner, the head of the prestigious Cambridge School of
intellectual historians. [2] He rejected it as a whole, not just that aspect
of it which involved the political scope of the Sienese frescos, an analysis of which was basically, he claimed, merely one argument in a
debate that went far beyond it: the relation between the Aristotelian
tradition of mediaeval thought and the genesis of republican ideology. This debate doubtless bypassed the strictly figurative power of
Lorenzetti's pictorial work, and the mass of subtle arguments and
scholarly references that Skinner drew on to divert attention from
what I myself feel are the essential issues at stake in the political painting of the Sala della Pace can seem intimidating. But since this controversy still to some extent shapes historiographical discussions of
the Sienese fresco commissioned by the Nine, it is probably worth
presenting a quick overview of it. I hope the reader will not mind if I
simplify matters to sketch out an argument that I have developed at
greater length elsewhere.[3]

The main thing we need to understand is that Skinner, who wishes
to write a history of liberty before liberalism, is part of a controversy
that is not merely scholarly but intellectual in the proper sense of the
word. This controversy concerns the very origins of humanism, and
is bound to have seemed politically crucial to an entire generation
of scholars who formed part of the Jewish emigration from Weimar
Germany.[4] This was the case with Hans Baron, Rubinstein's teacher:
Baron came up with the concept of 'civic humanism', which, in his
feverish history, he envisaged as 'the sole defence against the threat
of despotism'.[5] Baron insisted on the threshold year of 1400, which
in his view formed a rather clear break between the Middle Ages and
the Renaissance, and lauded the cultural revolution brought about
by Florentine thinkers such as Coluccio Salutati (1331–1406) and
Leonardo Bruni (1370–1444). These humanists had forged the idea of
republican liberty as a redoubtable weapon in the merciless ideological struggle between the 'commune' of Florence and the 'tyranny' of
the lords of Milan.[6] Before them, in his view, a republic was unthink-

able: communal governments had practised a policy in complete igno-
rance of its philosophical bases, and in any case revealed themselves
to be unable to affirm an 'independent lay ideology'.[7]

This fiercely contested thesis, both trenchantly expressed and even-
tually productive, dominated academic debate for a long time. Skinner
adopted and radicalized the criticisms formulated by Paul Oscar
Kristeller (another German exile),[8] and went on to argue vehemently
against the 'Baronian' idea that the Florentine civic humanism which
came into being around 1400 marked a clean break. Skinner defended
a much earlier date for the emergence of an urban consciousness of
republican liberty, one which was already evident in the communal
Italy of the first half of the thirteenth century. On this point, he was
doubtless followed by a certain trend in Italian historiography – a
trend that we might deem to be idealist, though it is still influential.[9]
This shift in perspective inspires the very architecture of Skinner's
great work of synthesis, *The Foundations of Modern Political
Thought*, the first chapters of which set out the connection between
'rhetoric and liberty' based on certain texts of the *ars dictaminis*.[10]
From this point of view, his 1986 paper on Lorenzetti, 'The Artist
as Political Philosopher', was, as it were, a 'defence and illustration'
of that central thesis. But what exactly was the *ars dictaminis*? In
the broadest sense of the term, it was the art of writing a composition, resting on a set of rhetorical techniques, most of them inherited
from ancient culture but reformulated so as to be better adapted to
mediaeval communication. Associated with the rhythmical prose of
the *cursus*, the *dictamen* comprised a 'caste-based ideology'[11] whose
aim was to heighten the aura of power with the solemn obscurity of
mysteries of state.

In the social and political context of communal Italy, the rise of the
ars dictaminis put its stamp on the central position of rhetoric in civil
life. For as soon as the stability of the political system rested on the
deliberations of councils and the ability of magistrates to convince the
citizens assembled together, the control of secular eloquence became
a major issue for government. The Podestà, those itinerant judges
who, selected from outside the commune to arbitrate in its conflicts,
became professionals of conciliation and persuasion from the thirteenth century onwards, seized on these oratorical techniques.[12] But
they were not the only ones to do so, and the political community
had to beware of unbridled uses of civic speech that might give too
great an authority to demagogues – a fear that haunted the Florentine
Dino Compagni, who, in his *Cronica* (1310–12), described how the
people had been corrupted by the *malizia* of the master of the art

of harangue.[13] That was why, as the thirteenth century gave way to the fourteenth, the question of eloquence took a more dramatic turn, moving into the sphere of a public ethics of political action.[14] There was doubtless something specific in communal regimes that made them confuse the *rector* with the *rhetor*, the just government with well-regulated speech, living well with speaking well. But it would be superficial to believe that this anxiety over language no longer concerns us today, now that we understand even more clearly that nothing is more profoundly political than the slow erosion of the common good of words.

Skinner decided to extract a doctrinal corpus from this continuum of texts. He brought together texts composed for the use of the Podestà (such as the anonymous compilation of the *Oculus pastoralis* from the 1220s, which was the pioneer example of such works), and also poems such as that by the judge Orfino da Lodi (*De regimine et sapientia potestatis*, 1245) and the collection of epistolary models and speeches put together by the Bolognese notary Guido Fava in 1238–9 (*Summa dictaminis*). Of a quite different level of importance is the *Liber de regimine civitatum* by the jurist Giovanni da Viterbo, probably also composed at the end of the 1230s; this work gave a blanket definition of *regimen* that was close to Foucault's view of governmentality.[15] Giovanni da Viterbo's clear commitment to a republican form of government was only partly evidenced in the great encyclopaedic work that Brunetto Latini produced in the langue d'oïl around 1260 (Latini, a Florentine diplomat, went into exile in France after the defeat of Montaperti), *Li Livres dou trésor*, which constitutes the *summa*, and the summit, of the great Italian literature of *vivere civile*.

This set of texts, all of them deeply rooted in the governmental practice of communal elites, holds a historical importance that is constantly being re-evaluated. Nonetheless, it would perhaps be going too far to consider it as the expression of a political theory.[16] This would be to disrespect the heterogeneity of genres, of languages, of target audiences, of political contexts, and of the social impact as measured in terms of the broad extent of the manuscript tradition:[17] whatever did a few short, confidential works have in common with Brunetto Latini's bestseller? But this hardly matters: for Skinner, everything is a matter of chronology. The sequence that began in the 1220s (*Oculus pastoralis*) and ended in 1260 (*Li livres dou trésor*) corresponded to the phase in which the *popolo* gradually extended its influence in the communal institutions. Now this sequence came before the great wave of complete translations of Aristotle's political and ethical works: the *Nicomachean Ethics* was circulating in its first complete Latin version only from the early 1250s, and William of Moerbeke completed his Latin translation of the *Politics* ten years later. So the *dictators* (as the authors of the *ars dictaminis* were known) had only an imperfect and indirect acquaintance with Aristotle.[18] On the other hand, they knew by heart Sallust, Seneca and, above all, the Cicero of *On Duties* and *On Invention*.

This was the really decisive factor as far as Skinner was concerned: he concluded that the ideology of republican autonomy developed in the early decades of the thirteenth century, and largely preceded the rediscovery of the moral and political works of Aristotle; or, more abruptly, that '[t]he political theory of the Renaissance, at all phases of its history, owes a far deeper debt to Rome than to Greece.'[19] The difference was an important one: it resided mainly in the very idea of community. Roman law had seen community as an artificial body constructed at the same time as the abstract idea of the juridical person, while Thomist theology envisaged it as a natural entity, in which the virtues of the social individual could be exercised. As Alain Boureau puts it, 'In Thomism, perfection consisted in a proper balance between the demands of life in society and the individual needs of freedom and responsibility.'[20] This balance could be achieved whatever the institutional definition of the political regime, once it tended towards the common good and respected the right of the community. When commenting on the typology of the four legitimate regimes (monarchy, aristocracy, democracy and mixed rule), most scholastic authors, such as Henry of Rimini and Thomas Aquinas, and even Marsilius of Padua, defended the overall idea that the best form of government varied with circumstances, and that there were several ways of creating the *res publica*.[21] With a few exceptions, such as Bartholomew of Lucca, only the neo-Ciceronianism of Brunetto Latini led to a defence of the strictly republican form of the *res publica*.[22]

Given all this, what is most important, in Skinner's view, is to show that what he considers to be the central personage in the composition on Lorenzetti's north wall is not the embodiment of the common good as Rubinstein saw it, but the Ciceronian *magnus vir sapiens* that Latini took as the hero of his *Rhetoric*.[23] This 'wise and superior man' (*On invention*, I, 2) persuaded people to abandon their brutal manners and live under the law. So he is the supreme legislator, who lives again in the person of the magistrates of the commune. For what else is the commune if not the political system in which the laws themselves govern insofar as they can find magistrates to embody them? As Giovanni da Viterbo writes: 'Those who preside over the affairs of republics have to be similar to the laws.' That is why they sit 'on a throne of glory' and hold their sceptre 'in a strong hand, with outstretched arm'.[24] Is this not what Lorenzetti represented? Hence Skinner's conclusion, as peremptory as a sentence that brooks no appeal: '[T]he regal figure has been misidentified by those who have seen it as a personification of the common good. The figure is, rather, a symbolic representation of the type of *signore* or *signoria* that a city needs to elect if the dictates of justice are to be followed and the common good secured.'[25]

Skinner's argument has been severely criticized by Italian historians (especially Maria Monica Donato),[26] and this is doubtless the point where it is most methodologically vulnerable. For Skinner, an allegory cannot refer to more than a single idea, and if the old bearded man represents the sovereignty of the law as it is embodied in the communal figure of the magistrate, this means that he cannot designate anything else, especially not the Thomist idea of the common good.[27] He probably derived this principle of non-contradiction from the iconographical rigours of the classical order whose historian he is. And this classical order rests on a demand for clarification and codification that involves the strictest assignation of allegorical personages to the textual traditions they are meant to illustrate. One example is the *Iconologia* of Cesare Ripa (1595), which disciplined the allegorical exuberance of the Renaissance, characterized by a liking for riddles, emblems and rebuses.[28] But in 1338, this still lay far in the future – we need only point to Lorenzetti himself, who, as we have seen, painted the *Sapientia* that sits above and inspires *Iustitia*. Skinner notes that this personification of wisdom is a reference neither to Aquinas (for whom it is practical, not speculative, reason which guides human law) nor to Cicero (for whom wisdom is a human attribute and not a heavenly power); and he concludes that the painter 'treats his authorities at this juncture with an unusual degree of licence'.[29] This is too far-fetched: why would anyone suppose that Lorenzetti might have needed to free himself from the weight of a philosophical culture in which he was in any case not completely at home? It is enough to realize that he was expressing a common political culture produced not by scholarly allusions but by a whole set of values, words and practices. In the language of communal Italy, *ragione* could almost equally mean both 'reason' and 'justice' – and this is how we need to understand the name of the Palazzo della Ragione that Giotto decorated in Padua. It is quite unnecessary to go back to scholarly treatises to find the idea that justice must be inspired by reason, as this was a self-evident truth of practical reason in the eyes of communal societies.

Interpreting a text by seeking not any doctrinal certainties, beliefs or ethical commitments *affirmed* within it, but rather the actions it seeks to produce – in other words to understand 'what he is actually *engaged on* when he says what he says':[30] this is the main element in a pragmatic hermeneutics. It also applies to images – at least if we *give them the initiative* and let them come to us. Look at the female figure sitting to the right of the great personage enthroned in majesty, between *Magnanimitas* and *Iustitia*, named in its *titulus* as *Temperantia* or Temperance. Draped in a lovely blue robe, in her right hand she raises an hourglass, while with her left hand she points to the sand that has already run out. This is an unusual symbolic attribute. Usually, temperance is represented holding two containers, pouring liquid from one into the other, often mixing water and wine – 'watering down' her wine, as we say. This was how Lorenzetti represented her in the fresco he painted on the walls of the church of San Francesco in Siena in 1326.[31] We might see this kind of iconography as corresponding to the Thomist conception of temperance as moderation ('the very name of this virtue signifies the power of moderating or tempering something', as Aquinas wrote in his *Summa Theologiae*, 2a–2ae). The motif of the hourglass refers, in Skinner's view, to another tradition, that of Cicero, who wrote, in his *On Duties*, that we must 'pronounce neither too broadly nor too rapidly'.[32] That is why Varro, in his treatise *De lingua Latina* (*On the Latin Language*) states that there is an etymological link between *tempus* and *temperantia*, and this is why an instrument for measuring time can be an adequate way of referring to the virtue of temperance.[33] To govern is to master time. The temperance painted by Lorenzetti thus points to a pragmatic conception of the exercise of power, one that is, if not exactly detached from an ethical demand, then at least more 'technical' in its principle.

Skinner's interpretation here is of a classical iconographic sort, since it is thanks to a textual source that he can decrypt the image. So his reading only half fulfils its programme: what is the image doing by here adopting a technical motif of temperance? After all, it is a far from anodyne motif, and it is one of great contemporary relevance: this is the first figurative representation of an hourglass, and the oldest documentary attestations of this theme do not date back before the early fourteenth century. Contrary to what common sense might suggest, what in those days were called 'sand glasses' (or 'sand clocks') were first used to check that mechanical clocks were regularly chiming out the hours. So the hourglass was an innovation of the first half of the fourteenth century, linked to the modern way of reckoning time and reliant on the revolution of regularly spaced hours that was part of the affirmation of urban identity.[34] In 1336, the Dominican Galvano Fiamma wrote an enthusiastic description (another first) of the mechanical clock perched on the campanile of San Gottardo in Corte, in Milan.[35] Thus the use of the theme of time mastered to designate the virtue of temperance cannot be seen just as a learned illustration of Cicero's text which Lorenzetti discovered all of a sudden between 1326 and 1338, but must also be seen as a way of bringing it to life in an accelerating political tempo connected mainly with the competition between cities (and between the political regimes they embodied) to appropriate the virtues of technical modernity.

So if we are to return to the image, we need to envisage the texts of political theory as resources to be exploited by an active iconography. What do we see? A man, imposing and venerable. His gaze is clear and direct, his features finely shaped, his white beard neatly trimmed: over the virtues surrounding him he sheds the calm beauty of his severity. This old man, the sole masculine allegory in the Sienese fresco, embodies the power of a 'virile majesty'.[36] He sits on his throne, and everything about his attitude, his frontal posture, his regalia (the sceptre, the royal robes), makes us think of a sovereign power. Everything alludes to this – and yet nothing clearly indicates it: so it is impossible to reduce Lorenzetti's composition to a precedent in political allegory. The best we can say is that the painter's *bellissima inventiva* takes several of its motifs from royal iconography – as on Frederick II's gate at Capua, where the emperor enthroned in majesty appears framed by the busts of figures embodying Justice, or, in another example, the effigy of Charles of Anjou on the Capitol in Rome.[37] Ernst Kantorowicz had this iconographic corpus in mind when he thought he could see, in the centre of the composition in Siena, 'a gigantic emperor-like figure':[38] this interpretation is probably wrong, but at least it highlights the fundamentally equivocal nature of the image.

This remark also applies to iconographical borrowings from that other main resource for legitimizing universal power, the institution of the Church. One can justifiably see this image has having several resemblances with well-known fourteenth-century motifs such as the persecuted Church.[39] But it would be to give it an exaggeratedly clerical meaning if we saw it as the main source for 'such a clearly profane political allegory'.[40] Admittedly, the theological virtues are hovering over the head of the great personage. To his right is *Fides*, carrying the Redeemer's cross: the very name *Fides* means both faith and fidelity, and binds the two aspects of obedience, spiritual and political, tightly together. On his left is *Spes*, Hope, with open hands hailing the sublime radiance of the face of God that she is contemplating. *Caritas*, finally, the keystone, displays her ardent heart as she summons the virtues: 'Charity is the mother of all virtues insofar as she informs all the virtues,' as Aquinas wrote (*Summa Theologiae*, 1–2 q. 62, a.4), since she signifies both love and the gift. However, this divine inspiration involves no clerical mediation: it illumines the head of the old man as well as the head of the young woman allegorizing justice, but these are not virtuous principles so much as they are the beneficial effects of their good government. Peace (*Pax*), Fortitude (*Fortitudo*, a lovely female warrior in shining armour), Prudence (*Prudentia*, pointing firmly to her phylactery with the names of the past, the present and future on it), Magnanimity (*Magnanimitas*, handing out money with one hand and with the other the crown of honour), Temperance (*Temperantia*, which is, like prudence, an art of mastering time), and finally *Iustitia*: all virtues that are not specifically Christian. They can be called political insofar as they proceed from the exercise of good government, and that is why they are all seated on the same level as the majestic personage whose 'assessors', in the proper sense of the word, they are.

So are we to call him a judge? He does wear, after all, not the sovereign's crown, but the ermine-trimmed cap of the Podestàs. However, a raking light here reveals a pentimento: the painter had initially set a laurel crown on the brows of this great personage. And while this laurel crown was clearly a pendant to the olive crown in the allegory of peace, it referred, indubitably given the Sienese figurative tradition, to imperial iconography.[41] It is high time to bring all these scattered elements together. If we absolutely need to *describe* the central allegory in Lorenzetti's composition, we will say that it points to communal government insofar as this is embodied in the sovereign figure of a venerable judge. In this respect, it corresponds to a certain Sienese tradition of representing the city magistrates (especially in the illuminated statutes).[42] But it also draws on the Giottesque model of the frescos in the palace of the Podestà in Florence, which, according to Vasari, already included (as we have seen) a figure of the commune 'sitting in the form of Judge [*in forma di giudice*], sceptre in hand', and surrounded by the four cardinal virtues.[43] Other visual codes add a wealth of ideological denotations to the image: it borrows from the symbols of authority (the old man's venerable beard), of majesty (the throne and the frontal pose), of sovereignty (the sceptre) and of sacredness (the theological virtues) – and the whole figure is reinterpreted within a communal framework (the royal crown becomes the ermine-trimmed cap of the Podestàs). This accumulation of symbols makes for ambiguity in reading, but it is precisely this ambiguity which *bears* meaning. For it makes visible what no theoretical text would say as powerfully: communal government, insofar as it is embodied in the magistrates who serve it, is a sovereign power.

The second level of denotation says that this government is not any random commune, but the commune of Siena. Over the great personage is a *titulus* whose meaning is barely discernible unless we remove a letter that has been intercalated by a clumsy piece of restoration: *C.S.C.C.V.* needs to be read as *C.S.C.V.*, *Commune Senarum Civitas Virginis*, the commune of Siena representing itself as the city of the Virgin.[44] The same abbreviations can be read in the allegory of the commune of Siena painted in 1344 on the tablet of a Biccherna (the tax department, the wooden bindings of whose accounts were decorated by the greatest artists in Siena) above the shoulders of a great personage very similar to that in the Sala della Pace.[45] On this image, which some art historians attribute to Lorenzetti, we see the throne and the frontal position, the venerable air, the beard and the regalia, and the ermine cap of the Podestà. We can also identify three motifs that appear on the fresco of the Palazzo Pubblico: the black and white costume of the personage dressed in the colours of the coat of arms of Siena; the seal of the commune, which he brandishes like a golden shield (the seal also bears the image of the Virgin); and a she-wolf at his feet, suckling twins. These are Senius and Aschius, sons of Remus, chosen as the mythical heroes of the city in one of its foundation legends at the very end of the thirteenth century.[46] The two brothers fled Rome after their father was killed by Romulus, and with them, on the black and white horses that Apollo and Diana had given them, they took the she-wolf of the Capitol: the very same figure that is depicted in the middle of the wall resembles a sculpture over the entrance to the well-governed city. The name *Senius*, which also refers, in Latin, to the city itself, echoes the *persona senex* who rules and embodies it.[47]

Once the code of denotations has been established, historians can take as much time as they like completing the never-ending range of connotations – and there is no reason why they should not draw on theoretical textual sources to do so. Skinner has demonstrated that this complex image could connote the neo-Ciceronianism of the orators who evoked the rigour of the laws, which they melded with the stature of the magistrate, who was at once the master and the servant of those laws.[48] This touch of *romanitas* is perfectly in line with the political ideology of the commune of Siena, which, in precisely those years, dreamed of itself as a new Rome, and even included within its statutes of 1336–8 the Justinian constitution of *Deo auctore*.[49] But this does

nothing to stop us completing the system of connotation by mention-
ing the Thomist notion of the *bene comune*; as Nicolai Rubinstein has
shown, this notion constituted a *common place* (in the proper sense
of the term) in communal ideology. This idea can be given real political shape only by concrete policies that implement it, especially in
the spheres of justice, fiscality and municipal government.[50] However,
it can be theoretically described, since the translation of Aristotle's
Politics made it possible after 1260 to describe this 'indefinite greatness', higher than the sum of particular interests, by conferring upon it
an aura of sacredness. It inspired a political theology which assumed
'a resolutely normative character', as promoted in the commentaries
on Aristotle between approximately 1270 and 1370: '[T]he common
good is the *object* of the political community: nothing can resist this
principle.'[51]

Indeed, nothing *can* resist it: Lorenzetti's political painting helps us
see and understand the royal authority exercised on political society
by the ideal, or rather the requirement, of the common good. Royal
authority is a form of political domination in the Aristotelian sense
– which does not mean that it is absolute. Etymologically, 'absolute' means 'unbound'. Here, however, the communal government
may admittedly be fully sovereign – it is *civitas sibi princeps*, 'the
city as ruler of itself' in the famous formula of the jurist Bartolus de
Saxoferrato,[52] like the prince or the emperor – but it remains linked
to justice, in a bond on which can be based the concord of the community. Always the rope, knotted to the wrist of the great personage
– while another, later allegory painted on a Biccherna tablet (1385)
adopts a more radical solution to express the nature of this power
that is both master and slave of the law by literally tying a rope round
his neck.[53] The government of the commune is a *dominus* to whom
citizens entrust their *libertas* and to whom they owe obedience. In so
doing, they become a political community without ceasing to experience themselves as free and distinct individuals. But at the same time
they also bind the communal government to the superior necessity
of defending the common good. This orientation towards the good
is, together with peace and prosperity, what keeps the community
together, not so as to sacralize it but to realize it politically. It is thus
that, in his *Defensor pacis*, Marsilius of Padua describes the unity of
the multitude, that *societas multorum* which would be doomed to
dispersal if a superior principle did not govern it, thus making it 'a
plurality of men which is called a unity'.[54]

Does the escutcheon of the painted writings not already say as
much? For too long we have ignored it, in vain, perhaps allowing

ourselves to be overwhelmed by the erudition of the commentators
when everything is here expressed in just a few lines. What we should
read, instead, lies at the bottom of the north wall of the allegories:
'This sacred virtue, wherever she rules, / leads to unity the multitude
of souls, / and these, gathered to this aim, / make the common good
their lord.' The poetic obscurity of the last formula has caused much
ink to flow (especially, as we have mentioned, on the meaning of the
word *per* in *un ben comun per lor signor si fanno*), but how can we not
see this is precisely the source from which the clarity of the meaning
arises? It resides entirely in an equivocation that can be expressed in
the words of painted poetry, as well as in the words of civic rhetoric.
The latter, in spite of all the efforts of the historians of ideas who
seek to organize it into contrasted political philosophies, can, in the
case of communal Italy, be reduced to something that Igor Mineo
has brilliantly characterized as 'the impossibility of thinking of "monarchy" and "republic" as antithetical forms'.[55] But the way political
regimes can be viewed as such hybrid formations, thereby turning the
commune into a signoria, is something that can be fully measured (as
we now know) only by the concrete history of the power practices of
the first third of the trecento.

It was with the means proper to painting that Lorenzetti succeeded
in expressing this tension, playing on the ambiguity of images that
drew on different resources of iconographic legitimation – even if he
subsequently revised his ideas if the meaning became too unambiguous, as was undoubtedly the case with the laurel wreath. For he then
had to confront the seduction exercised over people's minds by the
good government of the signoria, supported by skilful and convincing propaganda which made considerable use of political allegory.
One example is the funerary monument of Berardo Maggi, sculpted
shortly after the death of this man, both bishop and lord of the city of
Brescia, in 1308. He had himself represented on the bas-reliefs of the
lid of the sarcophagus that narrated his political life. He can be seen
among the citizens who are exchanging oaths and kisses of peace,
in a scene which is simultaneously one of pacification, submission
and triumph.[56] There is the same recourse to narrativity on the bas-
reliefs of the funerary mausoleum of the bishop and lord of Arezzo,
the Ghibelline Guido Tarlati, which were, as we have said (chapter
5), sculpted between 1329 and 1332 by the Sienese Agostino di
Giovanni and Agnolo di Ventura. It was Pier Sacone, Guido Tarlati's
own brother, who had gone to bring the two sculptors from Siena –
just as Pietro Lorenzetti, Ambrogio's brother, was leaving to work
in Arezzo.[57] This circulation of motifs and artists between commune

and signoria was also true, of course, in the case of Giotto, who was
working in Padua, Milan and Florence. The fresco that he painted
in the 1320s in the palace of the Podestà, now lost, represented the
commune 'in the form of Judge'. But this judge was being assailed by
the *rubatori*, the monopolists who had come to tear off his clothes, in
other words, to strip him of his majesty and confiscate the resources
of the commune – an image of civil discord and the self-annihilation
of the political community destined, according to Giorgio Vasari, to
frighten the people.[58] It was precisely this image of the commune
stripped bare (*comune pelato*) that contrasted with the image of
the *comune in signoria* on the funerary monument of Guido Tarlati
in Arezzo: a venerable figure enthroned in sovereignty, embodying
the restoration of the authority of the common good, with citizens
coming to acknowledge the triumph of this signorial achievement on
the part of the commune.

One could say the same about the funerary mausoleum of the lord
of Milan, Azzone Visconti, carved by the Pisan Giovanni da Balduccio
between 1342 and 1346, depicting Ambrose, saint and bishop, and
patron and protector of the city, as a victorious Roman general to
whom the allegories of the subjected cities, each accompanied by its
civic saint, bring their trophies as a testimony of submission.[59] It was
this soothing image of the *insignorimento* or signorial take-over of the
commune to which Ambrogio Lorenzetti needed to respond – and he
would do so with the same iconographic means that he used to adjust
his allegorical personification to the repertoires of the divine majesty,
imperial sovereignty and the civic values of the common good: that
is, by the equivocal borrowing of motifs. But these are clearly defined
here: pacification, submission and triumph. That is why we have to
agree with Rosa Maria Dessì when she states that the main subject of
the political allegories of the northern wall is pacification.[60] This pacification involved the submission of the adversaries of the commune
and the triumph of the public good over particular interests, but,
unlike the prince's peace, which was founded on the fear of discord,
it accomplished an ideal of social justice which kept conflict at bay
without eradicating it. This too was expressed with the greatest possible clarity in the verses of the political song of the *visibile parlare* of
the Sala della Pace: 'Therefore it is to him that are given in triumph /
taxes, tributes and signorias.'

This triumph is represented at the feet of the great personage not
in an allegorical form, but in a very clear allusion to the concrete conditions of the exercise of communal power when confronted with the
political emergencies of the times. If Lorenzetti painted the empire of

the commune, this latter must first be understood itself in the territorial dimension of the *pax senensis*. Here are the feudatories advanc-
ing towards the throne, in armour but bareheaded and submissive.
They bring the government of the commune their castle, as a trophy
– an evident symbol of the territorial incorporation of the signorias
of the Sienese land (but also perhaps the demonymic towers of the
noble party) into the political body of Siena.[61] A Roman-style political triumph, in which those 'wicked men who lived a long time ago
and who had acted badly'[62] were, as he thought, recognized by the
anonymous Sienese chronicler of the fourteenth century in the Sala
della Pace of the Palazzo Pubblico, in the manner of these collective
ignominious paintings which Giuliano Milano showed were a kind
of visual representation of the lists of the banished.[63] For here lay the
essential alternative for political communities torn apart by factional
struggles: to exclude their adversaries or to give themselves over to a
lord.[64]

Now what is there to recognize in this train of submissive men,
those who 'hate peace', as one reads in the escutcheon under the
allegories of the western wall? Less individuals than social types: by
allegorizing the vices of the enemies of the commune rather than por-
traying particular adversaries, political painting perpetuates its scope,
beyond the necessarily fleeting chronology of banishments, which
are by definition always transient. What is clearly visible here when
viewed through the eyes of the trecento is the way political society
was split between militia and *popolo*: everything about those who are
submitting on the left of the great personage – their demeanour, their
arms, their hairstyles and their beards – unambiguously connotes their
membership of the group of the *milites*, while the costume of the citizens bonded in harmony who march towards him on his right links
them to the business class of the *popolo*. Contrary to the aforementioned representations of signorial pacification, where the *dominus*
surpasses in his greatness and authority the bipartition of political
society which he neutralizes, the conflicts here remain a live issue. This
tension is constitutive of *regimi di popolo* such as the government of
the Nine: as a party regime, based on the exclusion of its opponents,
it aspires at the same time to represent the whole political community.
In the ordinary run of its political life, insofar as it is an unstable
system of parties, the commune constantly contradicted its founding
ideal of concord and unity, since the word '*popolo*' could designate
at the same time the whole of political space and one of its parts, the
abstract *princeps* who ruled the city by representing it in its unity, or
the body of the *cives* who obeyed him while counterbalancing him.[65]

'[T]hus, without war, / there follow for the city all effects / useful, necessary, and agreeable.' It was therefore necessary to go through the purgatory of words and concepts to emerge from hell. The small north wall of the allegories is the location of this passage. Not yet paradise, but what prepares for it and promises it. Not yet paradise, for paradise can only be realized in the brilliant colours of bodies at liberty, those of the talking beings which will soon be displayed along the eastern wall of the Sala della Pace. A woman sees it, and we see that woman. She is the most celebrated and beautiful of the allegorical personifications painted by Lorenzetti. She stands on the edge of the platform of the virtues, the first of the assessors of power who are enthroned there. Gently holding an olive branch, and resting her head on her right arm while leaning on an ornate cushion, she indolently contemplates the calm beauty of the panorama which unfolds on the eastern wall: the effects of *her* good government. For the Nine wanted to see depicted a great scene of pacification. And her *titulus* designates her as *Pax*. So here she is, sumptuous and sovereign and delightfully detached. Her light and immaculate dress, and also her classically inspired, softly drooping pose, distinguish her from her sisters. There is no hieraticism here: she looks like an ancient statue animated by a breath of life. But the modern eye is mistaken in taking her for a languid woman: under the cushion and under her right foot can be seen armour and a shield, the tarnishing of whose brilliant golds and silvers – which were much more present in Lorenzetti's work than is commonly believed[66] – certainly makes it less visible than it was originally.

Peace, in Lorenzetti's composition, is in a position of triumph or, more precisely, of rest after triumph. She therefore corresponds much less to the Thomistic thesis of peace as an absence of discord than to the Roman conception (found especially in Prudentius, whose *Psychomachia* was widely read in the Middle Ages) of peace as victory over discord. It is understandable, moreover, that the *dictatores*, confronted with an intensification of the factional conflicts that threatened to destroy civil peace, found a more energetic intellectual resource in this Roman conception. Examples include Orfino da Lodi, for whom peace represents the victorious outcome of 'battle and flight of discord', and Giovanni da Viterbo, who urges every magistrate to defend peace: that is, to 'free the community of evil men and ensure that he conquers them'.[67] It is she whom Lorenzetti painted here; everything seems accomplished. And yet . . . Her eyes are as green as unripe almonds. Sad and calm. What can she see that makes her so dreamy?

11

What Peace sees: narratives of spaces and talking bodies

Finally we come to the large spaces. Along the steepest slope of the written words as they stretch out, the eye glides effortlessly, making the vision of a pacified city seem even more extensive. Nothing blocks one's gaze, not even the clean line of the pink city walls cutting this interior wall into two equal parts. Here we see the sharp angles of the buildings, whose sudden jostling makes the urban densities seem so narrow, even though they agree to step back so that the urban crowd can gather; there we see the swell of the hills slowly sloping down towards the valley which cuts through the plain below, hills pricked with vines and clipped trees and crossed with paths and carefully aligned hedges. On both sides of the zigzagging city walls, people are walking and talking, unifying an entirely occupied space, in the streets and along the paths, albeit in different ways. So much so that a single landscape unfolds in the intensity of the careful attention we bring to its *enhancement* – in the sense of painters as well as of urban planners and agronomists.

Modern commentators distinguish between the effects of good government for the city, on the one hand, and for the *contado*, on the other. But the painter has grasped them all in one fell swoop, and we need to do the same, to pass through the walls as if breaking the spine of a book so that the image can finally be smoothed out, and so that the fine line which always hampers the light and bends the perspective can finally vanish. This is, in truth, impossible: the image is a nightmare for layout artists and it needs to be divided into sections if it is to fit into books. On the spot, it equally defies reading: we have to move, walk, turn round, retrace our steps, to embrace it in its totality; the very fact that it always exceeds the human capacity to grasp it should suffice to discourage any interpretation based on the implicit model of textuality. Unless, of course, we pick up that modern pen, the camera, and remember what Jean-Luc Godard said of the tracking shot. In 1960, Godard's *Le Petit Soldat* filmed a malaise in history, that of the generation marked by the war in Algeria. 'What I mainly want to show in this spy film,' the filmmaker explained, 'is the opposition between urban Geneva (Geneva is the most incredible, the most poetic city in Europe), and, just ten kilometres away, the wild slopes of Mont Salève, and show them meeting by means of a great tracking shot along the admirable little road of Collonges. But as I keep changing my mind, I don't know if I will.'[1]

Godard did not get round to it, but Lorenzetti did. This great tracking shot along the eastern wall of the Sala della Pace carries us away in a slow and broad movement, from left to right, which Western reading habits make quite natural. It descends the hill which the town gate surmounts, following the calm and sure steps of the noble cavaliers leaving it. Others, whose mounts are half-concealed by the buildings which block the prospect of the square in the centre of the busy city, follow in the same direction. But they cross the contrary movement of all those who, more modestly perched on their donkeys or accompanied by their pigs, are entering the city to bring to it all the food it needs. They are making their way up the slope, with more of an effort. So the tracking shot of the Sienese panorama is immediately thwarted, holding the gaze that runs across it and constantly bringing it back to the centre – as the wedding procession invites us, from the start of this vast lateral course, obliging us to turn back and retrace our steps to the left, near the corner of the north wall. We can grasp the measured pace of socially determined movement back and forth, sensing the economical breathing which gives it its regular rhythm.

The pulse of a city is taken at its gates. In the Middle Ages, the city walls defined the urban integrity of the *civitas* as a political, juridical and sacred space, set apart from the surrounding countryside. No city without a wall; this intangible principle of identification has the force of evidence of a coat of arms. Lorenzetti registered this fact explicitly: he represented this common place of civic culture – but he did so obliquely. With a bold and skilful use of perspective, raising the viewer's point of view above the city walls (even though this viewer is physically placed below the fresco), the painter produces an effect that shrinks the scene and collapses all the lines of perspective. All we can glimpse of the city gate is a small indentation partly concealed by the crenelated mass of its brick front (*rivellino*), so that the passage of those who enter and leave the city has to be deduced from the figurative construction rather than being displayed directly. Thus, with the same brush stroke, the painter of the Nine manages to represent opening and closure, the threshold effect which regulates the spatial functioning of a gate in the walls. In other words, in painting it from the side, Lorenzetti narrows its monumentality so as to emphasize its political use.

An urban gate, then – but which one? Since we no longer expect to find in this part of the work a realistic portrait of the city of Siena but rather the *veduta* of a well-governed city that resembles it, it is hardly surprising that we cannot accurately recognize any clearly identifiable monument. Most specialists agree, however, that the city gate depicted here is similar to the Porta Romana, or the Porta Tufi – at least one of the two gates on the south side of the city.[2] In 1323, the government of the Nine decided to enlarge the city walls.[3] They now ran for more than 6,600 metres, delimiting a closed area of about 165 hectares – for comparison, Genoa at that time covered 155 hectares, Pisa 185 hectares, Florence at least 430 hectares.[4] But the walls were actually built some way outside the mass of the city, and the whole of this surface was very far from being urbanized; even if Lorenzetti left a few vacant spaces, in particular near the walls, he depicted the urban fabric as much denser than it really was. The widening of the walls accentuated the irregularity of the urban form, stretched into a very narrow triangle along the backbone of the Via Francigena, which crossed it from north to south. The Porta Romana was the entry point of this thoroughfare of the trade linking Rome to France. It opened one of the three urban districts (*terzi*) – the oldest, the *Terzo di città*, corresponding to the old episcopal district in the south-west of the city – which fiscally and juridically divided the city, following a territorial division which projected itself out into the *contado*.

But it is precisely this projection of the cityscape beyond the walls of the old city that constitutes the most obvious political message of the painting in the Sala della Pace. The influence of the commune on its former diocese (the *contado*) was constitutive of, and strictly contemporary with, the affirmation of urban government as early as the twelfth century. But it extended beyond that, incorporating rural communities, signorias and small towns into what the documents of this practice called the 'district'. The essential instrument of this territorialization of urban power was the policy of road creation and maintenance. As a daughter of the road, Siena very soon developed (being among the first in communal Italy to do so) a systematic and coordinated plan to build a radiating network of roads and paths which, from the thirteenth century, it enlarged and paved, guaranteeing their maintenance, control and security. Subjected to the same

statutory rules and defended by the same magistrates since the creation of the *judex viarium* in 1291, this 'reticular' policy applied
equally to the streets of the city and to the roads of its countryside,
both of which were defined, together with the bridges that spanned or
connected them, as public roads.[5]

'Without fear, let every man walk safely'; let everyone walk the
roads freely and unhindered – this is what was promised by the seduc-
tive and stern figure of *Securitas* hovering over the gate we are discussing: *Senza paura ogn'uom franco camini*. And since it is difficult
for us now not to hear in the echo of its Latin name the unpleasant
stridency of CCTVs, car alarm fitters and private security companies,
let us say that this *Securitas* did not promise the security measures of
today but rather a general sense of security as it was still understood
in the Enlightenment, where public tranquillity was also achieved by
the care people took to preserve themselves from the arbitrary actions
of the state. The well-governed city was nothing but this: a discreet
state that still fiercely insisted on ensuring that the individuals who
composed it could enjoy the freedom to circulate and trade. And that
is why Mercury, god of commerce and travel, but also of all human
exchanges, was figured in the blazon on the threshold of the city, over
Securitas. What we really need, yet again, is a cinematic approach.
For while the northern wall, at least as regards its upper part, remains
largely stuck in the stiff and solemn recitative of its hieratic virtues,
everything here is full of movement – and it is in this very movement that we need to recognize the energy of a policy focused on the
common good.

This policy became a particularly acute issue just as Lorenzetti
was at work on his painting. The government of the Nine was then
engaged in a difficult and costly enterprise of territorial expansion
in Maremma. Whether we see the gate in the Sala della Pace as an
indirect representation of the Porta Romana or the Porta Tufi, it is
the southern border of the Sienese state, strategic for its political survival, which is here shown. For the city of Siena was far from being
at the geographical centre of the territorial limits of the land it ruled.
To the north, impinging on the hills of Chianti in a defensive march
of barely ten kilometres, it very quickly came up against the borders
of the Florentine state. Its spread was limited to the south-east by
the mountainous area of the Peaks and the Amiata, and it was therefore in the south-west, towards the foothills of the Apennines (Colline
Metallifere) and the barren clayey hills, which slowly bend towards
the marshes of the Maremma bordering the Tyrrhenian Sea, that the
'Sienese advance' reached its greatest territorial extent.[6] If, as has been

suggested, the 'dark' part of Lorenzetti's fresco contains some allusion
to the harshness of this war of expansion, from the capture of Massa
Marittima (1335) to that of Grosseto (1338), its peaceful section
shows the converse side of the same policy. For to gain a foothold
in this old land of *incastellamento*, with its dense scatter of hill-top
castles that polarized the rural habitat and reinforced the signorial
power of well-established lineages, the municipality of Siena resorted
to the force of right as much as to the violence of might. After the
agreement signed in 1203 with the Aldobrandeschi counts, the city
progressed step by step, contractualizing its relations of domination
and interdependence with the *castelli* of the local powers.

It is not so much a portrait of a country as a painting of history
that Lorenzetti creates: the accelerated history of a process, the same
in short as that which is everywhere on display in the Sala della Pace,
but shifting the emphasis from one wall to another, narrating the
pacification of a political society through recourse to justice. So we
may conclude that it is a question of making spatial justice visible:
the geographical integration of a political territory into an economic
region, in an incorporation of which the organization of public road
networks is one of the most powerful government instruments. This
economic region extended beyond the *contado*, from the walls to the
sea. In the foreground is a bridge crossed by donkeys loaded with
bales of wool. Marking a boundary of the well-governed territory, it
is built of the same red bricks as the city walls, and its median spur
breaks the current of the river – the Ombrone? – that it spans. By
following this watercourse, we reach the shores where a building is
labelled by a *titulus* as 'Talam' – namely the port of Talamone, which
Siena bought in 1303 from the San Salvatore abbey of Mount Amiata,
and which realized the Sienese dream of gaining access to the sea.
Situated on a promontory where the Uccellina mountains fall towards
the Tyrrhenian Sea south of Grosseto, Talamone was the object of
systematic urban planning, as is shown by an exceptional document.
This is a plan of subdivision drawn up in 1306 and kept in one of the
registers of the Commune (the *Caleffo nero*), which depicts the building plots granted to the inhabitants.[7] This depiction is an example of
the administrative use of documentary recording, as carried out by
Sienese painters when, it will be remembered, they went off to paint
castles just as they were made part of the Sienese state.

Lorenzetti does not show us the stages of this unpredictable, contradictory and reversible history. Contrary to the topographical portraits of the *castelli in palazzo*, whose essentially perishable images
were added to or subtracted from the pictorial space of the palace as

political fortunes waxed and waned, the rather ghostly silhouettes of the castles that dominate the hills are protected by their only fragile referential value. Only Talamone is named, pointing to another fig-urative order: that of the precision of portolan charts. For the port opens onto the vast world whose expanding horizons Lorenzetti painted in the neighbouring Hall of the Great Council, called the Sala del Mappamondo as a result of the presence of this circular rep-resentation of the universe that Ghiberti described as a *cosmografia*.[8] But on this side of the wall, Lorenzetti paints history at a standstill, caught in the sudden shrinking of the number of places offered to the traveller's gaze by a landscape that passes by – that tracking shot again – as he observes it while journeying along the road, in the very movement of his steps or the trot of his horse, when the foreground is concealed and the distances are fixed and clear. In 1920, the painter Fernand Léger wrote: 'A landscape crossed or broken by a car or a fast train loses in descriptive value, but gains in synthetic value.'[9] We are now familiar with faster speeds and other modes of transport that produce visually more abrupt syntheses which complicate time as much as space. In Lorenzetti's peaceful landscapes, people sow at the same time as they reap; some thresh the wheat while others take in the swathes, and those tending the vines are very close to others who, at the first rain, bring their flocks in to shelter. Thus the compo-sition brings together in a single scene the whole range of works and seasons, like the 'eurythmic world' painted in illuminated calendars.[10]

Happy is the countryside that has no history? You might think so when you see the quiet and prosperous peasants of this world of plenty, docilely playing their roles as walk-on parts as they populate the 'backdrop for a true economic idyll'.[11] The latter seems to form a rural extension of the wedding procession which, in the city, opens the felicitous composition and which is similar to the decoration (very common in Tuscan art) of a wedding chest painted in 1335 for the Bulgarini family, perhaps by Lorenzetti himself.[12] We see love and fecundity: for while the coat of arms of Venus surmounts the young bride as she rides towards the happiness of her wedding, the labour of the fields is logically placed under the sign of a beautiful endless summer. A charming young girl, too, in her allegory, crowned with tender green, and carrying in her hand a sickle and a sheaf of wheat. And look at all those fine folk emerging from the city: two riders on horseback, the first one turning round to a servant who carries his livery, and brandishing a hawk on his gloved fist, while the second is a girl with blonde tresses trotting straight towards the hillslope accom-panied by two dogs. Both are going hunting, and not on any old hunt:

they are hunting with birds, which, unlike the grand hunting parties in the forest where the big game is pursued with a pack of dogs, takes place without moving, out in the open, often in proximity to bodies of water. There are a few dogs here, just to raise the game, which is then attacked by the raptors. Hunting with birds is open to women; it is an aristocratic ritual of territorial marking which consists in turning a cultivated space into a controlled wilderness; it is something that courtly culture charges with a mystical and erotic symbolism.[13] This is discreetly suggested by the scene of the peasants who, in the foreground, are using crossbows to hunt the birds in the vineyard.

And how should we interpret the ways people's eyes meet at the city gates? Here, young aristocrats meet merchants leading their convoy of donkeys loaded with linen and food. Pigs, chickens, oxen, mules, sheep: on this part of the Lorenzetti fresco there are fifty-nine animals for fifty-six humans – not counting the magpies hiding in the vine.[14] It is because this animal world penetrates deep into the city, here represented as a fair freely open to the women and men of the *contado* who have come to sell their surplus – here poultry, there cereal cakes. They walk and they talk: two peasants, one wearing a bonnet and the other a straw hat, are deep in conversation as they walk behind their donkeys, whose bundles are marked with symbols that help the illiterate to identify their goods or owners. Turning towards each other, gesticulating persuasively, they are directing their steps towards the city, that space of the regulated word; and it is as if their trading becomes more and more intense as they approach the gate. Indeed, when we see them we think: it is life itself which is represented here, throbbing, chaotic life – interwoven narratives made up of spaces and words.

But the proliferation is only apparent, for an order is emerging, one which, yet again, radiates out from the urban space. More than for the peasants who work there, this 'ideal' countryside is primarily ideal for the urban dwellers who live off it; it is 'this well-populated *contado* covered with a dense network of settlement centres',[15] which, in the view of Gabriella Piccinni, makes the rural area a paradise when seen from the city. This paradise was, first of all, the paradise of urban investment as it transformed the agrarian economy of communal Italy. Its historians have long studied the details of this part of the fresco to emphasize the exceptional density of its documentary value. In it, they can see the variety of farming methods (such as one ploughman with a swing plough, another with a common plough); the refining of a shrubby polyculture combining fallow plots with planted plots; the care taken to demarcate fields and roads; the trellises and rows of vines; the pergola; the orchard and the hooped shrubs; and the ponds lined with rushes. They can also recognize the subtle typology of agricultural buildings – from the wine press to the stable, by way of the straw hut – and the masters' houses with their tile roofs, preceded by a courtyard surrounded by a low wall or extending into an awned gallery.[16] But they can also discern the spatial gradient of an agriculture that is all the more intensive and speculative in that it borders the outskirts of the city: vineyards and orchards climb the hillsides that are topped by the city walls, while the fallow lands and the brushwood gradually spread over the flat fields of grain closer to the border country. There, the castles are perched higher, more clearly fortified, and have less room for dwellings between them.

The geography of the city's dominance over its countryside is better understood when we take into account the effects of the monetarization of the agrarian economy and all its consequences: the debts owed by rural communities to the urban elites, who invested heavily in land ownership, transforming agrarian contracts as they developed short-term leases (*mezzadria*), and the reparcelling and restructuring of a community's farming areas (finages, or *appoderamenti*). In short, what liberal historiography has long celebrated as the 'conquest of the *contado*', which freed the peasants from their feudal servitude and at the same time allowed them to gain access to urban modernity, can now be better understood in all its ambivalence: 'a whole society throws itself upon the earth' – beginning, as we have seen, with the political society which filled the magistracies of the government of the Nine – and those who cultivated it moved from one dependency to another.[17] The financial context of the 1330s further accelerated the process, as the crisis in international banking investment shifted speculation massively to the land market.[18] For the system which now combined the city and its countryside into an economically integrated region took its place in wider exchange circuits: if we see the wool for the drapery industry arriving in the city, the silks in which Lorenzetti clothed the richest of his fellow-townsfolk necessarily came from farther afield.

It is not surprising that the joyous energy of the school of 'world history' has not spared the Sienese fresco, and that some historians want to see Talamone extending as far as Tabriz and the Silk Road. Was Lorenzetti a painter of the 'Mongol peace', without which the rise of Western cities since the thirteenth century would remain incomprehensible? Some writers are emboldened to take the plunge, thinking they have recognized on the potter's stall in the centre of the well-governed city the blue glazes of Yuan porcelain imported from southern China, or have seen the strange conical hat of the rider passing

behind a wall as a Turco-Mongolian cap.[19] Comparing the silhouettes of the Lorenzetti hills with those, also in monochrome, which
the vizier Rashid al-Din had had painted in his workshops in Tabriz
where illuminators from Afghanistan and Armenia worked is probably a very risky intellectual operation. But at least it has the merit
of troubling the illusory obviousness of a panorama that has always
been celebrated as marking the official birth of a pictorial modernity
– one which credits Europe with an exaggerated reputation for accuracy in the depiction of and sensitivity to landscapes.

'None will deny Ambrogio Lorenzetti the envied title of first landscape painter in the history of Western art.'[20] If we wanted to, we
could harvest granaries full of similarly peremptory sentences from
the general bibliography relating to the (obviously European) invention of the landscape. In these accounts, the Sienese fresco is generally
related to the famous letter which Petrarch wrote on his ascent of
Mount Ventoux, a letter dated 26 April 1336, but which was probably written in the middle of the year 1353. Just as this text deploys
a subtle metaphorical network which can hardly be reduced to the
mere aesthetic vibration of the landscape, so it would be mistaken
to sink into the blissful contemplation of an allegedly new sensibil-
ity to natural beauties.[21] For these beauties, as Piero Camporesi has
shown, become perceptible at the end of the Middle Ages only if they
are related to new practices of space as suggested by the title of his
book *Belle contrade*.[22] *Contrada* in Italian designates both a territorial section of the city (say a district) and a part of the land that is
natural in the sense that it is inhabited, humanized and transformed.
In other words, nature as considered by the moderns (as an organic
cluster of mere objects denied any social life since the 'great division'
of naturalist cosmology described by Philippe Descola[23]) is nowhere
to be seen in Lorenzetti's painting. He painted, from end to end, a
constructed landscape, a land occupied, subjected to human will; and
he placed the house and the hill opposite one another like two buildings flaunting the same colours of urbanity.

'The sides of these hills went sloping gradually downward to the
plain on such wise as we see in amphitheatres, the degrees descend
in ordered succession from the highest to the lowest, still contracting
their circuit,' as Boccaccio wrote in the sixth day of his *Decameron*.[24]
If the hills are theatres, it is the houses that, symmetrically, make the
urban panorama a landscape. Not as a stage setting; they play the
main roles. Sharp corners, openings, small columns, entablatures and
divided windows, battlements and chimneys, awnings, loggias, shop-
keeper's benches – and also contrasting materials and textures, grey

and red facing one another, in a crazy perspective: on this side, over three-quarters of the painted surface is covered with this playful use of volumes, which, by dint of being observed in the mattness of their different pigments, become at once fully abstract (there is nothing here but painting) and obstinately alive (there is nothing here but movement). A city under construction, clearly; it is depicted not in the firm assurance of an orderly plan and the accomplishment of a perfect form, but as a permanent work in progress.[25] Beware wet paint: the masons are the first to draw your gaze, trowel in hand, perched on their scaffold, holding over their heads their plaster and baskets full of bricks. There is no symmetry here, and not much beauty: we must not expect concord to build cities with a cord. The *dritta corda* is used here for the partitioning of the spaces of the city, not for their monumentalization. For inside the city walls, too, the defence of public roads is an essential issue. But what do the urban statutes of 1309 say about the tasks of the road officials? They must *sciampare* – that is, enlarge and expand. They must *diriziare* – that is, straighten and direct. But above all they must *acconciare* and *racconciare*, adjust and readjust.[26]

This is *precisely* what Lorenzetti painted. Recent research suggests that his urban scenography combines six staggered viewpoints over groups of houses that urban archaeologists believe they can still find in the city of today. So the painter seems to have created a purely abstract image of the urban landscape from a variety of positions, creating the formal artifice of a *visione* through the conjunction of *vedute*.[27] The happy city is the one where territories and temporalities are matched precisely. It cannot be reduced to the symbolic form of perspective envisaged as a space geometrically unified by a single vanishing point. Unlike the famous 'ideal city' of Urbino, which 'offers nothing to view that can be narrated',[28] there are many things to be narrated in this mutual adjustment of places, and this is because temporality here is as split as the pictorial field is diffracted into an impossible vision. Not a space and a *historia* in the sense that Alberti gave, a hundred years later, in his *De Pictura* (1436), to the art of painting, which had now become an art of ordered persuasion, but instead, places, bodies and narratives. So Lorenzetti's pictorial space can be said to be fundamentally Aristotelian in the sense that it represents nothing but 'the sum of places occupied by bodies'.[29] For the *locus* of Aristotle is defined as 'the primary container of each body' (*Physics*, IV, 209b1). Undoubtedly inspired by the arts of memory, this conception of space prior to Alberti's reduction, by which a unified space is combined into a single history, is that of a juxtaposition of

'local boxes' where figures and narratives take their places, as analysed in the case of Giotto by Jean-Philippe Antoine.[30]

From this point of view there is also a sort of pictorial synonymy
between the hill and the valley, on the one hand, and the building
and the street, on the other. For in Sienese painting, voids begin to
be treated as plenums: they no longer merely represent the interval
between two inanimate and compact objects, but acquire the plen-
itude of a place[31] – a place that can properly be called a common
place. At the same time, volumes grow like shells to accommodate
so many scenes of speech. In front of the wedding procession, two
young women watch the bride passing by. Are they envious? One
gently places her two hands on the neck and shoulders of the other.
Behind, two young men make exactly the same gesture. What are they
saying to each other? And look, there are others in the background,
holding each other by the arm, speaking as if in an aside. In front of
them, three men are seated under a portico, leaning on a bench, probably absorbed in a game of dice. Are the two children watching them
commenting on the game? It must be remembered here that one of
the most common political metaphors used in the late Middle Ages to
designate the space of political domination was the chessboard: you
have to move to improve your position, but not every piece has the
same ability to move, and the one that is 'taken' is out of the game. A
place, a body in each place, words and movements – but what game
is being played here?

The game, of course, of the plurality of urban voices. To the right
of the square where people are dancing, we can sense the animation
of the exchanges in the shop selling footwear; this flanks the school,
where the master's studious voice echoes as he looks down on his
attentive pupils from the top of his desk. Here we could reconstruct
the full range of voices and all the chatter that comprise the sound
landscape of cities. But the sharp corners of the buildings truncate bits
of narrative, cutting into the silhouettes of the figures as if breaking
off a conversation. What we have here is not the univocal unfolding of a single urban phrase – the discourse that the city holds on
itself – but the polyphonic chorus of the words that resonate there:
'The totality of all that is said in the city, the mass of all that the city,
even without its own knowledge, propagates in its midst.'[32] Stronger
than strength itself is this incidental and discrete propagation which
manages without the vehemence of propaganda. What can you hear?
First and foremost, the dignity of toil. The university masters, these
mercenaries of the verb, were the first to know how to defend the
value of intellectual labour, that singular form of work. But in an

urban society as intensely educated as was that of the Italian cities, people sold their knowledge: the schoolmasters managed their business like dealers in drapery or china.

Here, too, the coats of arms and the symbols that frame the fresco highlight its significance. In the lower register are represented the seven liberal arts: the symbols of the trivium under the allegories of the north wall (grammar, dialectic and rhetoric) remind us that the political order is founded on rhetoric and that in a political system based on persuasion, the art of governing is first and foremost the art of not confusing one word with another. As for the east wall, it is emphasized by the frieze of the medallions of the quadrivium (arithmetic, geometry, music and astronomy), to which are added the medallion of philosophy and the Sienese coat of arms. As the historian Uta Feldges-Henning has shown, this symbolic representation is surmounted by scenes from the city at work – as opposed to the idle city on the 'bad' side of the fresco, where only the armourer has opened his shop. We can interpret it as a systematic representation, but a representation in deeds and *in vivo*, of the mechanical arts. These are understood by means of the classification by Hugh of Saint Victor that was still widely used in the late Middle Ages (found, for example, in the *Summa Theologica* of Antoninus of Florence).[33] Thus there are five looms linked to the art of wool (*Lanificium*), but also *Armatura* (which includes *Architectura*), *Navigatio* and, of course, the various components of *Agricultura*. The symbolic evocation of the liberal arts and the 'realistic' depiction of the mechanical arts thus form a system in which the former alerts us to the scope of the latter. The meaning of this representation is political: to incorporate the mechanical arts into the portrait of the well-governed city is already, in itself, to favour the most modest activities.

But at the same time, things are, surprisingly, simpler. We would need to express them with the cold and ardent clarity of the philosopher Jean-Claude Milner when he defends a politics of speaking beings: no other justification can be found for the good government of men and women than that which consists in exercising no constraint on their bodies.[34] Once talking beings can move around and exchange things freely, once they are allowed to live fully in their own places, and to occupy in all sovereignty the place they choose in language, then the ideal of the common good is realized. The requirement may seem minimal; it nevertheless configures the very space of the political, that space in which discussion cannot lead to people being put to death. This, and this when you think about it, differentiates the two walls facing each other. Does this mean that the sharing out of this diversity of common places in one and the same public space is impossible? Probably not, and this is also shown by the confrontation between the two walls of the Sala della Pace. Along the west wall, tyranny spreads darkness over the dead earth and desolation over a city eaten away by hatred. Whence comes the deep anguish which, even beyond what is represented, grips the spectator? John White reveals the reason, one that is all the more powerful because it can long pass unnoticed: the pictorial space itself seems dismembered, disconnected, strident: 'Nothing fits. Nothing continues from one building to the next. Nothing is made easy.'[35] In the well-governed city too, 'every building is obliquely set'. But this distortion obeys a principle of order: 'Each recedes from this one centre, the dividing line of which is marked by the street that runs upward through the houses beyond the left-hand boundary of the foreground inlet.'[36] The inclination of the roofs gives the impression that the houses are arranged on terraces, in the theatrical manner of the hills of Boccaccio; it is a political performance that is played out to the solemn rhythm of the strange choreography occupying the heart of the city.

As White goes on to say, 'the diminution both of figures and of architecture has been seen as radiating from the centre of the city'.[37] Hence the impression of strangeness created by the vision of this urban scene: shapes and figures do not only diminish in depth (which is in accordance with the visual effect of the perspective), but also laterally, accompanying in a decrescendo the viewer's gaze as it leaves the marvellous urban scene. Are we looking for a political message in Lorenzetti's fresco? Here is one message, clear and imperious: anyone who enters the city grows; anyone who moves away from it becomes smaller. The nobles are leaving the city to go hunting? That diminishes them. Peasants from the *contado* are leading their black pigs to the urban market? They gain a new stature. There is no need to interpret in order to understand: it is through the barely noticed distortion in perception that the idea creeps into the spectator's mind. This singular eloquence of representation, which is persuasive without being demonstrative, is perfectly adequate to the thing represented. It is also possible to define the symbolic efficiency of architecture (or, in general, urban design) in the manner of Walter Benjamin, as 'the prototype of an artwork that is received in a state of distraction and through the collective'.[38]

To produce this effect, the Sienese artist uses all the proper means of painting: the composition of spaces, and also the play on light and the saturation of colours. For White has also shown that the 'outward radiation, already noted as inherent in the structure of each building,

1 West wall, left part, in front of the troop of soldiers crossing the bridge: houses on fire.

2 West wall, right part, in the city at war: citizens being assaulted by the soldiers.

·AVARITIA·   ·VANAGLORIA·

TYRANNIDIS

IO·   ·FRA·   ·VS·   AV

IVSTI

4 West wall, right part, far right section of the court of vices: allegories of Division and War.

(Overleaf) 5 West wall, left part.

(Opposite) 3 West wall, right part, the court of the vices: allegory of Tyranny under the figures of Avarice, Pride and Vainglory, and with Fraud and Fury at either side. Lower foreground: Justice bound.

TIMOR

ERE ELBENTROPIO TOVESTA TERRA
ASSE LAGIUSTITIA ATYRANNIA
E DOVESTA VIA
ASSA ALCUN SEGA DUBBIO DIMOTE
VOR SIROBBA CONTRO DELE PORTA

...NA E GRAN SOSPETTO · GUERRE RAPINE TRADIMENTI ET GANI·PREMANSI SIGNORIA SOPRA·OLLEI · VONGASI LA MORTE

CRVDE... LITAS · PRODI...TI...

...I TIRBBE LADDOL SIE P SVO MERTO · DI

LAOQVE STA LEGATA LA...
...ICORDA · DE TIRA ADRITT...
SORMONTI · LA OVAL D'OM...
INI OPRA DISCORDA · TORI...
SON DA COGLIOTI · ODEST...
GIARDINI ANE CIASCVN OMD...
CHI · SFORCA O ROBBA O CHI...
I COLTA GIACE

LIBERTAS

IVSTI

TO · DISCACCIATE · DISERTO · IN SIEME · CON QUALUNQUE · SIA

GATA LA IUSTITIA · NESSUNO ALBE · COMVNE GIAMAY
ADRITTA CORDA · DO CONVIE CHE TIRANNIA
VA · D ADEMPIR LA SUA NEQVITIA · NVLLO DOLER
A · DALLA MISVRA LORDA · DE VITII CHE CO LEI

7 West wall, right part, under the court of vices: allegory of Justice bound with her truncated *titulus* (*Iusti-*), and inscription running at her feet (*la vuol se per suo merto . . .*) over the escutcheon (*La dove sta legata la iustitia . . .*). Echoes and symmetries of sound and meaning here reinforce the visual correspondences.

(Previous page) 6 West wall, right part.

(Opposite) 8 East wall, left part: builders working on the roofs of the houses over the shops of the footwear maker and the schoolmaster

(Overleaf) 9 East wall, left part: the square in the city centre and the group of dancers

SENÇA PAVRA OGNVOM FRANCO CAMINI·
ELAVORANDO SEMINI CIASCVNO·
MENTRE CHE TAL COMVNO·
MANTERRA QVESTA DONA ISIGNORIA·
CHEL ALEVATA AREI OGNI BALIA·

11 East wall, right part, above the door to the hall, allegory of *Securitas*.

(Overleaf) 12 East wall, left part.

(Opposite) 10 East wall, right part, in the centre of the composition: hills and country landscapes.

VOLGIETE GLIOCCHI A RIMIRAR COSTEI VOI CHE REGGIETE CHE QVI FIGVRATA 7 PSVE CIELLEC

ECHA DAMA OGNVOM FRANCO CAMINI
ELAVORANDO SEMINI CIASCVNO ·
MENTRE CHE TAL COMVNDO ·
MANTERNA QVESTA DONNA I SIGNORIA
CHEL ALEVATA ARCI OGNI BALIA ·

QVESTA NITV KEPIV ᐧDALTRA BISPREGE · ELLA GVARDE ᐧDIFEDE · CHI LEI ONORA 7 LOR INTRICA 7 PASCIE · ᐧDA LA SVO LVCIE

ERITAR COLOR COPERA BENE · 7 ACLINIOVI VAR OEBITE PENE

(Previous page) 13 East wall, right part.

14 North wall.

(Overleaf) 15 North wall: allegories of Justice and Concord: the procession of councillors; allegories of Peace, Strength and Prudence.

SAPIENTIA

CONCORDIA

AMBROSIVS · L

ENTII · DESENIS · HIC PINXIT · VTRINOVE

16 North wall, platform of the virtues: allegory of Peace.

(Opposite) 17 North wall, platform of the virtues: great personage with allegory of Prudence at his side.

(Overleaf) 18 North wall, platform of the virtues: allegories of Magnanimity and Temperance. Lower foreground: triumph of the feudatories, and prisoners.

MAGNANIMITAS · TENPERANTIA

is also expressed by figures, and by movement, and by light' – striking the right side of all the buildings to the left of this line of demarcation, and vice versa.[39] Scholars have competed in their ingenious attempts to explain this truly supernatural distribution of light in Lorenzetti's fresco. For Chiara Frugoni, Divine Wisdom is the source of the light that obliquely illuminates the main wall from the north wall; Jack Greenstein inclines instead to seeing the gaze of Peace as the source of the light shed over the peaceful city; as for Roger Tarr, he sees the 'golden shield' of the venerable figure in which the image of the Virgin appears as a kind of fictitious sun.[40] These subtle hypotheses have one point in common, namely their idealism: only the smaller scenes in the allegories are able to illuminate the urban scene. It needs a huge effort to reject the obviousness and simplicity of the hypothesis of immanence: the heart of the city is the source of light, because it is public space itself that radiates.

We are once again at the heart of what Lorenzetti's fresco has to tell us politically. If this government is good, it is not because it is inspired by a divine light but because its effects are just and harmonious, because they spare bodies, respect their places, hear their words. The city, in its very materiality, is a source of authority. It is light and moderation, the measure of all things. Lorenzetti does not just paint urban objects, he represents the social uses that make sense of places. This applies to the heart of the city, a solemn, theatrical space, the scene of a meditative gathering. The buildings themselves seem to move back in order to observe the dance, which gives space its rhythm and regulates the intensity of civil life. As you approach this incandescent heart, the light becomes brighter and you gain in stature. Lorenzetti is thus simultaneously depicting the hollowing of the centre of the city and the accomplishment of its political order. That is to say, he paints, precisely, the fundamentally abstract and rigorously concrete place comprised by public space in an Italian city in the late Middle Ages. This square is not only empty of houses, it is full of meaning. And since it is painted in fresco in the Palazzo Pubblico of Siena, and since, in order to see it, it is necessary to cross the public square on which the palace stands, the painted space can also be read *through* the built space, as through a prism. The Siena *campo*, both a shell and a fan, is like the *orchestra* of a Greek amphitheatre curled up in the hollow of the hills. In it, a quarrel is being enacted which mimics the original disorder of the city. It is high time to go and see it. Let us join the dance.

12

Well, now you can dance

When he entered the Sala della Pace of the Palazzo Pubblico of Siena, the Swiss historian Jacob Burckhardt saw what others before him, and others after him, could not fail to see: the sky, the seasons, the sun and the moon, the sea just visible in the distance, the abundance of work and days, but above all a world divided into two – on one side a city at war, on the other a city at peace. It was the end of the nineteenth century, and the views of Burckhardt, the author of the famous study *The Civilization of the Renaissance in Italy* (1860), were not yet limited by an interpretative tradition which, once established, led him towards certain texts in order to exclude others. Thus he was free to let the image come to him, and to witness the echoes which it awakened in his memories and readings, as if at the sight of some unexpected encounter. And he said to himself, as it were: 'But this painting in motion, this image which is like the world the warrior holds in his fist when he goes into battle, is the shield of Achilles.'[1] As we read in the *Iliad*:

> On it [the shield] he made also two fair cities of mortal men. In the one there were marriages and feastings, and by the light of the blazing torches they were leading the brides from their rooms through the city, and loud rose the bridal song. And young men were whirling in the dance, and with them flutes and lyres sounded continually.[2]

The reference to this surprising coincidence is to be found in a manuscript left unfinished on Burckhardt's death.[3] It had no impact up until its recent rediscovery.[4] But what are we to do with it? You can always count on philologists to pour cold water on novel and audacious interpretations. The text of the Homeric epic was not available in the trecento, except in the abridged Latin adaptation of the *Ilias Latina* composed by the Roman senator Publius Baebius Italicus in the first century AD; this was the starting point for the whole mediaeval tradition (notably through the *Roman de Troie* by Benoît de Sainte-Maure). But in this work the description (*ekphrasis*) of the shield of Achilles, with a bit of Ovid thrown into the mixture, is unrecognizable. Petrarch avidly searched for a more direct path to Homer and claimed to have a manuscript of it, but it is very probably the little prose summary attributed to Ausonius that he actually possessed;[5] Boccaccio said that he had 'privately heard' readings of Homer's poem at the Neapolitan court of Robert I, but it was not until 1362 that he obtained a first Latin translation of the *Iliad* from Leonzo Pilato.[6] In short, the traces are too fleeting, too late and too far away from Siena.

Are we following a false trail here? Probably: but there is always something to be learned from wandering from the straight path. Burckhardt's intuition allows us to link the Sienese fresco to its Greco-Roman antecedents. This does not mean that we need to see this as anticipating an improbable Renaissance: the antiquarian obsessions of the city of Siena in 1338 were not in the least expressive of a desire to rediscover the past, but rather were directed towards reviving its energy and novelty. For this past was not past; it was still there, fresh and available, as the continual present of political action. Lorenzetti may have found in the descriptions of Greek and Roman paintings in Pliny the Elder's *Natural Histories* a challenge and an encouragement, and not just a repertory of antiquarian motifs.[7] To see the scenes painted in the Sala della Pace in this light amounts to politicizing our gaze. Homer's description not only brings together the city and the cosmos, the centre of the *polis* and its territory (*chora*): it associates the dance of the city at peace with the original dispute or *stasis*. This fundamental duality spreads dramatically through the city at war, which is completely torn apart. But the resolution of this conflict is found not in the return to unity, but in a tripartite political geometry which structures the whole *ekphrasis* of the shield of Achilles.

Homer refers to a gathering on the square where a quarrel arose. We do not see such a quarrel on the walls of the Palazzo Pubblico in Siena. But we now know what the contrast between the two walls reveals: not *polemos*, the struggle against a powerful external enemy, but *stasis*, the sedition that led to the divided city. So we need to seek this *stasis*, to face it, to go out to meet it. If it can be located anywhere, it is not on the margins, but at the very heart of political space. For it is its very principle: 'The city-state created [. . .] a public space, centering on the *agora* [public square] and its common hearth, the place where problems of general interest were argued and where power was no longer located in the palace but in the center, *es meson*.'[8] In the heart of the palace, therefore, the Nine wanted a depiction of the very place where all power escaped their grasp, for that is where it is located, in the centre, at the disposal of all, in an empty figure which Vernant turned into the beating heart of his simultaneously political and poetic vision of the world.[9] This dispute, therefore, should be sought in the centre, where we dance. It should be sought, that is to say (as the Homeric detour invites us), in the rhythm of the dance, beyond unity and division into two or three parts.

One, two, three, four. In the centre of the stage, dressed in a black robe and open-mouthed, someone with a large tambourine is singing. To the right of this static figure are two silhouettes seen from behind, displaying to the viewer the supple curve of their necks. Then three other characters, profiled, their fingers just lightly touching, with a slight swing of the hips. They are dancing. The round is completed, to the left of the singer, by four other young people in the same posture. But it is not a round, or at least not a closed round. It is a *ridda*, for it winds along and passes under the bridge formed by the clasped hands of the two last dancers, so that some recognize the sinuous shape on the ground as the S of the city of Siena.[10] One, then two, then three, then four characters: ten in all, according to a numerical sequence of Pythagorean origin that Plato discussed at the beginning of the *Timaeus* and whose mediaeval commentators liked to plumb for its hidden meaning. And among these ten characters are one singer and nine dancers. Just as there are nine virtues on the north wall and nine vices on the west; and just as, on leaving the Palazzo Pubblico by the square of the *campo*, you find nine segments paved with bricks on the square. Here, carried away by the rhythm of this silent dance, you start to count, confusing the pictorial field with the space of the city, and discerning in this tempo something like a basso continuo which sings, in a discreet but insistent way, the omnipresence of the *Nove* in the city they govern. By the force of number, a certain strangeness insinuates itself into an apparently banal scene that has long been reduced to the ordinary life of peaceful days in a mediaeval city. Young girls dancing in the street: nothing more than that.

Because they *are* young girls – or are they? Since at least the eighteenth century, no one has doubted it: those long robes and fine features can only be beautiful young girls – virgins, indeed, add some commentators, holding forth learnedly about feminine grace and the realism of the painter who knows how to sketch from life scenes of the urban daily round. This way of judging the identity of characters from their faces and determining their sex based solely on our impressions as modern spectators is obviously not without risk. Notwithstanding *The Da Vinci Code*, a personage painted in fresco at the end of the Middle Ages may well strike *us* as a woman; but this may not have been the idea in the painter's mind or that of his contemporaries. The mediaeval image is coded: it distributes discreet signs that make it possible to identify characters, positions and postures according to a limited number of symbolic attributes. A king will not be king just because he looks royal, but because he wields certain insignia of sovereignty. And what applies to political functions or social status is equally valid for gender. As the American historian Jane Bridgeman has shown, all the female characters in Lorenzetti's Sala della Pace are characterized by a set of criteria which can be listed. These are: the curve of the ankle, the roundness of the breasts, and above all the long blonde hair that appears either braided down the back (such as the female rider leaving the scene on the left, or the allegory of Concord) or plaited or wrapped in a bun (like the lady going hunting to the right, or the allegory of Peace). All these signs are missing in the 'dancers' with their short hair and flat chests.[11]

Without doubt, then, the dancing women are dancing *men*. And we might even add that they are professional dancers. It is well known that, on certain great occasions, the municipalities used *giullari*, itinerant artists, who, in the midst of musicians, storytellers and other entertainers, occupied the forefront of civic celebrations and private festivities. The Sienese statutes of 1309 attempted to regulate this activity, in particular by subjecting their participation in wedding ceremonies to prior authorization, and strictly limiting the practice of public dances.[12] For they were suspicious of their restless movements, even if these were for professional reasons. A century later, when severe moralists such as Matteo Palmieri in his *Della Vita Civile* and Gianozzo Alberti in his *Della Famiglia* attempted to re-establish the order of the Church Fathers in all its solemnity and rigor, the denunciation of the extravagance and effeminacy of the *giullari* became a commonplace of political discourse, as expressed repeatedly in the sermons of Bernardino of Siena. As a result, the sense of the scene changes: it is not the innocent and spontaneous round of young girls in bloom, but the *danza ad arco*, the codified performance of dancers employed by communal governments to participate in a complex form of political ritual that, like the Palio's famous horse races, involved placing power at the centre of public space.

We still need to understand the meaning of this transgression. Why did the painter clothe his dancers like nymphs, even if this risked flouting all the social rules of propriety and moderation so strictly laid down in the sumptuary laws of the government of the Nine?[13] Why set this disorder in the representation of gender at the very heart of the pictorial field? The pose and costume *alla ninfa* remind us of the obsessions of Aby Warburg, who sought in *Pathosformeln* (formulae of emotion) the expressions of feelings that swept away Western art as soon as it summoned up the ghosts of the ancient image so as to reactivate the intensity of an emotional gesture. Or, to put it another way, as does Georges Didi-Huberman: what are the corporeal forms of surviving time?[14] What survives here, for us, in the choreographed slowness of this serpentine *ridda*, is in no way a free effusion of souls, but the obligatory expression of a political emotion. So we must scrutinize the strange patterns that decorate the silk dresses of the dancers. The purple is invaded by insects with elongated bodies equipped with two pairs of wings that can be seen, depending on your mood, as dragonflies or damselflies – in any case *odonatoptera*. There is no doubt, however, as to the identity of the things swarming all down the frazzled yellow robe: they are indeed larvae. If one considers them as the caterpillars of the preceding insects, then the dance takes on the mythological dimension of a ceremony of the great metamorphoses that preside over political renewal.[15] But it cannot be denied that its overall tonality evokes less the overflowing joy of spring rites than the typical torpor expressed in Charles Baudelaire's poem 'Harmonies du soir' ('Evening Harmonies'), with their 'melancholy waltz and languorous dizziness'.

For even if it is easy to convince oneself that dragonflies are not moths and that the purple robe is not really moth-eaten, it is difficult not to see that the yellow dress of the person standing closest to the edge of the fresco is falling to pieces: with the worms that pullulate through it, this makes a most disturbing foreground. Worms and moths are the symbols of *tristitia*, the vice of sadness and moroseness which Christian moralists had long targeted. Such an affection of the soul was no longer merely the prerogative of monks whose accumulation of black bile provoked acedia, a sin specific to their condition.[16] Melancholy was no longer confined to the seclusion of the cloisters, but had poured out into the public space: this is why the authors of the *ars dictaminis* (Albertano da Brescia and Guido Fava in particular), those theorists of how to live well in society, drew on and politicized the system of sins developed by the Church. In civil life too, we must struggle against *tristitia* by expressing our *gaudium*

– joy, in other words, but joy considered as the political necessity of collective emotion. It involves a public body posture, offered to everybody's gaze, demonstrating social feeling in an expressive and codified way. Already during the High Middle Ages, '*Tristitia* and *Laetitia* were public bodily postures intended to manifest respectively political hostility and friendship.'[17] Controlling sad passions is a duty, since they eat away at concord in the heart of civic space, like the worm in the fruit.

Quentin Skinner has noted the way in which Antiquity portrayed such emotions in the *tripudium*, a majestic triple dance. Seneca, in his *Tranquillity of the Mind*, sketches a portrait of Scipio, an unbending warrior who nonetheless had no hesitation in dancing 'in the style of the *tripudium*, the manly style in which the heroes of olden times used to dance at the times of games and festive celebrations'. Thus, a dance of peace and victory, as solemn and grave as that of the Homeric heroes, illuminates the whole urban scene with an unreal light, while at the same time opening up a wide and available space, echoing the words exchanged, and acting as the setting for gestures that are controlled and ritualized, as if suspended by a feeling of respectful joy – in short, the place of the political. In 1310, a Podestà congratulated the citizens of Padua who had overcome their divisions: '[Y]our letters of peace brought immense *gaudia* [joy] to our hearts and led to the festive dancing of the *tripudium* with high exultation among the whole populace of Padua.'[18] Peace, joy, dance: in Lorenzetti's ideal city, politics is like a waltz in triple rhythm. But it is a melancholy and slow waltz, with a somewhat forced joy, with an anxiety which spreads like a shock wave fleeing its epicentre from the group of dancers to the whole of the urban panorama, which is polarized as a result.

And since we are now preparing to take leave of it, since, at the moment when we pass through the entrance under the red bridge in the painting, spanning as it does the river flowing off into the sea, we will doubtless take one last backward glance to the side of the 'bad' wall eroded by the worsening condition of the pigments, reflecting that, ever since we decided to set off from here on our long crossing, we have never been completely free of anxiety. Hell, purgatory, paradise – yes, no doubt; but if we consider things in that order, paradise is irremediably lost in the mist. Siena, 1338. Will the danger be warded off? Images do not have that power. And as for those which decorate the walls of this extraordinary site of painting, the Sienese palace, so long regarded as the triumphal expression of a communal civilization at its apogee, we now see more clearly that these images express its doubts, its contradictions, and especially the slow subversion of civic values that made a crisis inevitable. In this respect, it was strictly contemporary with the Florentine chronicle of Giovanni Villani, in particular his famous twelfth book: Andrea Zorzi has shown that Villani saw the events in Florence between 1333 and 1342 – with their grim train of fires, shipwrecks, catastrophic weather and fateful celestial signs – as symptomatic of 'the anguish of the republic'.[19] This anguish has the same face as the *Timor* of Lorenzetti, or the *Trionfo della morte* by Buonamico Buffamalco in Pisa: not the fear of a coming tyranny, but of that signorial seduction which is always lurking under the honest justifications of the commune as soon as the latter conceives of itself as the political form of an original misunderstanding. How to ward off *that* fear? The political strength of images consists precisely in keeping nothing out of sight.

Peace can see this. From her platform, so beautiful in her immaculate dress, she sees all of this: both sides, both peace and war, but also the fact that there are not only two sides, and that war always casts its shadow over peace. She has triumphed over the wicked, she lies stretched out nonchalantly on her trophies, and everything seems complete. But this is not how Lorenzetti paints things. He does not depict the great division sealed by the end of history, the secularized version of the Last Judgment. He draws Petrarch's *bivium*, that fraught moment when the roads fork, when men have to decide which way to look, while in front of them stretch the vanishing lines of the effects their choices will entail. Some of these are predictable, and it is the task of the painter of the Nine to alert us to this fact, for in politics there must always be an alternative, one that is reasonably and deliberately thought through. But others are not so predictable. History continues, which means that there will always be inevitably uncertain political decisions to be made. We need to be alerted to this, too; it must be set in full view of those who are willing to take the trouble to look. Peace sees all of this.

That is why a little of the *tristitia* which is slowly fraying the clothes of the dancers has splashed onto the sweet face of Peace, like the benefits of the moon poured over the woman in love depicted in Baudelaire's poem. I thought she was dreamy, just dreamy. In a brief and luminous article, Pierangelo Schiera states his compelling objections.[20] This woman, with her head bowed, too heavy to be supported by a languid fist, has all the attributes of the melancholy pose as defined since Antiquity. She is the melancholy of power, since in her solitude, however populous it may be, she understands that there are no good fights in politics except those which will never be entirely won. She has triumphed, yes, but she knows henceforth that triumph is impossible. We can very well decide not to see this – or rather, we do not really decide, but at the same time we really do not see. She is there, before our eyes, she has seen and she knows, but we prefer to look away. And yet, once we have seen her, we shall never be able to forget her. Like the *Angelus Novus* painted by Paul Klee, by which Walter Benjamin was so obsessed. This is the Angel of History. He looks towards the past, 'the pile of debris before him grows skyward'. But he will not remain there to take care of the dead, for a storm drives him towards this future, on which he turns his back. 'This storm is what we call progress.'[21]

One could read in the eyes of Peace the frightened announcement of all our storms, for we stand before her face in the same way that we stand in front of time. Let us come to a proper conclusion, by merely sustaining her gaze in the immediate aftermath of her melancholy victory. On 29 May 1339, Ambrogio Lorenzetti received the balance of his final payment: 55 florins. His painting was evidently considered to be complete, and it had probably been judged by experts to be in accordance with the expectations of its sponsors. The 351 members of the Great Council, who had met a month earlier, had certainly seen it, but it was in the Sala del Mappamondo, facing the *Maestà*, that they had gathered. For the occasion was a solemn one: on this 24 April the Podestà read to them a long petition written by a group of merchants and bankers. They had drawn up an alarming report on the credit crisis raging in Siena. The Nine were to abolish imprisonment for debt, otherwise, they claimed, the whole of the city might end up in gaol.[22] Gabriella Piccinni has recently traced all the stages of this complex financial history, which constitutes the decisive background of Siena's political upheavals. Since the major bank failures of the years 1316–17, marked by the bankruptcies of the Forteguerri, Malavolti, Gallerani and Tolomei, the whole credit system had been weakened. The main Sienese *casati* reinvested huge amounts of their speculative capital in the public debt and land ownership, abandoning productive investment – a strategy to which the Piccolomini and the Salimbeni had already resorted. From 1332 onwards, the monetary requirements of the great monarchies – especially France and England – continued to deplete the credit market. It must be said that 1338 was also the first year of what historians call the Hundred Years War. Artisans and entrepreneurs in Siena had no choice but to turn to usurers, impoverishing and undermining the labour market.

The political decisions taken by the Nine from 1339 onwards were fraught with consequences, and also revealed the social contradictions of the regime: they systematically chose to provide assistance to the financial and banking oligarchy, aggravating public debt – though this indebtedness was precisely the reason behind the banks' fortune – and abandoning support for economic activity. Ideologically, the regime of the Nine demanded a government of the *mezza gente* (middling sort) based on a twofold political exclusion: that of the most powerful of the tycoons, and that of the most modest of the *popolo minuto*. Lorenzetti had painted only merchants in his depiction of the councillors roped together, and only *milites* among the powerful subjects; he had seen the wealthy aristocrats leaving the city and honest workers entering it. But in reality, it was the latter who suffered the hardest consequences of the crisis, before suffering the cataclysm of the Black Death. The Lorenzetti brothers, as we know, did not survive.

On 23 April 1355, Emperor Charles IV of Luxembourg entered a dramatically weakened city of Siena. But on that day, the political ritual, though minutely prepared, turned into a riot.[23] Did those in power manipulate the common people, as liberal historiography has long maintained, or was it the Sienese *Ciompi* (labourers and artisans) who carried out 'the first insurrection of what is usually called the pre-proletariat',[24] as the Marxists claimed? In any case, this revolt opened a period of great political instability for Siena, marked first by the expansion of the regime's social base (with the government of the Twelve), then by various attempts to impose order by the city's *Grandi*, under the leadership of the Salimbeni, and finally the takeover of the *Riformatori*, who in 1368 rejected a second imperial intrusion into communal institutions.

Still, in the streets of Siena, one cry had clearly been heard: '*Viva lo 'nperadore e muoia li Nove*' – 'Long live the emperor and death to the Nine!'[25] It was the noon of 25 March 1355 and the chronicler presents this clamour as a unanimous appeal for the lordship of a single man as against a regime supposed to defend all the civic virtues of communal resistance. A cry, in short, which contradicted all that Lorenzetti had painted seventeen years before. The rebels did not kill the Nine, but they did attack their archives. They made for the seat of the *Arte della Lana*, the tax registers of the Biccherna, and also went to the Palazzo Pubblico. Here they burned books, and perhaps it was this fire that damaged the left end of the west wall of the fresco, since, to judge from old plans, the rooms where the books and the administration's registers were kept were just behind the wall where Lorenzetti painted the ravages of war. Flame on flame: the painting of the fire burned in its turn. Other books and archives were thrown out of the windows and consumed by fire, that evening, in the square of the *campo*. An ass then roamed the whole city, under the gibes of the crowd, which had hung on its tail the communal box containing the names of the men likely to be elected to the magistracies.[26] It was the last day of the government of the Nine, ending in a somewhat sinister ritual of political derision. A sad piece of choreography, no doubt, but one which diverted the violence of the insurgents – for, according to the chronicler Donato di Neri, if they had not burned their books, 'they would have cut the Nine into pieces'.[27]

So, is the history of Lorenzetti's fresco definitively complete? No, of course not: it goes on. Is it belied by history? Obviously not: it insists. With the fall of the Nine, only the most immediately contextual part of its message becomes outdated. The rest, everything else, remains active. Its meaning has continually been updated. Among the *Riformatori* who took power in 1368 was the painter Andrea Vanni, brother of Lippo, to whom Caterina Benincasa, a Dominican mystic known today as Catherine of Siena, wrote from Rome to exhort him to hold fast to his political programme: she desired him, she said, to be just and to foster justice and order in Siena.[28] Art historians believe they can see Andrea Vanni's hand in repainted sections at the corner of the north wall and the eastern wall, from the great personage to the wedding procession.[29] How far will he have tried to adapt Lorenzetti's figures to the political changes in which he was himself involved? In fact, it is impossible to say. But we must be sure of one thing: if we go to Siena, if we cross the square of the *campo* to enter the Palazzo Pubblico, if we climb the stairs and cross the rooms which now lead to the one called the Sala della Pace, we will see a painting which dates neither from the moment when Lorenzetti painted it, nor from the times when Vanni and others after him retouched it, nor even from the time when Bernardino of Siena spoke of it, but which, from the very moment when the gaze we bring to bear on it makes it contemporary with us, becomes what Mallarmé called our 'beautiful today'.

Epilogue

Vanishing point

From Empoli, the train glides nonchalantly along between gentle low hills. It lingers at each station. Just a few kilometres further on, and a new name looms. We recognize it, for it has already played its part in the old musical score that we have been trying to read: Castelfiorentino, Certaldo, Poggibonsi. Where is the *buon governo*? The landscape is weary, soiled by a dull, lifeless yellow that seems to have given up the struggle: the colour of the collective habitat in the working-class outskirts of Italian cities. In Granaiolo, the train almost brushes along the broken windows of a massive, hollow factory, a large blackened corpse. What is truly recognizable here, once we can no longer trust in the sonorous echo of toponyms? Of course, there are a few hills topped by their villas with their flared roofs, the sky-lines dotted with cypresses arranged in such an exaggeratedly artistic way that one always wonders whether it is nature that is imitating painting or vice versa. Castles, especially, sumptuously displayed, appear furtive and trembling behind the curtain of the trees, as similar to one another as ghosts.

I return to Siena with the ever-renewed hope of understanding something. One should neither expect anything from contemplation, nor hope for any sudden inspiration. That is not how things happen; they happen incidentally, obliquely, with the sad smile of some doleful pop song. So this slow, stealthy approach suits me: and you can also circumvent fear by slowing your pace, opening yourself to surprises and unexpected contacts. I have returned to Siena, but I slow down, I linger, I do not rush. I wait; I count on nothing but the virtues of waiting, intent on deferring my goal so as to broaden my vision and adopt the point of view of the locale. So I have to organize things. I spent last night a few miles from the city, and now I set off. For it is on foot that one must climb the hill. And take the measure of the facetious tyranny of slopes, never violent but sustained, insidious and above all changeable: their sudden jolts shake the fabric of the landscape.

One morning, in the early warm hours of a Sunday after the horse racing at the Palio, I came to a better understanding of the authority of the gate – here, the Porta Tufi – where it suddenly looms up after a bend in the road. I have also seen the incisive line of the city walls which divide the landscape, sharply and clearly, plunging abruptly downwards towards the tranquil turf of the gardens. You can find a similar angle in Lorenzetti, resolute and cutting, in spite of the little-girl pink with which he painted the walls of his happy city. And it is this same plunge that the walker can inflict on himself when, buffeted by the waves made by the streets at the edge of the *campo* where they roll and bounce in a swell that finally disorientates him, he suddenly sees a *chiasso* tumbling down. Through this narrow lane which pierces the mass of the buildings, a section of brick chevrons suddenly appears. He recognizes them easily, and slips into the opening of the walls which gradually allows the blue cut of the sky to impose its presence. Then he raises his eyes to the area of redder brick, which can only be those of the palace. It is here; once again the square has vanquished the distracted visitor; it lures him like a magnet and seizes hold of him.

On that day, even though people had continued to trample over it since the Palio, the *tuffo* still bore the fierce prints of the horses that had run their race, that brutal spasm, a manifestation of pure, foolish force so ignorant of any rules – a rider can even slash his opponent's face with his whip – that not even the motley clowning of the fake mediaeval costumes can make it more amiable. Drums and pennants, this whole circus is there only to pull the wool over the eyes of those who come to see it. But it would be better if they did not understand what was really happening when time – compressed since the early hours by the throng that has been basking in the warm July sun (and on whose faces lurks the sudden possibility of that pure hatred found whenever crowds assemble) – relaxes as soon as the rope sags to allow the horses to dash forward. Thundering round the conch shell that comprises, in the hollow of the hills of Siena, the most delicate and the most theatrical of cavities, out surges the raging certainty of the males: a hymn to suddenness. It's always over too soon – and then they spend hours drinking, strolling and mulling over the events.

I lower my eyes towards the compacted sand: you need only see how the imprint of the hoofs is hollowed out asymmetrically when approaching the sharp angles of a track that comes up short along-side the façade of the palace to understand the violence of the shock when the horses gallop up, lurching but intent on winning. The day before yesterday, one of them slammed into the barriers, swinging its puppet rider into the air, and its heart seized up. The *fantino* suffered broken bones, but it was the death of the horse that made the Sienese weep. By filling the square with the press of their agglutinated bodies, they verify each year the extravagant singularity of the shape that the city here adopts. Now they start to dismantle the wooden walls that obstructed the space between each marble plot, thus giving the square its rhythm: the workers are busy, their gestures are precise, and it is a fine spectacle to see them regaining possession of these places – their places. This is how Lorenzetti's fresco unfolds: it is not trades that it depicts – none of those vaguely nauseating allegories that pompously exalt the labour of the humble; no, it is men and women at work whom one sees, individuals absorbed in the joys and pains of labour. Everything calls you in, and this invitation is nothing but life itself. So we must enter the palace.

But not right now. I take a detour to the gallery of the Pinacoteca, intending to go round the fresco. To capture it from a distance and to breathe in the pictorial atmosphere of that moment: Siena, 1338. Here, then, is Ambrogio Lorenzetti among the cohort of his predecessors and his successors. He has renounced nothing, not even the brilliance of gold, which clearly covers the background of his *Annunciation*, and boldly begins to prick the ear of the Virgin in ecstasy with a fine droplet of divine light. Did he not, more than any other Sienese painter, display writing in his painting? The infant Jesus, the saints and the Madonna, all brandish brilliant phylacteries, sometimes pointing at them with a precise finger, where the reddened initial of a beautiful Gothic script invites us to read. This whole Sienese painting is there, gazing at you, as if frozen in the unreasonable admiration of a few ancient masters who made its reputation but prevented it from pursuing its history.

There is no history of art in Siena; just art, and the insistence of images. Here they are, all the paintings, lined up as if on parade – and you reflect that, basically, a museum is the exact opposite of those sites of painting where, as in the Palazzo Pubblico, images exist only in the space that holds them captive. But once they are no longer held by those places, then these images can drift in their quiet insolence towards the delirium of our reveries. I walk past the canvases to catch the eyes of those depicted. There are the eyes of the Madonnas which fix you with their stare in Simone Martini – almond-shaped, hazelnut in colour: delicious, crisp fruit. Conversely, the eyes of Bernardino of Siena, painted by Sano di Pietro, but also by Sassetta, are hollow and dry; they maliciously perforate a white face, cracked and curled like a parchment. Sassetta always depicts him with his body elongated like a flame, but strangely this flame is black, as if the preacher were consumed by a dark fire which, without even giving him the grace of a dazzling burst of conflagration, directly transformed his flesh into ash. Here he is, pointing to the monogram of Jesus, staring at the spectator, imposing on him or her the disquieting spectacle of an asceticism which nobody likes to see.

Where do our desires come from, and our blindness? What keeps the force of images within us? For such a long time, I did not want to see the melancholy figure of Peace, and thereby spared myself the splendid bitterness of the political lesson that she continues to give us. This was not for want of being warned. How many times had I read the injunctions of the painted writings? 'Turn your eyes to gaze, / you who rule, on the woman who is depicted here.' So I went back. In the Sala della Pace, for several hours – I do not think I have ever looked at something as long as those three painted walls – I turn round and round, I go and I come, I continue my exercises in disorientation. I am alone, most of the time. Visitors pass by, few stay long. A model of the reconstituted city provides a diversion, as well as a UNESCO panel calling for 'Education for Peace and Non-Violence for the Children of the World', with the melancholic figure of Peace becoming a soothing logo: *simbolo di Siena, messaggero del mondo*. A strange denial of the brutality of the scenes depicted in it, all the ingredients of the insipid tourist mentality combined in a comical way: infantilization, depoliticization, the so-called global village.

There is still nobody here. So I decide to take some notes, trying to recover the calm evidence of a few visual impressions. I then start to feel that everything here is about slopes, recesses and heights. I need, more than I had thought, to raise my head to see figures which, now, do not appear so large. My eye-line is a little below the medallions and the escutcheons – so we are under the feet of the councillors. Vivid spots around the great personage, in the happy city (of course), contrast with the more tarnished colours. Gilded touches strike the eye in the relative penumbra – especially those on the dancers' tambourines. Everything is stretched out, elongated, perplexing. Less evidently beautiful, perhaps, than in my memory. But at the same time everything also seems simpler. On the one hand, the freedom to move around, to converse, to learn, to exchange, to dance, to quarrel, to love, to flirt, to shut oneself away, to be bored – and power cannot risk this, nor can the Church or the civil government, since all the confused heap of principles, symbols and allegories is reserved for the north wall, the one that fascinates the ideologues, the one to which we ought simply to be indifferent if we so wish, responding to it with a polite neutrality. For on the other wall, all is confused and mingled – war and city, the council of tyrannical rulers and their frightened subjects – and oppression only aims at one thing, precisely and obstinately: to constrain speaking beings, to hamper their recalcitrant bodies.

And if anyone were to come along to convince me that all these people are perhaps only the agitated dream of the woman in her reverie on the north wall, I would probably be ready to believe it. And why just the woman in majesty, after all? In the streets and on the roads there are many of these little characters whom you can catch wandering or meditating. They have stopped there and put down their tools, like this man near the mill watching the water flowing and shimmering. Only a foolish historicist would have reduced this crowd to life as it was seven centuries ago: it is so much simpler to recognize in it that eternal struggle which disturbs our idylls and stirs the enigmatic fantasies inside our skulls. There is always a psychoanalyst laughing behind the historian's back and whispering in his ear: each of us is two cities confronting one another. How can we escape this obsession? On the south wall, the only open window in the room looks out over the sumptuous landscape visible from the loggia, on the upper floor: today, the marketplace which is lodged in a notch between two hills, and from which the Sienese countryside can be discerned – with the massive and peaceful presence of the Certosa di Maggiano in the distance. So the Nine sat with their backs to the *campo*, and to the land they ruled. I turn around again and try to measure the sightlines. The only figure who has sufficient height to contemplate this landscape in its entirety is the venerable old man, whose golden shield perhaps reflects the light that comes in through the window, appearing like a second sun with a dull, withdrawn lustre.

Here we are at his feet, facing the fourth wall, the one we never look at. It is decorated with a modern fresco, continuing the dull ornaments that run along the first level of the walls, and representing architectural shapes in grisaille – in particular, four niches of missing statues. Some historians have imagined that this south wall was also painted with narrative scenes. This is a superfluous hypothesis, which nothing in the documentation justifies: what is lacking in the present state of the fresco that was described and that we can no longer see? Nothing, absolutely nothing. Nothing is lacking in Lorenzetti's painting. Not even its destroyed parts, which have inflicted a wound on its 'bad' part but contain no mystery. Not even the insolent beauty of the Sienese landscape that slips through the only window obstructed by heavy curtains. Still nobody. I am definitely alone – I might as well make sure of it. I open the window wide. The light pours into the Sala della Pace. And above all, it is as if everything were linked in concord. To the left, on the happy, disciplined side, Lorenzetti painted the hills that lean towards the sea. To the right, on the bad side, they have a similar curve. Through the window I can see the horizon stretching across the hills as they pull a straight rope between the two cities. *Dritta corda.* Stop looking for a fourth wall: between the paintings of the fertile country and those of the dead earth, the landscape takes responsibility for making the connection. Vanishing point; no way out: only one world.

I had finally found the off-screen dimension that comprises the force of images. So I went back and walked past the rear of the Palazzo Pubblico. It is from its reverse side that we can best understand the discrete art of the overhang that creates the properly political charm of this site. For this is all that power is: this ability to make us raise our eyes to what looks down on us and concerns us. The front façade of the palace hangs below the *campo* and imposes itself on the side of the market square that it dominates in a much more abrupt cliff, opening majestically onto the deep and tranquil breathing of the relief, where the hills lazily move back. The whole of this complex system of slopes takes its meaning here, behind the palace, in the axis of the eyes of the Nine. From below, the great, scowling judge watches us. We live under his gaze. The visual impression is that which grabs you when you look up at the rear side of the Capitol in Rome – but I am especially reminded of the palace of Urbino, yet again, and the grip of a place's aura. It is time to get back on the streets, to wander, to get lost in the red brick volutes of the city. For in spite of its great airs – and this always rather irritating manner of stamping every corner of the street, every door-frame, every portion of the sky, with its white and black escutcheon – Siena remains free and cheerful. It is the joy of steep slopes and sudden bends in the road, the joy of the rippling of streets, stirred into quickness like a tablecloth being shaken after a family meal.

Appendices

The square of the *campo* and the Palazzo Pubblico in its urban environment

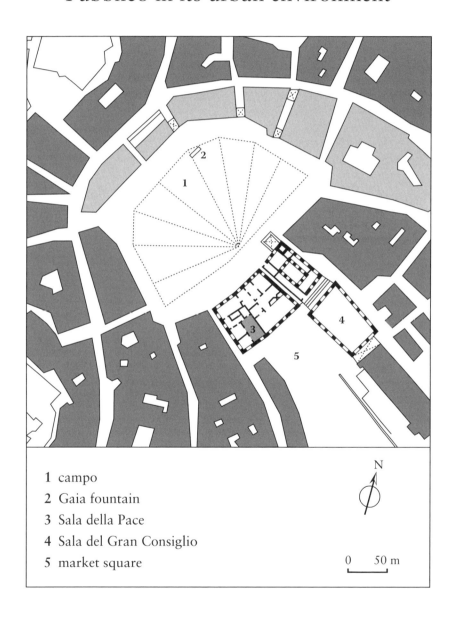

1 campo
2 Gaia fountain
3 Sala della Pace
4 Sala del Gran Consiglio
5 market square

N

0   50 m

Arrangement of the rooms on the first floor of the Palazzo Pubblico

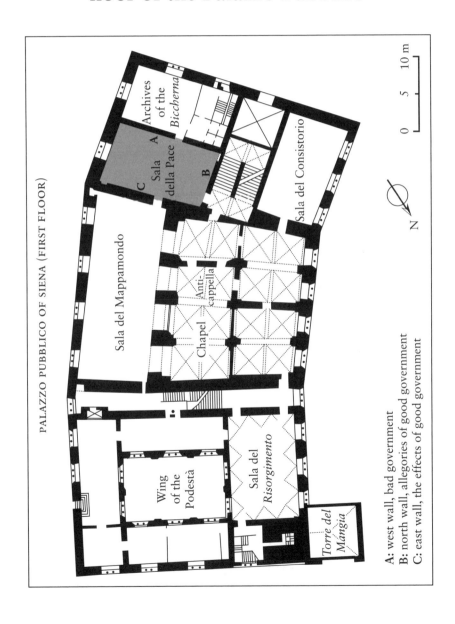

PALAZZO PUBBLICO OF SIENA (FIRST FLOOR)

Sala del Mappamondo

Sala della Pace

A
B
C

Archives of the *Biccherna*

Sala del Consistorio

Chapel

Anti-cappella

Wing of the Podestà

Sala del Risorgimento

Torre del Mángia

N

0 5 10 m

A: west wall, bad government
B: north wall, allegories of good government
C: east wall, the effects of good government

The fresco of the Sala della Pace: silhouettes, inscriptions, identifications

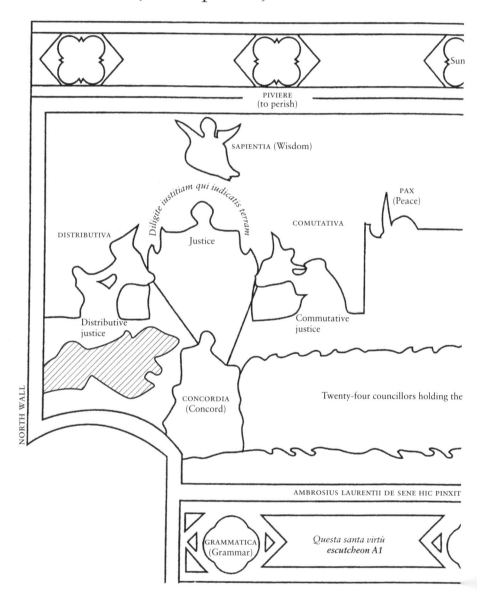

Key:
In CAPITALS: *tituli* designating the allegories and the artist's signature
In *italics*: other inscriptions, escutcheons and scrolls
In roman: main identifications
In cross-hatching: main areas destroyed

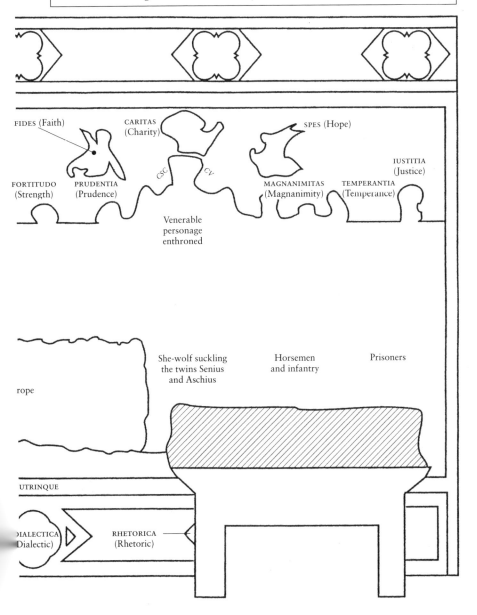

FIDES (Faith)

CARITAS (Charity)

SPES (Hope)

IUSTITIA (Justice)

FORTITUDO (Strength)

PRUDENTIA (Prudence)

CSC   *CV*

MAGNANIMITAS (Magnanimity)

TEMPERANTIA (Temperance)

Venerable
personage
enthroned

She-wolf suckling
the twins Senius
and Aschius

Horsemen
and infantry

Prisoners

rope

UTRINQUE

DIALECTICA (Dialectic)

RHETORICA (Rhetoric)

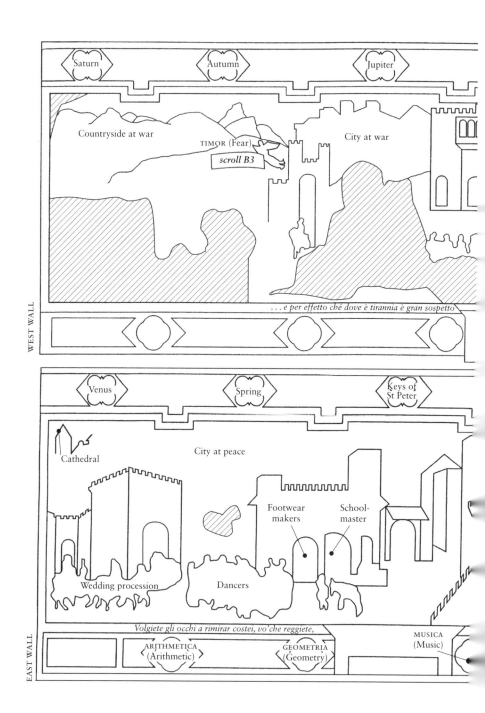

WEST WALL

Saturn

Autumn

Jupiter

Countryside at war

TIMOR (Fear)

scroll B3

City at war

. . . e per effetto ché dove è tirannia è gran sospetto

EAST WALL

Venus

Spring

Keys of St Peter

Cathedral

City at peace

Footwear makers

School-master

Wedding procession

Dancers

Volgiete gli occhi a rimirar costei, vo'che reggiete,

ARITHMETICA (Arithmetic)

GEOMETRIA (Geometry)

MUSICA (Music)

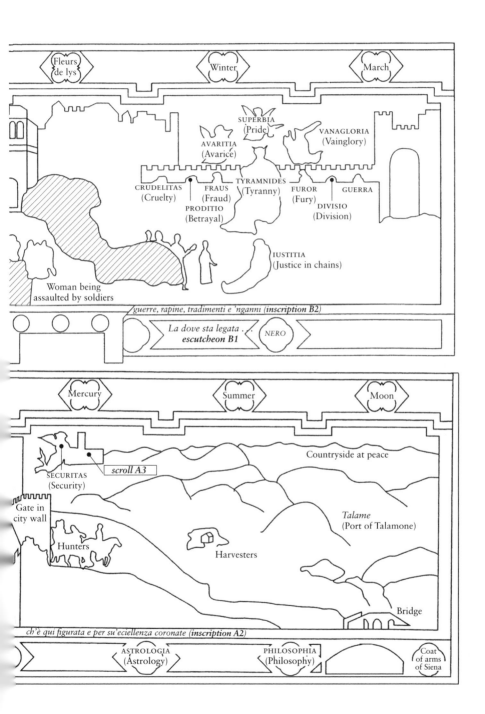

Fleurs de lys — Winter — March

SUPERBIA (Pride)

AVARITIA (Avarice)

VANAGLORIA (Vainglory)

CRUDELITAS (Cruelty)

FRAUS (Fraud)

TYRAMNIDES (Tyranny)

FUROR (Fury)

GUERRA

PRODITIO (Betrayal)

DIVISIO (Division)

IUSTITIA (Justice in chains)

Woman being assaulted by soldiers

guerre, rapine, tradimenti e 'nganni (**inscription B2**)

La dove sta legata . . . **escutcheon B1**

NERO

Mercury — Summer — Moon

SECURITAS (Security)

scroll A3

Countryside at peace

Gate in city wall

Talame (Port of Talamone)

Hunters

Harvesters

Bridge

ch'è qui figurata e per su'eciellenza coronate (**inscription A2**)

ASTROLOGIA (Astrology)

PHILOSOPHIA (Philosophy)

Coat of arms of Siena

Inscriptions in the vernacular: transcription, edition and translation[1]

A1 – North wall, escutcheon under the 'allegories of good government'

QUESTA SANTA UIRTU LADOVE REGGE. INDUCE ADUNITA LIANIMI MOLTI. (E)QUESTI ACCIO RICCOLTI. UN BEN COMUN PERLOR SIGROR SIFANNO. LOQUAL P (ER) GOUERNAR SUO STATO ELEGGE. DINO(N) TENER GIAMMA GLIOCHI RIUOLTI DALO SPLENDOR DEUOLTI. DE LE UIRTU CHE(N)TORNO ALLUI SISTNNO.

 P(ER) QUESTO CONTRIUNFO ALLUI SI DANNO. CENSI TRIBUTI (E) SIGNORIE DITERRE. PER QUESTO SENÇA GUERRE. SEGUITA POI OGNI CIUILE EFFETTO. UTILE NECESSARIO E DIDILETTO.

Questa santa virtù, là dove regge,
induce ad unità li animi molti,
e questi, a cciò ricolti,
a ben comun per lor signor si fanno,
lo qual, per governar suo stato, elegge
di non tener giamma' gli ochi rivolti
da lo splendor de' volti
de le virtù che 'ntorno a llui si stanno.
Per questo con triunfo a llui si danno
censi, tributi e signorie di terre,
per questo senza guerre
seguita poi ogni civile effetto,
utile, necessario e di diletto.

This sacred virtue, wherever she rules,
leads to unity the multitude of souls,

and these, gathered to this aim,
make the common good their lord,
who, in order to govern his state, chooses
never to take his eyes from the splendour of the faces
of the virtues that stand around him.
Therefore it is to him that are given in triumph
taxes, tributes and signorias,
thus, without war,
there follow for the city all effects
useful, necessary, and agreeable.

A2 – East wall, inscription running under the 'effects of good government'

VOLGIETE GLIOCCHI ARIMIRAR COSTEI VOCHE REGGIETE CHE QVI
FIGVRATA. (E) P(ER)SVE CIELLE(N)ÇIA CORONATA. LAQVAL SE(M)PRA
CIASCVN SVO [...
....…....] DELA CITTA DVE SERVATA
• QVESTA VI(R)TV KEPIV DALTRA RISPRENDE. ELLA GVARD(A)E DIFENDE
• CHI LEI ONORA (E) LOR NVTRICA (E) PASCIE. DA LA SVO LVCIE NASCIA
• EL MERITAR COLOR COPERAN BENE. (E) AGLINIQVI DAR DEBITE PENE.

Volgiete gli occhi a rimirar costei,
vo' che reggiete, ch'è qui figurata
e per su'eciellenzia coronata,
la qual sempr'a a ciascun suo [dritto rende.
Guardate quanti ben' vengan da lei
e come è dolce vita e riposata
quella] de la città du' è servata
questa virtù ke più d'altra risprende.
Ella guarda e difende
chi lei onora e lor nutrica e pascie;
da la suo lucie nascie
el meritar color c'operan bene
e agl'inqui dar debite pene.

Turn your eyes to gaze,
you who rule, on the woman who is depicted here
and who for her excellence is crowned,
who always renders to each one his or her due.
Gaze at all the benefits that stem from her,
how sweet and restful is the life

of this city where respect is paid to this virtue
which more than any other shines.
She keeps and protects
those who honour her, she nourishes and calms them.
From her light arises
the reward of those who do good
and the punishment due to evildoers.

A3 – East wall, scroll of *Securitas*

SENÇA PAVRA OGNVOM FRANCO CAMINI.
ELAVORANDO SEMINI CIASCVNO.
MENTRE CHE TAL COMVNO.
MANTERRA QVESTA DO(N)NA I(N) SIGNORIA.
CHEL ALEVATA AREI OGNI BALIA.

Senza paura ogn'uom franco camini,
e lavorando semini ciascuno,
mentre che tal comuno
manterrà questa donna in signoria,
ch'el à levata a' rei ogni balia.

Without fear, let every man walk safely
and let everyone cultivate and sow
as long as this commune
remains under the signoria of this lady
for she has taken all power from the guilty.

B1– West wall, escutcheon under the 'allegories of bad government'

LADOUE STA LEGATA LA IUSTITIA. NESSUNO ALBE(N) COMUNE GIAMAY
SACORDA. NE TIRA ADRITTA CORDA. P(ER)O CONVIE(N) CHE TIRANNIA
SORMONTI. LA QVAL P(ER) ADEMPIR LA SVA NEQVITIA. NULLO UOLER
NE OP(ER)AR DISCORDA. DALLA NATURA LORDA. DA UITII CHE
CO(N) LEI SON QVI CO(N)GIONTI. QUESTA CACCIA COLOR CALBEN
SON PRONTI. (E) CHIAMA ASE CIASCVN CAMALE I(N) TENDE. QVESTA
SEMPRE DIFENDE. CHI SFORÇA O ROBBA O CHI ODIASSE PACE. VNDE
OGNITERRA SVA I(N) CULTA GIACE.

Là dove sta legata la iustitia,
nessuno al ben comun già mai s'acorda,

né tira a dritta corda:
però convien che tirannia sormonti,
la qual, per adempir la sua nequitia,
nullo voler né operar discorda
dalla natura lorda
de' vitii che con lei son qui congionti.
Questa caccia color c'al ben son proni
e chiama a sé ciascun c'a male intende;
questa sempre difende
chi sforza o robba o chi odiasse pace,
unde ogni terra sua inculta giace.

Wherever justice is bound in chains,
nobody can ever be in harmony with the common good
or pull the rope straight:
thus it is that tyranny takes the upper hand,
for it, in order to accomplish its misdeeds,
accords both in thought and deed
with the corrupt nature
of the vices that accompany it.
It chases away all those who are preparing to do good
and attracts all those who tend to evil,
it always defends
those who rape or steal, or those who hate peace,
thus all its lands remain uncultivated.

B2 – West wall, inscription running under the 'effects of bad government'

[..] E P(ER)
EFFETTO. CHE DOUE E TIRANNIA E GRAN SOSPETTO. GUERRE RAPINE
TRADIMENTI EN GANNI. PRENDANSI SIGNORIA SOPRA DLLEI. (E)
PONGASI LAMENTE (E) LO INTELLETTO [..
....] HI TURBAR LA UUOL SIE P(ER)
SUO MERTO. DISCACCIATE DISERTO. IN SIEME CON QUALUNQUE SIA
SEGUACIE. FORTIFICMDO LEI P(ER) UOSTRA PACE.

.... *[-ei]*
.... *e per effetto*
ché dove è tirannia è gran sospetto
guerre, rapine, tradimenti e 'nganni.
Prendasi signoria sopra di lei

e pongasi la mente e lo 'ntelletto
[in tener semper a iustizia suggietto
ciascun per ischifar sì scuri danni,
abbattendo e' tiranni;
e c]hi turbar la vuol sie per suo merto
discacciat' e diserto
insieme con qualunque sia seguacie,
fortificando lei per vostra pace.

....
.... and in fact
for where there is tyranny, great are mistrust,
wars, thefts, betrayals and frauds.
Let lordship be taken over her
and let each man busy his spirit and his intelligence
with always subjecting everyone to justice,
to forestall such black damage
and strike down tyrants;
and may anyone who seeks to trouble her be, for all his reward,
sent away and undone,
he and all those who follow him,
thus fortifying justice for your peace.

B3 – West wall, scroll of Timor

P(ER) VOLERE ELBENPROPIO I(N)QVESTA TERRA
SO(M)MESSE LAGIVSTITIA ATYRANNIA.
UNDE P(ER) QVESTA VIA.
NO(N) PASSA ALCVN SE(N)ÇA DVBBIO DIMO(R)TE.
CHE FVOR SIROBBA ET DENTRO DALEPORTE.

Per voler el ben propio, in questa terra
Sommess'è la giustizia a tyrannia,
unde per questa via
non passa alcun senza dubbio di morte,
ché fuor si robba e dentro de le porte.

Because all seek their own good alone, here
justice is in thrall to tyranny.
thus by this path
no one passes without fearing death
because everything shrinks away, inside and outside the gates.

Notes

Prologue

1   See the diagram of the whole fresco on pp. 138–41 below.

Chapter 1 'I thought of these images, painted for you'

1   Rosa Maria Dessì, 'Pratiche della parola di pace nella storia dell'Italia urbana', in *Pace e guerra nel basso medioevo. Atti del XL Convegno storico internazionale, Todi, 12–14 ottobre 2003* (Spoleto: Centro italiano di studi sull'alto medioevo, 2004), pp. 271–312; see also Rosa Maria Dessì, 'L'invention du "Bon Gouvernement". Pour une histoire des anachronismes dans les fresques d'Ambrogio Lorenzetti (XIVe–XXe siècle)', *Bibliothèque de l'École des Chartes*, 165, 2007, pp. 129–80.
2   Enzo Carli, 'Luoghi ed opere d'arte senesi nelle prediche di Bernardino del 1427', in *Bernardino predicatore nella Società del suo tempo (16° Convegno del Centro di studi sulla spiritualità medievale, Todi 9–12 ottobre 1975)* (Todi: L'Accademia Tudertina, 1976), pp. 155–82.
3   Bernardino da Siena, *Prediche volgari sul Campo di Siena 1427*, ed. Carlo Delcorno (Milan: Rusconi, 1989), 2 vols, p. 1254.
4   Michel Sennelart, *Les Arts de gouverner. Du regimen médiéval au concept de gouvernement* (Paris: Seuil, 1995).
5   Bernardino da Siena, *Le prediche volgari. La predicazione del 1425 in Siena*, ed. Ciro Cannarozzi (Florence: Libreria Editrice Fiorentina, 1940), 3 vols, pp. 276–7.
6   Nirit Ben-Aryeh Debby, 'War and Peace: The Description of Ambrogio Lorenzetti's Frescoes in Saint Bernardino's 1425 Siena Sermons', *Renaissance Studies*, 15 (3), 2001, pp. 272–86; Lina Bolzoni, '"Come tu vedi dipinto": la predica e le pitture cittadine', in *La rete delle immagini*.

Predicazione in volgare dalle origini a Bernardino da Siena (Turin: Einaudi, 2002), pp. 67–190.

7 Didier Boisseul, *Le Thermalisme en Toscane à la fin du Moyen Âge. Les bains siennois de la fin du XIIIe siècle au début du XVIe siècle* (Rome: École française de Rome, 2002).

8 Edna Carter-Southard, 'Ambrogio Lorenzetti's Frescoes in the Sala della Pace: A Change of Name', *Mitteilungen des Kunsthistorischen Institutes in Florenz*, 24, 1980, pp. 361–5.

Chapter 2 *Nachleben*: the watchful shadows

1 'Cronaca senese dei fatti riguardanti la città ed il suo territorio di autore anonimo del secolo XIV', in *Cronache senesi*, ed. Alessandro Lisini and Fabio Iacometti, *Rerum Italicarum Scriptores*, XV–6, new edn (Bologna: N. Zanichelli, 1933–5), p. 78.

2 Michele Cordaro, 'Le vicende costruttive', in Cesare Brandi (ed.), *Palazzo Pubblico di Siena. Vicende costruttive e decorazione* (Milan: Pizzi-Monte dei Paschi di Siena, 1983), pp. 29–143.

3 Gaston Bachelard, *The Poetics of Space*, trans. Richard Kearney (London: Penguin, 2014), p. 132.

4 Rosa Maria Dessì, 'L'invention du "Bon Gouvernement". Pour une histoire des anachronismes dans les fresques d'Ambrogio Lorenzetti (XIVe–XXe siècle)', *Bibliothèque de l'École des Chartes*, 165, 2007, pp. 129–80 (pp. 138–9, n. 27).

5 Roberto Guerrini, '*Dulci pro libertate*. Taddeo di Bartolo: il ciclo di eroi antichi nel Palazzo Pubblico di Siena (1413–1414). Tradizione classica ed iconografi a politica', *Rivista storica italiana*, 112, 2000, pp. 510–68.

6 Marianna Jenkins, 'The Iconography of the Hall of the Consistory in the Palazzo Pubblico, Siena', *Art Bulletin*, LIV, 1972, pp. 430–51.

7 Edna Carter-Southard, 'Ambrogio Lorenzetti's Frescoes in the Sala della Pace: A Change of Name', *Mitteilungen des Kunsthistorischen Institutes in Florenz*, 24, 1980, pp. 361–5; Robert Gibbs, 'In Search of Ambrogio Lorenzetti's Allegory of Justice: Changes to the Frescoes in the Palazzo Pubblico', *Apollo*, 159 (447), 1999, pp. 11–16.

8 Lorenzo Ghiberti, *I Commentarii*, ed. Lorenzo Bartoli (Florence: Giunti, 1998), p. 89.

9 Giorgio Vasari, 'Life' of Giotto, in Vasari, *Lives of the Most Eminent Painters, Sculptors and Architects*, Vol. 1, *Cimabue to Agnolo Gaddi*, trans. Gaston du C. de Vere, available online at http://www.gutenberg.org/files/25326/25326.txt.

10 Dessì, 'L'invention du "Bon Gouvernement"', p. 142.

11 Ibid., pp. 148–9.

12 Rosa Maria Dessì, 'Da Toso Pichi ad Aristotele: visioni risorgimentali

del "Buon Governo" di Lorenzetti', *Rivista storica italiana*, 122 (3), 2010, pp. 1146–70.

13 Georges Didi-Huberman, 'Before the Image, Before Time: The Sovereignty of Anachronism', in Claire Farago and Robert Zwijnenberg (eds), *Compelling Visuality: The Work of Art in and Out of History* (Minneapolis: University of Minnesota Press, 2003), pp. 31–44.

14 Cesare Brandi, 'Chiarimenti su "Buon Governo" di Ambrogio Lorenzetti', *Bollettino d'Arte*, 40, 1955, pp. 119–23.

15 Dessì, 'L'invention du "Bon Gouvernement"', p. 146.

16 Rosa Maria Dessì, 'Il bene comune nella comunicazione verbale e visiva. Indagini sugli affreschi del "Buon Governo"', in *Il bene comune: forme di governo e gerarchie sociali nel basso medioevo. Atti del XLVIII Convegno storico internazionale, Todi, 9–12 ottobre 2011* (Spoleto: Centro italiano di studi sull'alto medioevo, 2012), pp. 89–130.

17 Dessì, 'L'invention du "Bon Gouvernement"', p. 172.

18 Georges Didi-Huberman, *The Surviving Image: Phantoms of Time and Time of Phantoms: Aby Warburg's History of Art*, trans. Harvey Mendelsohn (University Park: Pennsylvania State University Press, 2017 [2002]).

Chapter 3 The Nine

1 Hayden Maginnis, 'Chiarimenti documentari: Simone Martini, i Memmi e Ambrogio Lorenzetti', *Rivista d'arte*, 51, 1989, pp. 3–23..

2 Roberto S. Lopez, 'Économie et architecture médiévales. Ceci aurait-il tué cela?', *Annales ESC*, 7, 1952, pp. 433–8. For a discussion of these ideas, see Patrick Boucheron, 'È possibile un investimento disinteres-sato? Alcuni considerazioni sul finanziamento delle cattedrali nelle città dell'Italia centro-settentrionale alla fine del Medio Evo', *Città e storia*, 4, 2009, pp. 1–16.

3 Fabrizio Nevola, *Siena: Constructing the Renaissance city* (New Haven, CT, and London: Yale University Press, 2007).

4 Fabio Gabbrielli, *Siena medievale. L'architettura civile* (Siena: Protagon Editori, 2010).

5 Duccio Balestracci, 'L'acqua a Siena nel Medioevo', in Jean-Claude Maire Vigueur and Agostino Paravicini Bagliani (eds), *Ars et Ratio. Dalla torre di Babele al ponte di Rialto* (Palermo: Sellerio, 1990), pp. 19–31.

6 William Bowsky, 'The *Buon Governo* of Siena (1287–1355): A Medieval Italian Oligarchy', *Speculum*, 37, 1962, pp. 368–81 (p. 375).

7 Nicolai Rubinstein, 'Le allegorie di Ambrogio Lorenzetti nella Sala della Pace e il pensiero politico del suo tempo', *Rivista storica italiana*, 109, 1997, pp. 781–802 (p. 783). For other hypotheses, see Aloïs Riklin, *Ambrogio Lorenzettis politische Summe* (Berne: Stämpfli Verlag AG, 1996), p. 73.

8 Furio Brugnolo, '"Voi che guardate …" Divagazioni sulla poesia per pittura del Trecento', in Claudio Ciociola (ed.), *Visibile parlare'. Le scritture esposte nei volgari italiani dal Medioevo al Rinascimento* (Naples: ESI, 1997), pp. 305–39 (p. 323).
9 Quentin Skinner, *Visions of Politics*, Vol. 2, *Renaissance Virtues* (Cambridge: Cambridge University Press, 2002), p. 70.
10 Giovanni da Viterbo, *Liber de regimine civitatum*, ed. Gaetano Salvemini, in *Biblioteca juridica medii aevi*, Vol. 3 (Bologna: Biblioteca Juridica Medii Aevi, 1901), pp. 215–80 (p. 252).
11 Milani, Giuliano, *L'esclusione dal comune. Conflitti e bandi politici a Bologna e in altre città italiane tra XII e XIV secolo* (Rome: ISIME, 2003), p. 172.
12 Julien Théry, 'Faide nobiliaire et justice inquisitoire de la papauté à Sienne au temps des Neuf: les *recollectiones* d'une enquête de Benoît XII contre l'évêque Donosdeo de' Malavolti (ASV, Collectoriae 61A et 404A)', in Susanne Lepsius and Thomas Wetzstein (eds), *Als die Welt in die Akten kam. Prozeßschriftgut im europäischen Mittelalter* (Frankfurt: Klostermann, 'Rechtsprechung', 2008), pp. 275–345.
13 Paolo Cammarosano, 'Il comune di Siena dalla solidarietà imperiale al guelfismo: celebrazione e propaganda', in Paolo Cammarosano (ed.), *Le forme della propaganda politica nel due e nel trecento* (Rome: École française de Rome, 1994), pp. 455–67.
14 Mario Ascheri, 'Legislazione, statuti e sovranità', in *Antica legislazione della Repubblica di Siena* (Siena: Il Leccio, 1993), pp. 1–40 (p. 18).

Chapter 4 Ambrogio Lorenzetti, *famosissimo e singularissimo maestro*

1 Daniel Russo, 'Le Nom de l'artiste, entre appartenance au groupe et écriture personnelle', in Dominique Iogna-Prat and Brigitte Bedos-Rezak (eds), *L'Individu au Moyen Âge. Individuation et individualisation avant la modernité* (Paris: Aubier, 2005), pp. 235–46 (pp. 237 and 239).
2 Lorenzo Ghiberti, *I Commentarii*, ed. Lorenzo Bartoli (Florence: Giunti, 1998), pp. 87–9.
3 Richard Krautheimer, *Lorenzo Ghiberti* (Princeton, NJ: Princeton University Press, 1956), p. 220.
4 Giorgio Vasari, 'Life' of Giotto, in Vasari, *Lives of the Most Eminent Painters, Sculptors and Architects*, Vol. 1, *Cimabue to Agnolo Gaddi*, trans. Gaston du C. de Vere, available online at http://www.gutenberg.org/files/25326/25326.txt.
5 'Written on a sheet of parchment in Italian, written by the hand of master Ambrogio.' See Valerie Wainwright, 'The Will of Ambrogio Lorenzetti', *The Burlington Magazine*, 117, 1975, pp. 543–4.

6   Enrico Castelnuovo (ed.), *Ambrogio Lorenzetti: il Buon Governo* (Milan: Electa, 1995), p. 19.

7   Quentin Skinner, 'Ambrogio Lorenzetti: The Artist as Political Philosopher', *Proceedings of the British Academy*, 122, 1986, pp. 1–56.

8   Randolph Starn and Loren Partridge, *Arts of Power: Three Halls of State in Italy, 1300–1600* (Berkeley, Los Angeles and Oxford: University of California Press, 1992), p. 318, no. 83.

9   Thanks to Étienne Anheim for his most useful explanations of the structure of payments.

10 Étienne Anheim, 'Expertise et construction de la valeur artistique (XIVe–XVe siècle)', *Revue de synthèse*, 132, 2011, pp. 13–31 (p. 28).

11 Hayden Maginnis, *The World of the Early Sienese Painter* (University Park: Pennsylvania State University Press, 2001), pp. 65–9.

12 Chiara Frugoni (ed.), *Pietro e Ambrogio Lorenzetti* (Florence: Le Lettere, 2004).

13 Alessandro Angelini, 'I restauri di Pietro di Francesco agli affreschi di Ambrogio Lorenzetti nella "Sala della Pace"', *Prospettiva*, 31, 1982, pp. 78–82.

14 Agnolo di Tura del Grasso, 'Cronache senesi', ed. Alessandro Lisini and Fabio Iacometti, *Rerum Italicarum Scriptores*, XV-6, new edn (Bologna: N. Zanichelli, 1933–5), p. 518.

15 Alessandro Tomei, (ed.), *Le biccherne di Siena: arte e finanza all'alba dell'economia moderna* (Rome: Retablo, 2002).

16 Erwin Panofsky, *Perspective as Symbolic Form*, trans. Christopher S. Wood (New York: Zone Books, 1991), p. 57; Daniel Arasse, *L'Annonciation italienne* (Paris: Hazan, 1999), pp. 59–92 (p. 59).

17 Frugoni (ed.), *Pietro e Ambrogio Lorenzetti*, pp. 91–5.

18 Daniel Arasse, *Histoires de peintures* (Paris: Denoël, 2004), p. 67.

19 Guido Castelnuovo and Carole Mabboux, 'I letterari e l'epidemia del 1348', in Sergio Luzzatto and Gabriele Pedullà (eds), *Atlante delle letteratura italiana*, Vol. 1, *Dalle origini al Rinascimento*, ed. Amedeo De Vincentiis (Turin: Einaudi, 2010), pp. 221–3.

20 Mario Luzi, *Earthly and Heavenly Voyage of Simone Martini*, trans. Lugi Bonaffini (Los Angeles: Green Integer, 2003 [1994]), p. 249.

Chapter 5 On each side: allegory, realism, resemblances

1   Jonathan Riess, 'Uno studio iconografico della decorazione ad affresco del 1297 nel Palazzo dei Priori a Perugia', *Bollettino d'Arte*, 66, 1981, pp. 43–58.

2   Patrick Boucheron, 'Connotations, accentuations, signatures. Remarques conclusives', *Annali di Storia moderna e contemporanea*, 16, 2010 (*Atti del Convegno: Immagini, culti, liturgie: le connotazioni politiche del messaggio religioso*), pp. 473–81.

3 Nicolai Rubinstein, 'Political Ideas in Sienese Art: The Frescoes by Ambrogio Lorenzetti and Taddeo di Bartolo in the Palazzo Pubblico', *Journal of the Warburg and Courtauld Institutes*, 21, 1958, pp. 179–207.
4 Maria Monica Donato, '"Cose morali, e anche appartenenti secondo e' luoghi": per lo studio della pittura politica nel tardo medioevo toscano', in Paolo Cammarosano (ed.), *Le forme della propaganda politica nel due e nel trecento* (Rome: École française de Rome, 1994), pp. 491–517.
5 These are the four cardinal virtues. Giorgio Vasari, 'Life' of Giotto, in Vasari, *Lives of the Most Eminent Painters, Sculptors and Architects*, Vol. 1, *Cimabue to Agnolo Gaddi*, trans. Gaston du C. de Vere, available online at http://www.gutenberg.org/files/25326/25326.txt.
6 Donato, '"Cose morali"', pp. 510–17.
7 Jonathan Riess, 'Justice and Common Good in Giotto's Arena Chapel Frescoes', *Arte cristiana*, LXXII, 1984, pp. 69–80.
8 Georgina Pelham, 'Reconstructing the Programme of the Tomb of Guido Tarlati, Bishop and Lord of Arezzo', in Joanna Cannon and Beth Williamson (eds), *Art, Politics, and Civic Religion in Central Italy, 1261–1352* (Aldershot: Ashgate, 2000), pp. 71–115.
9 Hubert Damisch, *The Origin of Perspective*, trans. John Goodman (Cambridge, MA: MIT Press, 1994), p. 194.
10 Jean-Philippe Genet, 'Revisiter Assise: la lisibilité de l'image médiévale', in Corinne Péneau (ed.), *Itinéraires du savoir de l'Italie à la Scandinavie (Xe–XVIe siècle). Études offertes à Élisabeth Mornet* (Paris: Publications de la Sorbonne, 2009), pp. 391–419.
11 Hans Belting, 'The Coat of Arms and the Portrait: Two Media and the Body', in *An Anthropology of Images: Picture, Medium, Body*, trans. Thomas Dunlap (Princeton, NJ: Princeton University Press, 2011 [2001]), pp. 62–83.
12 Jean Wirth, *L'Image à la fin du Moyen Âge* (Paris: Cerf, 2011), p. 67.
13 J.-B. Pontalis, *Le Dormeur éveillé* (Paris: Gallimard, 2004), p. 13.
14 Enzo Carli, *La pittura senese del Trecento* (Milan: Electa, 1980), p. 208.
15 Avraham Ronen, 'Due paesaggi nella Pinacoteca di Siena già attribuiti ad Ambrogio Lorenzetti', *Mitteilungen des Kunsthistorischen Institutes in Florenz*, 50 (3), 2006, pp. 367–400.
16 Uta Feldges, *Landschaft als topographisches Porträt. Der Wiederbeginn der europäischen Landschaftsmalerei in Siena* (Berne: Benteli, 1980).
17 Max Seidel, '"Castrum pingatur in palatio", 1. Ricerche storiche e iconografiche sui castelli dipinti nel Palazzo Pubblico di Siena', *Prospettiva*, 28, 1982, pp. 17–41 (pp. 36–7).
18 Odile Redon, *L'Espace d'une cité. Sienne et le pays siennois (XIIIe–XIVe siècles)* (Rome: École française de Rome, 1994), p. 163.
19 Anne-Laure Imbert, 'Un miroir pour la Commune: les peintures de bataille à Sienne entre Tre- et Quattrocento', in Philippe Morel (ed.), *Le*

Miroir et l'espace du prince dans l'art italien de la Renaissance (Rennes and Tours: Presses universitaires de Rennes and Presses universitaires François-Rabelais, 2012), pp. 257–81.

20 Maria Monica Donato, 'Testi, contesti, immagini politiche nel tardo Medioevo: esempi toscani. In margine a una discussione sul *Buon Governo*', *Annali dell'Istituto storico italo-germanico in Trento*, 19, 1993, pp. 305–55.

21 Andrea Brogi and Francesca Bianciardi, *Nella Siena ritrovata di Ambrogio Lorenzetti* (Siena: NIE, 2005).

22 Max Seidel, *Dolce vita. Ambrogio Lorenzettis Porträt des Sienneser Staates*, Basel, 'Vorträge der Aeneas-Silvius-Stiftung an der Universität Basel', 33, 1999.

23 Hans Belting, 'The New Role of Narrative in Public Painting of the Trecento: *Historia* and Allegory', *Studies in the History of Arts*, 16, 1985, pp. 151–68 (p. 159).

24 Roland Barthes, 'The Reality Effect', in *The Rustle of Language*, trans. Richard Howard (Berkeley and Los Angeles: University of California Press, 1989), pp. 141–8.

25 Petrarch, *Familiares*, XXIII, 19, quoted in Michael Baxandall, *Giotto and the Orators: Humanist Observers of Painting in Italy and the Discovery of Pictorial Composition 1350–1450* (Oxford: Clarendon, 1971), p. 33.

Chapter 6 *Esto visibile parlare*: the walls speak to us

1 Hans Belting, 'Media and Bodies: Dante's Shadows and Greenaway's TV', in *An Anthropology of Images: Picture, Medium, Body*, trans. Thomas Dunlap (Princeton, NJ: Princeton University Press, 2011 [2001]), pp. 128–43.

2 Dante, *Purgatory*, trans. Robin Kirkpatrick (London: Penguin, 2007), canto 26 lines 22–4.

3 Ibid., canto 10, lines 38–40 and lines 94–6.

4 Claudio Ciociola (ed.), '*Visibile parlare*'. *Le scritture esposte nei volgari italiani dal Medioevo al Rinascimento* (Naples: ESI, 1997).

5 Alessandro Bagnoli, *La Maestà di Simone Martini* (Milan: Silvana Editoriale, 1999).

6 Joachim Poeschke, *Italian Frescoes: The Age of Giotto, 1280–1400* (New York: Abbeville Press, 2005), p. 279.

7 Hans Belting, 'The Madonnas of Siena: The Image in Urban Life', in *Likeness and Presence: A History of the Image before the Era of Art*, trans. Edmund Jephcott (Chicago: University of Chicago Press, 1994 [1990]), pp. 377–408 (p. 408).

8 Luciano Bellosi, *Duccio. La Maestà* (Paris: Gallimard, 1999 [1998]).

9 Odile Redon (ed.), *Les Langues de l'Italie médiévale* (Turnhout: Brepols, 2002), p. 113.

10   Furio Brugnolo, '"Voi che guardate . . ." Divagazioni sulla poesia per pittura del Trecento', in Ciociola (ed.), *'Visibile parlare'*, pp. 305–39; Emanuele Coccia and Sylvain Piron, 'Poésie, sciences et politique. Une génération d'intellectuels italiens (1290-1330)', *Revue de Synthèse*, 129 (4), 2008, pp. 551–86.

11   Wolfgang Schild, 'Gerechtigkeitsbilder', in Wolfgang Pleister and Wolfgang Schild (eds), *Recht und Gerechtigkeit im Spiegel der europäischen Kunst* (Cologne: DuMont Buchverlag, 1988), pp. 86–171 (p. 138).

12   Brugnolo, '"Voi che guardate . . ."', p. 322.

13   Roberto Guerrini, *'Dulci pro libertate.* Taddeo di Bartolo: il ciclo di eroi antichi nel Palazzo Pubblico di Siena (1413–1414). Tradizione classica ed iconografi a politica', *Rivista storica italiana*, 112, 2000, pp. 510–68 (p. 543).

14   Rosa Maria Dessì, *'Diligite iustitiam vos qui iudicatis terram* (Sagesse, I, 1): sermons et discours sur la justice dans l'Italie urbaine (XIIe–XVe siècle)', *Rivista internazionale di diritto comune*, 18, 2007, pp. 197–230.

15   Rosa Maria Dessì, 'La giustizia in alcune forme di comunicazione medievale. Intorno ai protesti di Giannozzo Manetti e alle prediche di Bernardino da Siena', in Ginetta Auzzas, Giovanni Baffetti and Carlo Delcorno (eds), *Letteratura in forma di sermone. I rapporti tra predicazione e letteratura nei secoli XIII–XVI* (Florence: Leo S. Olschki, 2003), pp. 201–32 (p. 224).

16   Mario Ascheri and Cecilia Papi, *Il 'Costituto' del Comune di Siena in volgare (1309–1310). Un episodio di storia della giustizia?* (Siena: Aska, 2009).

17   Laura Neri, 'Culture et politique à Sienne au début du XIVe siècle: le Statut en langue vulgaire de 1309–1310', *Médiévales*, 22–3, 1992, pp. 207–21 (p. 207).

18   Bram Kempers, *Painting, Power and Patronage: The Rise of the Professional Artist in the Italian Renaissance*, trans. Beverley Jackson (London: Allen Lane, 1992 [1987]), p. 139.

19   Enrico Castelnuovo, *Un pittore italiano alla corte di Avignone: Matteo Giovannetti e la pittura di Provennza nel secolo XIV* (Turin: Einaudi, 1991 [1962]).

20   Étienne Anheim, 'La Forge de Babylone. Pouvoir pontifical et culture de cour sous le règnc de Clément VI (1342–1352)', Ph.D. thesis, École pratique des hautes études, 2004.

21   Maria Monica Donato, 'Immagini e iscrizioni nell'arte "politica" fra Tre e Quattrocento', in Ciociola (ed.), *'Visibile parlare'*, pp. 341–96.

22   Roger Chartier, 'Pouvoirs et limites de la représentation. Marin, le discours et l'image', in *Au bord de la falaise. L'histoire entre certitudes et inquiétude* (Paris: Albin Michel, 1998), pp. 173–90 (p. 184).

23   Louis Marin, *On Representation*, trans. Catherine Porter (Stanford, CA: Stanford University Press, 2001 [1994]).

24   Quentin Skinner, *Visions of Politics*, Vol. 2, *Renaissance Virtues*

(Cambridge: Cambridge University Press, 2002), p. 81. But see also Brugnolo, '"Voi che guardate . . ."', pp. 318–19, n. 37, arguing against the ideas put forward in Skinner's 'Ambrogio Lorenzetti: The Artist as Political Philosopher', *Proceedings of the British Academy*, 122, 1986, pp. 1–56. See, further, Maria Monica Donato, 'Testi, contesti, immagini politiche nel tardo Medioevo: esempi toscani. In margine a una discussione sul *Buon Governo*', *Annali dell'Istituto storico italo-germanico in Trento*, 19, 1993, pp. 305–55 (pp. 321–33).

25 B2 and A2 respectively of the transcription below (see p. 141).

26 Furio Brugnolo, 'Le iscrizioni in volgare: Testo e commento', in Enrico Castelnuovo (ed.), *Ambrogio Lorenzetti: il Buon Governo* (Milan: Electra, 1995), pp. 381–91 (p. 382).

27 Brugnolo, '"Voi che guardate . . ."', pp. 320 and 325.

28 *Meglio à con povertà secure stare/che per le guerre ad tanto dubio andare.* Quoted in Rosa Maria Dessì, 'Il bene comune nella comunicazione verbale e visiva. Indagini sugli affreschi del "Buon Governo"', in *Il bene comune: forme di governo e gerarchie sociali nel basso medioevo. Atti del XLVIII Convegno storico internazionale, Todi, 9–12 ottobre 2011* (Spoleto: Centro italiano di studi sull'alto medioevo, 2012), pp. 89–130 (p. 96, no. 25).

29 Brugnolo, '"Voi che guardate . . ."', p. 322.

30 Maria Monica Donato, '"Quando i contrari son posti da presso . . ." Breve itinerario intorno al Buon Governo, tra Siena e Firenze', in Giuseppe Pavanello (ed.), *Il Buono e il Cattivo Governo. Rappresentazioni nelle Arti dal Medioevo al Novecento* (Venice: Marsilio, 2004), pp. 21–43 (p. 35); Maria Monica Donato, 'Dal "Comune rubato" di Giotto al "Comune sovrano" di Ambrogio Lorenzetti (con una proposta per la "canzone" del Buon Governo)', in Arturo Carlo Quintavalle (ed.), *Medioevo: immagine e racconti. Atti del convegno internazionale di studi (Parma, 2002)* (Milan: Electa, 2005), pp. 489–509 (pp. 502–4).

31 Riccardo Scrivano, 'Bindo di Cione del Frate', *Dizionario biografico degli Italiani*, Vol. 10 (Rome: Fondazzione Treccani, 1968), pp. 495–6; Juan Carlo D'Amico, *Le Mythe impérial et l'allégorie de Rome. Entre Saint-Empire, Papauté et Commune* (Caen: Presses universitaires de Caen, Cahiers de Transalpina, 2009).

32 Donato, 'Dal "Comune rubato" di Giotto', p. 492.

33 Jorge Luis Borges, 'The Aleph' (1949), in *The Aleph and Other Stories*, trans. Andrew Hurley (London: Penguin, 1998), pp. 118–33 (p. 129).

Chapter 7 Guernica in the lands of Siena

1 'Cronaca senese dei fatti riguardanti la città ed il suo territorio di autore anonimo del secolo XIV', in *Cronache senesi*, ed. Alessandro Lisini and

Fabio Iacometti, *Rerum Italicarum Scriptores*, XV–6, new edn (Bologna: N. Zanichelli, 1933–5), p. 78.

2 Michele Cordaro, 'Le vicende costruttive', in Cesare Brandi (ed.), *Palazzo Pubblico di Siena. Vicende costruttive e decorazione* (Milan: Pizzi-Monte dei Paschi di Siena, 1983), pp. 29–143; Joseph Polzer, 'Ambrogio Lorenzetti's War and Peace Murals Revisited: Contribution to the Meaning of the Good Government Allegory', *Artibus et historiae*, 45, 2002, pp. 63–105 (pp. 68–70).

3 Dennis Romano, 'A Depiction of Male Same-Sex Seduction in Ambrogio Lorenzetti's *Effects of Bad Government* Fresco', *Journal of the History of Sexuality*, 21 (1), 2012, pp. 1–15.

4 Bernardino da Siena, *Le prediche volgari. La predicazione del 1425 in Siena*, ed. Ciro Cannarozzi (Florence: Libreria Editrice Fiorentina, 1940), 3 vols, pp. 276–7; Andrea Zorzi, 'L'angoscia delle repubbliche. Il "timor" nell'Italia comunale degli anni trenta del Trecento', in Andrea Gamberini, Jean-Philippe Genet and Andrea Zorzi (eds), *Languages of Political Society: Western Europe, 14th–17th Centuries* (Rome: Viella, 2011), pp. 287–324 (p. 304).

5 Chiara Frugoni,(ed.), *Pietro e Ambrogio Lorenzetti* (Florence: Le Lettere, 2004), p. 180; Zorzi, 'L'angoscia delle repubbliche', p. 304.

6 Jérôme Baschet, *Les Justices de l'au-delà. Les représentations de l'enfer en France et en Italie (XIIe–XVe siècle)* (Rome: École française de Rome, 1993).

7 Nicole Loraux *The Divided City: On Memory and Forgetting in Ancient Athens*, trans. Corinne Pache with Jeff Fort (New York: Zone Books, 2002), pp. 93–122.

8 Aeschylus, *Eumenides*, ll. 976 and 984–6.

9 Jean-Claude Bonne, *L'Art roman de face et de profil. Le tympan de Conques* (Paris: Le Sycomore, 1984), p. 258.

10 Claude Lefort, 'Machiavel et la *verità effetuale*', in *Écrire. À l'épreuve du politique* (Paris: Calmann-Lévy, 1992).

11 Élisabeth Crouzet-Pavan, *Enfers et paradis. L'Italie de Dante et de Giotto* (Paris: Albin Michel, 2001), pp. 121ff.

12 Jean-Claude Maire Vigueur, *Cavaliers et Citoyens. Guerre, conflits et société dans l'Italie communale, XIIe–XIIIe siècles* (Paris: Éditions de l'EHESS, 2003), p. 66.

13 Giorgio Vasari, 'Life' of Lorenzetti, in Vasari, *Lives of the Most Eminent Painters, Sculptors and Architects*, Vol. 1, *Cimabue to Agnolo Gaddi*, trans. Gaston du C. de Vere, available online at http://www.gutenberg.org/files/25326/25326.txt.

14 Ibid. Translation modified.

15 Diana Norman, 'Pisa, Siena and the Maremma: A Neglected Aspect of Ambrogio Lorenzetti's Paintings in the Sala dei Nove', *Renaissance Studies*, 11 (4), 1997, pp. 310–42 (pp. 330–5).

16 Rosa Maria Dessì, 'Il bene comune nella comunicazione verbale e visiva.

Indagini sugli affreschi del "Buon Governo"', in *Il bene comune: forme di governo e gerarchie sociali nel basso medioevo. Atti del XLVIII Convegno storico internazionale, Todi, 9–12 ottobre 2011* (Spoleto: Centro italiano di studi sull'alto medioevo, 2012), pp. 89–130 (pp. 108–11).

17 Fritz Saxl, 'I figli dei planeti', in Salvatore Settis (ed.), *La fede negli astri. Dall'antichità al Rinascimento* (Turin: Einaudi, 1985), pp. 274–9.

18 Jack M. Greenstein, 'The Vision of Peace: Meaning and Representation in Ambrogio Lorenzetti's *Sala della Pace* Cityscapes', *Art History*, 11, 1988, pp. 492–510 (p. 499).

19 Colin Cunningham, 'For the Honour and Beauty of the City: The Design of Town Halls', in Diana Norman (ed.), *Siena, Florence and Padua: Art, Society and Religion, 1280–1400* (New Haven, CT, and London: Yale University Press, 1995), Vol. 2, pp. 29–54 (pp. 50–3).

20 Carlo Ginzburg, 'The Sword and the Lightbulb: A Reading of *Guernica*', in *Fear, Reverence, Terror: Five Essays in Political Iconography* (Calcutta: Seagull. 2017), pp. 165–242.

Chapter 8 The seductions of tyranny (what the image conceals)

1 Nicolai Rubinstein, 'Le allegorie di Ambrogio Lorenzetti nella Sala della Pace e il pensiero politico del suo tempo', *Rivista storica italiana*, 109, 1997, pp. 781–802 (p. 792).

2 Diego Quaglioni, *Politica e diritto nel Trecento italiano. Il 'De Tyranno' di Bartolo da Sassoferrato (1314–1357)* (Florence: Leo S. Olschki, 1983).

3 Barbara Morel, 'Justice et bien commun. Étude comparée de la fresque du bon gouvernement d'Ambrogio Lorenzetti et d'un manuscrit juridique bolonais', *Mélanges de l'École française de Rome, Moyen Âge*, 113 (1), 2001, pp. 685–97.

4 Renaud Villard, *Du bien commun au mal nécessaire. Tyrannies, assassinats politiques et souveraineté en Italie, vers 1470–vers 1600* (Rome: École française de Rome, 2008), p. 95.

5 Giovanni Maria Gianola, 'L'*Ecerinis* di Albertino Mussato tra Ezzelino e Cangrande', in Giorgio Gracco (ed.), *Nuovi studi ezzeliniani* (Rome: Istituto storico italiano per il Medio Evo, 1992), Vol. 2, pp. 536–74.

6 Albertino Mussato, *Écérinide. Épîtres métriques sur la poésie. Songe*, ed. and trans. Jean-Frédéric Chevalier (Paris: Les Belles Lettres, 2000), pp. 2, 5 and 28.

7 Giorgio Agamben, *The Omnibus Homo Sacer*, trans. Daniel Heller-Roazen (Stanford, CA: Stanford University Press, 2017 [1995]), p. 42.

8 Christiane Klapisch-Zuber, *Retour à la cité. Les magnats de Florence, 1340–1440* (Paris: Éditions de l'EHESS, 2006).

9 Dante, *Purgatory*, trans. Robin Kirkpatrick (London: Penguin, 2007), canto 11, lines 91–6.

10 Creighton Gilbert, 'The Fresco by Giotto in Milan', *Arte Lombarda*, 47–8, 1977, pp. 31–72.
11 Giuliano Milani, *L'esclusione dal comune. Conflitti e bandi politici a Bologna e in altre città italiane tra XII e XIV secolo* (Rome: ISIME, 2003); Sergio Raveggi, 'Appunti sulle forme di propaganda nel conflitto tra magnati e popolani', in Paolo Cammarosano (ed.), *Le forme della propaganda politica nel due e nel Trecento* (Rome: École française de Rome, 1994), pp. 469–89 (p. 480).
12 Carla Casagrande and Silvana Vecchio, *I sette vizi capitali. Storia dei peccati nel Medievo* (Turin: Einaudi, 2000).
13 Quentin Skinner, *Visions of Politics*, Vol. 2: *Renaissance Virtues* (Cambridge: Cambridge University Press, 2002), p. 46.
14 Patrick Boucheron, 'È possibile un investimento disinteressato? Alcuni considerazioni sul finanziamento delle cattedrali nelle città dell'Italia centro-settentrionale alla fine del Medio Evo', *Città e storia*, 4, 2009, pp. 1–16.
15 Patrick Boucheron, 'Connotations, accentuations, signatures. Remarques conclusives', *Annali di Storia moderna e contemporanea*, 16, 2010 (*Atti del Convegno: Immagini, culti, liturgie: le connotazioni politiche del messaggio religioso*), pp. 473–81.
16 Jean-Claude Maire Vigueur, 'Échec au Podestàt. L'expulsion de Comacio Galluzzi Podestàt de Todi (17 juillet 1268)', *Bollettino della deputazione di storia patria per l'Umbria*, 92, 1995, pp. 5–41 (p. 12).
17 Sergio Raveggi, 'Sienna nell'Italia dei guelfi e dei ghibellini', in Gabriella Piccinni (ed.), *Fedeltà ghibellina, affari guelfi. Saggi e riletture intorno alla storia di Siena fra Duecento e Trecento* (Pisa: Pacini, 2008), Vol. 1, pp. 29–61.
18 Andrea Zorzi, 'Siena nella trasformazione dell'Italia comunale. A proposito di *Fedeltà ghibellina, affari guelfi. Saggi e riletture intorno alla storia di Siena fra Duecento e Trecento*, a cura di G. Piccinni (Pisa, Pacini 2008)', *Bullettino senese di storia patria*, 115, 2008, pp. 266–305.
19 Renato Lugarini, 'Il ghibellino: Provenzano Salvani tra mito e dimensione storica', in Gabriella Piccinni (ed.), *Fedeltà ghibellina, affari guelfi. Saggi e riletture intorno alla storia di Siena fra Duecento e Trecento* (Pisa: Pacini, 2008), Vol. 2, pp. 467–97.
20 See above, p. 26.
21 Giorgio Chittolini, '"Crisi" e "lunga durata" delle istituzioni comunali in alcuni dibatti recenti', in Luigi Lacchè, Carlotta Latini, Paolo Marchetti and Massimo Meccarelli (eds), *Penale, giustizia, potere. Metodi, ricerche, storiografie. Per ricordare Mario Sbriccoli* (Macerata: EUM, 2007), pp. 125–54; Andrea Zorzi, *Le signorie citadine in Italia (secoli XIII–XV)* (Milan: Mondadori, 2010).
22 Giovanni Tabacco, *The Struggle for Power in Medieval Italy: Structures of Political Rule*, trans. Rosalind Brown Jensen (Cambridge: Cambridge University Press, 1989 [1974]).

23 Andrea Zorzi, 'Un segno della "mutazione signorile": l'arroccamento urbano', in Patrick Boucheron and Jean-Philippe Genet (eds), *Marquer la ville. Signes, empreintes et traces du pouvoir dans les espaces urbains (XIIIe–XVIIe siècle)* (Paris and Rome: Publications de la Sorbonne and École française de Rome, 2013), pp. 23–40.

24 Patrick Boucheron, 'Tout est monument. Le mausolée d'Azzone Visconti à San Gottardo in Corte de Milan (1342–1346)', in Dominique Barthélemy and Jean-Marie Martin (eds), *Liber largitorius., Études d'histoire médiévale offertes à Pierre Toubert par ses élèves* (Geneva: Droz, 2003), pp. 303–26.

25 Dante, 'Letter to Cangrande della Scala', trans. James Marchand, available online at http://faculty.georgetown.edu/jod/cangrande.english.html.

26 Dante, *Paradise*, trans. Robin Kirkpatrick (London: Penguin, 2007), canto 9, lines 28–30.

27 See above, p. 41.

28 Diana Norman (ed.), '"Love Justice, You Who Judge the Earth": The Paintings of the Sala dei Nove in the Palazzo Pubblico, Siena', in *Siena, Florence and Padua: Art, Society and Religion, 1280–1400*, 2 vols (New Haven, CT, and London: Yale University Press, 1995), Vol. 1, pp. 145–67, p. 328, no. 38.

29 Gian Maria Varanini, 'Propaganda dei regimi signorili. Le esperienze venete del trecento', in Paolo Cammarosano (ed.), *Le forme della propaganda politica nel due e nel trecento* (Rome: École française de Rome, 1994), pp. 311–434.

30 Rubinstein, 'Le allegorie di Ambrogio Lorenzetti', pp. 795–6.

31 Amedeo De Vincentiis, 'Politica, memoria, oblio a Firenze nel XIV secolo. La tradizione documentaria della signoria del duca d'Atene', *Archivio Storico Italiano*, CLXI, 2003, pp. 209–48.

32 Klapisch-Zuber, *Retour à la cité*, p. 114.

Chapter 9 Concord with its cords

1 Dominique Fourcade, 'en laisse', in *en laisse* (Paris: P.O.L., 2005), pp. 37–51 (p. 37).

2 Cicero, *Scipio's Dream*, cited in St Augustine *The City of God*, trans. Henry Bettenson (London: Penguin, 1972), p. 72. See Quentin Skinner, *Visions of Politics*, Vol. 2, *Renaissance Virtues* (Cambridge: Cambridge University Press, 2002), p. 51.

3 Furio Brugnolo, '"Voi che guardate . . ." Divagazioni sulla poesia per pittura del Trecento', in Claudio Ciociola (ed.), *'Visibile parlare'. Le scritture esposte nei volgari italiani dal Medioevo al Rinascimento* (Naples: ESI, 1997), pp. 305–39 (p. 316); Chiara Frugoni, *Una lontana città. Sentimenti e immagini nel Medioevo* (Turin: Einaudi, 1983), pp. 147–8.

4 Jacques Heers, 'Les Villes d'Italie centrale et l'urbanisme: origines et affirmation d'une politique (environ 1200–1350)', *Mélanges de l'École française de Rome, Moyen Âge*, 101 (1), 1989, pp. 67–93 (p. 91); Duccio Balestracci and Gabriella Piccini, *Siena nel Trecento, assetto urbano e struttura edilizia* (Siena: CLUSF, 1977), p. 57.

5 Joseph Polzer, 'Ambrogio Lorenzetti's War and Peace Murals Revisited: Contribution to the Meaning of the Good Government Allegory', *Artibus et historiae*, 45, 2002, pp. 63–105 (p. 77).

6 See above, pp. 40–1.

7 Chiara Frugoni, *L'affare migliore di Enrico. Giotto e la cappella Scrovegni* (Turin: Einaudi, 2008), pp. 301–4.

8 Bertrand Cosnet, 'Les Personnifications dans la peinture monumentale en Italie au XIVe siècle: la grisaille et ses vertus', in Marion Boudon-Machuel, Maurice Brock and Pascale Charron (eds), *Aux limites de la couleur. Monochromie et polychromie dans les arts (1300–1600)* (Turnhout: Brepols, 'Études renaissantes', 2011), pp. 125–32.

9 Maria Monica Donato, 'Testi, contesti, immagini politiche nel tardo Medioevo: esempi toscani. In margine a una discussione sul *Buon Governo*', *Annali dell'Istituto storico italo-germanico in Trento*, 19, 1993, pp. 305–55 (p. 335).

10 Skinner, *Visions of Politics*, Vol. 2, *Renaissance Virtues*, pp. 76.

11 Maria Monica Donati, 'Ancora sulle "Fonti" nel *Buon Governo* di Ambrogio Lorenzetti: dubbi, precisazioni, anticipazioni', in Simonetta Adorni Braccesi and Mario Ascheri (eds), *Politica e cultura nelle repubbliche italiane dal Medioevo all'età moderna: Firenze, Genova, Lucca, Siena e Venezia, Atti del Convegno Siena 1997* (Rome: Istituto Storico Italiano per l'età moderna e contemporanea, 2001), pp. 43–79 (pp. 55–8).

12 Ibid., p. 56.

13 Mario Sbriccoli, 'La Triade, le bandeau, le genou. Droit et procès pénal dans les allégories de la Justice du Moyen Âge à l'âge moderne', *Crime, Histoire et Sociétés*, 9 (1), 2005 (available online: http://chs.revues.org/382), para. 32.

14 Maria Monica Donato, 'Il pittore del Buon Governo: le opere "politiche" di Ambrogio in Palazzo Pubblico', in Chiara Frugoni (ed.), *Pietro e Ambrogio Lorenzetti* (Florence: Le Lettere, 2004), pp. 201–55 (p. 217).

15 Andrea Zorzi, 'La justice pénale dans les États italiens (communes et principautés territoriales) du XIIIe au XVIe siècle', in Xavier Rousseaux and René Lévy (eds), *Le Pénal dans tous ses états. Justice, États et sociétés en Europe (XIIe–XXe siècles)* (Brussels: Publications des facultés universitaires Saint-Louis, 1997), pp. 47–63.

16 Mario Sbriccoli, 'Justice négociée, justice hégémonique. L'émergence du pénal public dans les villes italiennes des XIIIe et XIVe siècles', in Jacques Chiffoleau, Claude Gauvard and Andrea Zorzi (eds), *Pratiques sociales et politiques judiciaires dans les villes de l'Occident à la fin du Moyen Âge* (Rome: École française de Rome, 2007), pp. 389–421.

17 Maria Monica Donato, 'La "bellissima inventiva": immagini e idee nella Sala della Pace', in Enrico Castelnuovo (ed.), *Ambrogio Lorenzetti: il Buon Governo* (Milan: Electa, 1995), pp. 23–41 (p. 24).

Chapter 10 With the common good as lord

1 Nicolai Rubinstein, 'Political Ideas in Sienese Art: The Frescoes by Ambrogio Lorenzetti and Taddeo di Bartolo in the Palazzo Pubblico', *Journal of the Warburg and Courtauld Institutes*, 21, 1958, pp. 179–207 (p. 184).
2 Quentin Skinner, 'Ambrogio Lorenzetti: The Artist as Political Philosopher', *Proceedings of the British Academy*, 122, 1986, pp. 1–56.
3 Patrick Boucheron, '"Tournez les yeux pour admirer, vous qui exercez le pouvoir, celle qui est peinte ici". La fresque dite du Bon Gouvernement d'Ambrogio Lorenzetti', *Annales HSS*, 6, 2005, pp. 1137–99.
4 Riccardo Fubini, 'Renaissance Historian: The Career of Hans Baron', *Journal of Modern History*, 64, 1992, pp. 541–74 (especially p. 560).
5 Hans Baron, *The Crisis of the Early Italian Renaissance* (Princeton, NJ: Princeton University Press, 1955), p. 357.
6 Anthony Molho, 'Hans Baron's Crisis', in David S. Peterson and Daniel E. Bornstein (eds), *Florence and Beyond. Culture, Society and Politics in Renaissance Italy: Essays in Honour of John M. Najemy* (Toronto: Center for Reformation and Renaissance Studies, 2008), pp. 61–90.
7 George Holmes, 'The Emergence of an Urban Ideology at Florence', *Transactions of the Royal Historical Society*, 23, 1973, pp. 111–34 (p. 124).
8 Paul Oscar Kristeller, 'Humanism and Scholasticism in the Italian Renaissance', in Michael Mooney (ed.), *Renaissance Thought and Its Sources* (New York: Columbia University Press, 1979), pp. 85–105.
9 Mari Ascheri, *Le città-stato. Le radici del municipalismo e del repubblicanesimo italiani* (Bologna: Il Mulino, 2006).
10 Quentin Skinner, 'Rhetoric and Liberty', in *The Foundations of Modern Political Thought*, Vol. 1, *The Renaissance* (Cambridge: Cambridge University Press, 1978), pp. 23–48.
11 Benoît Grévin, *Le Parchemin des cieux. Essai sur le Moyen Âge du langage* (Paris: Seuil, 2012), p. 261.
12 Enrico Artifoni, 'I Podestà professionali e la fondazione retorica della politica comunale', *Quaderni storici*, 63, 1983, pp. 687–719.
13 Dino Compagni, *Dino Compagni's Chronicle of Florence*, trans. Daniel E. Boorstein (Philadelphia: University of Pennsylvania Press, 1986).
14 Paolo Cammarosano, 'L'Éloquence laïque dans l'Italie communale (fin du XIIe–XIVe siècle)', *Bibliothèque de l'École des Chartes*, 158, 2000, pp. 431–42.

15 Michel Sennelart, *Les Arts de gouverner. Du regimen médiéval au concept de gouvernement* (Paris: Seuil, 1995), pp. 25–6.

16 Ronald Witt, *In the Footsteps of the Ancients: The Origins of Humanism from Lovato to Bruni* (Leiden: Brill, 2003); and Ronald Witt, *The Two Latin Cultures and the Foundation of Renaissance Humanism in Medieval Italy* (Cambridge: Cambridge University Press, 2007).

17 Enrico Artifoni, 'L'Éloquence politique dans les cités communales (XIIIe siècle)', in Isabelle Heullant-Donat (ed.), *Cultures italiennes (XIIe–XVe siècle)* (Paris: Cerf, 2000), pp. 269–96 (pp. 275ff).

18 Cary J. Nederman, 'The Meaning of "Aristotelianism" in Medieval Moral and Political Thought', *Journal of the History of Ideas*, 57, 1996, pp. 563–85.

19 Quentin Skinner, *Visions of Politics*, Vol. 2, *Renaissance Virtues* (Cambridge: Cambridge University Press, 2002), p. 92.

20 Alain Boureau, 'On ne doit pas parler la bouche pleine. Un épisode d'histoire politique non thomiste (Bourdieu, Foucault, Sennelart)', *L'Atelier du Centre de recherches historiques*, 1, 2008 (available online: http://acrh.revues.org/316), para. 3.

21 James M. Blythe, *Ideal Government and the Mixed Constitution in the Middle Ages* (Princeton, NJ: Princeton University Press, 1992).

22 Brunetto Latini, *Trésor*, ed. Pietro G. Beltrami, Paolo Squillacioti, Plinio Torri and Sergio Vatteroni (Turin: Einaudi, 2007), p. 80.

23 Peter von Moos, 'La retorica nel Medioevo', in *Lo spazio letterario del Medioevo*, Vol. 1, *Medioevo latino, la produzione del testo* (Rome: Salerno, 1993), pp. 231–71 (p. 245).

24 Giovanni da Viterbo, *Liber de regimine civitatum*, ed. Gaetano Salvemini, in *Biblioteca juridica medii aevi*, Vol. 3 (Bologna: Biblioteca Juridica Medii Aevi,1901), pp. 215–80 (p. 238).

25 Skinner, *Visions of Politics*, Vol. 2, *Renaissance Virtues*, p. 80.

26 Maria Monica Donato, 'Testi, contesti, immagini politiche nel tardo Medioevo: esempi toscani. In margine a una discussione sul *Buon Governo*', *Annali dell'Istituto storico italo-germanico in Trento*, 19, 1993, pp. 305–55; and Maria Monica Donato, 'Ancora sulle "Fonti" nel *Buon Governo* di Ambrogio Lorenzetti: dubbi, precisazioni, anticipazioni', in Simonetta Adorni Braccesi and Mario Ascheri (eds), *Politica e cultura nelle repubbliche italiane dal Medioevo all'età moderna: Firenze, Genova, Lucca, Siena e Venezia*, Atti del Convegno Siena 1997 (Rome: Istituto Storico Italiano per l'età moderna e contemporanea, 2001), pp. 43–79.

27 Skinner did in fact move closer towards the idea of multiple meanings, as shown in 'Ambrogio Lorenzetti's "Buon Governo" Frescoes: Two Old Questions, Two New Answers', *Journal of the Warburg and Courtauld Institutes*, 72, 1999, pp. 1–28.

28 Antonella Fenech Kroke, *Giorgio Vasari, la fabrique de l'allégorie. Culture et fonction de la personnification au Cinquecento* (Florence: Leo S. Olschki, 2011).

29 Skinner, *Visions of Politics*, Vol. 2, *Renaissance Virtues*, p. 71.

30 Quentin Skinner, *La Vérité et l'historien* (Paris: Éditions de l'EHESS, 2012 [2010]), p. 53.

31 Chiara Frugoni (ed.), *Pietro e Ambrogio Lorenzetti* (Florence: Le Lettere, 2004), p. 192.

32 Cicero, *Ethical Writings I (De Officiis* [etc.]), trans. Andrew P. Peabody (Boston: Little Brown, and Company, 1887), para. 37, available online at http://oll.libertyfund.org/titles/cicero-on-moral-duties-de-officiis.

33 Skinner, *Visions of Politics*, Vol. 2, *Renaissance Virtues*, pp. 85–6.

34 Anthony Turner, '"The Accomplishment of Many Years": Three Notes towards a History of the Sand-Glass', *Annals of Science*, 39, 1982, pp. 161–72; Gerhard Dohrn-van Rossum, *History of the Hour: Clocks and Modern Temporal Orders*, trans. Thomas Dunlap (Chicago and London: University of Chicago Press, 1996).

35 Patrick Boucheron, 'Tout est monument. Le mausolée d'Azzone Visconti à San Gottardo in Corte de Milan (1342–1346)', in Dominique Barthélemy and Jean-Marie Martin (eds), in *Liber largitorius. Études d'histoire médiévale offertes à Pierre Toubert par ses élèves* (Geneva: Droz, 2003), pp. 303–26 (pp. 310–11).

36 Jean Wirth, *L'Image à la fin du Moyen Âge* (Paris: Cerf, 2011), p. 285.

37 Joachim Poeschke, *Italian Frescoes: The Age of Giotto, 1280–1400* (New York: Abbeville Press, 2005), p. 292.

38 Ernst Kantorowicz, *The King's Two Bodies: A Study in Medieval Political Theology*, preface by William Chester Jordan; introduction by Conrad Leyser (Princeton, NJ: Princeton University Press, 2016 [1957]), p. 113.

39 Rosa Maria Dessì, 'Il bene comune nella comunicazione verbale e visiva. Indagini sugli affreschi del "Buon Governo"', in *Il bene comune: forme di governo e gerarchie sociali nel basso medioevo. Atti del XLVIII Convegno storico internazionale, Todi, 9–12 ottobre 2011* (Spoleto: Centro italiano di studi sull'alto medioevo, 2012), pp, 89–130 (p. 93).

40 Wirth, *L'Image*, p. 284.

41 Max Seidel, 'Vanagloria. Studi sull'iconografi a degli affreschi di Ambrogio Lorenzetti nella "Sala della Pace"', in *Arte italiana del Medioevo e del Rinascimento*, Vol. 1, *Pittura* (Venice: Marsilio, 2003 [1997]), pp. 293–340 (pp. 79ff.).

42 Giulia Orofino, 'Decorazione e miniatura del libro comunale: Siena e Pisa', in *Atti della Società ligure di storia patria*, 103, 1989 (*Civiltà Comunale: libro, scrittura, documento*), pp. 463–91 (p. 482).

43 Giorgio Vasari, 'Life' of Giotto, in Vasari, *Lives of the Most Eminent Painters, Sculptors and Architects*, Vol. 1, *Cimabue to Agnolo Gaddi*, trans. Gaston du C. de Vere, available online at http://www.gutenberg.org/files/25326/25326.txt.

44 Aloïs Riklin, *Ambrogio Lorenzettis politische Summe* (Berne: Stämpfli Verlag AG, 1996), p. 13; Maria Monica Donato, 'Immagini e iscrizioni

nell'arte "politica" fra Tre e Quattrocento', in Claudio Ciociola (ed.), *'Visibile parlare'. Le scritture esposte nei volgari italiani dal Medioevo al Rinascimento* (Naples: ESI, 1997), pp. 341–96 (p. 393).

45 Alessandro Tomei (ed.), *Le biccherne di Siena: arte e finanza all'alba dell'economia moderna* (Rome: Retablo, 2002), pp. 150–1.

46 Dietmar Popp, 'Lupa senese: zur Inszenierung einer mythischen Vergangenheit in Siena (1260–1560)', *Marburger Jahrbuch für Kunstwissenschaft*, 24, 1997, pp. 41–58.

47 Edna Carter-Southard, *The Frescoes in Siena's Palazzo Pubblico, 1289–1539: Studies in Imagery and Relations to Other Communal Palaces in Tuscany* (London and New York: Garland Publishing, 1979), p. 60.

48 Skinner, *Visions of Politics*, Vol. 2, *Renaissance Virtues*.

49 Mario Ascheri, 'Legislazione, statuti e sovranità', in *Antica legislazione della Repubblica di Siena* (Siena: Il Leccio, 1993), pp. 1–40 (p. 19).

50 Patrick Boucheron, 'Politisation et dépolitisation d'un lieu commun. Remarques sur la notion de "bien commun" dans les villes d'Italie centro-septentrionale entre commune et signoria', in Élodie Lecuppre-Desjardin (ed.), *'De Bono Communi'. Discours et pratique du Bien Commun dans les villes d'Europe occidentale (XIIIe–XVIe siècle)*, *Urban History*, 22 (Turnhout : Brepols, 2010), pp. 237–51.

51 Bénédicte Sère, *Penser l'amitié au Moyen Âge. Études historiques des commentaires sur les livres VIII et IX de l'Éthique à Nicomaque (XIIIe–XVe siècle)* (Turnhout: Brepols, 2007), p. 238.

52 Diego Quaglioni, *Politica e diritto nel Trecento italiano. Il 'De Tyranno' di Bartolo da Sassoferrato (1314–1357)* (Florence: Leo S. Olschki, 1983), p. 157.

53 Tomei (ed.), *Le biccherne di Siena*, pp. 165–6.

54 Marsilius of Padua, *The Defender of the Peace*, ed. and trans. Annabel Brett (Cambridge : Cambridge University Press, 2005). On this text, see Anthony Black, 'Society and the Individual from the Middle Ages to Rousseau: Philosophy, Jurisprudence and Constitutional Theory', *History of Political Thought*, 1, 1980, pp. 145–66.

55 E. Igor Mineo, 'Liberté et communauté en Italie (milieu XIIIe–début XVe siècle)', in Claudia Moatti and Michèle Riot-Sarcey (eds), *La République dans tous ses états. Pour une histoire intellectuelle de la république en Europe* (Paris: Payot, 2009), pp. 215–50 (p. 217).

56 Jean-François Sonnay, 'Paix et bon gouvernement: à propos d'un monument funéraire du *Trecento*', *Arte medievale*, IV (2), 1990, pp. 189–91.

57 Patrick Boucheron, 'Paroles de paix et seigneurs de guerre en Italie dans le premier tiers du XIVe siècle: quelques problèmes iconographiques', in Sylvie Caucanas, Rémy Cazals and Nicolas Offenstadt (eds), *Paroles de paix en temps de guerre* (Toulouse: Privat, 2006), pp. 165–79 (p. 172). See above, p. 101.

58 Maria Monica Donato, '"Cose morali, e anche appartenenti secondo e' luoghi": per lo studio della pittura politica nel tardo medioevo toscano',

in Paolo Cammarosano (ed.), *Le forme della propaganda politica nel due e nel Trecento* (Rome: École française de Rome, 1994), pp. 491–517 (p. 510).

59 Boucheron, 'Tout est monument'.
60 Dessì, 'Il bene comune nella comunicazione verbale e visiva', pp. 94–5.
61 See above, pp. 43–4.
62 'Cronaca senese dei fatti riguardanti la città ed il suo territorio di autore anonimo del secolo XIV', in *Cronache senesi*, ed. Alessandro Lisini and Fabio Iacometti, *Rerum Italicarum Scriptores*, XV–6, new edn (Bologna: N. Zanichelli, 1933–5), p. 78.
63 Giuliano Milani, 'Prima del Buongoverno. Motivi politici e ideologia popolare nelle pitture del Broletto di Brescia', *Studi medievali*, 49 (1), 2008, pp. 19–85 (pp. 82–5).
64 Lorenzo Tanzini, 'Emergenza, eccezione, deroga: tecniche e retoriche del potere nei comuni toscani del XIV secolo', in Massimo Vallerani (ed.), *Tecniche di potere nel tardo medioevo. Regimi comunali e signorie in Italia* (Rome: Viella, 2010), pp. 149–81 (p. 172).
65 Mineo, 'Liberté et communauté en Italie (milieu XIIIe–début XVe siècle)', p. 234.
66 Max Seidel, *Dolce vita. Ambrogio Lorenzettis Porträt des Sienneser Staates*, Basel, 'Vorträge der Aeneas-Silvius-Stiftung an der Universität Basel', 33, 1999.
67 Skinner, *Visions of Politics*, Vol. 2, *Renaissance Virtues*, p. 45.

Chapter 11 What Peace sees: narratives of spaces and talking bodies

1 Quoted in Antoine de Baecque, *Godard. Biographie* (Paris: Grasset, 2010), p. 157.
2 Andrea Brogi and Francesca Bianciardi, *Nella Siena ritrovata di Ambrogio Lorenzetti* (Siena: NIE, 2005), p. 87.
3 Duccio Balestracci and Gabriella Piccini, *Siena nel Trecento, assetto urbano e struttura edilizia* (Siena: CLUSF, 1977), pp. 30–7.
4 Étienne Hubert, 'La Construction de la ville. Sur l'urbanisation dans l'Italie médiévale', *Annales HSS*, 59 (1), 2004, pp. 109–39 (p. 119).
5 Thomas Szabó, 'Le rete stradale del contado di Siena. Legislazione statutaria e amministrazione comunale del Duecento', *Mélanges de l'École française de Rome. Moyen Âge*, 87 (1), 1975, pp. 141–86.
6 Odile Redon, *L'Espace d'une cité. Sienne et le pays siennois (XIIIe–XIVe siècles)* (Rome: École française de Rome, 1994), pp. 137ff.
7 David Friedman, 'Talamone, 1306', in Marco Folin (ed.), *Rappresentare la città. Topografi e urbane nell'Italia di antico regime* (Reggio Emilia: Diabasis, 2010), pp. 57–76.
8 Marcia Kupfer, 'The Lost Wheel Map of Ambrogio Lorenzetti', *Art Bulletin*, 78 (2), 1996, pp. 287–310 (p. 301).

9   Quoted in Marc Desportes, *Paysages en mouvement. Transports et perception de l'espace XVIIIe–XXe siècle* (Paris: Gallimard, 2005), p. 8.
10 Perrine Mane, 'Les travaux et les jours', in Jacques Dalarun (ed.), *Le Moyen Âge en lumière. Manuscrits enluminés des bibliothèques de France* (Paris: Fayard, 2002), pp. 139–71 (p. 158).
11 Joachim Poeschke, *Italian Frescoes: The Age of Giotto, 1280–1400* (New York: Abbeville Press, 2005), p. 292.
12 Alberto Colli (ed.), *Il cofano nuziale istoriato attribuito ad Ambrogio Lorenzetti* (Milan: Electa, 2000).
13 Alain Guerreau, 'Chasse', in Jacques Le Goff and Jean-Claude Schmitt (eds), *Dictionnaire raisonné de l'Occident médiéval* (Paris: Fayard, 1999), pp. 166–78.
14 Charles-Marie de La Roncière, Philippe Contamine and Robert Delort, 'Le Paysage rural autour de Sienne et en Toscane', in *L'Europe au Moyen Âge*, Vol. 3, *Fin XIIIe siècle–fin XVe siècle* (Paris: Armand Colin, 1971), pp. 135–45.
15 Gabriella Piccinni, 'La campagna e le città (secoli XII–XIV)', in Alfio Cortonesi, Gianfranco Pasquali and Gabriella Piccinni, *Uomini e campagna nell'Italia medievale* (Rome and Bari: Laterza, 2002), pp. 123–89 (p. 167).
16 Giovanni Romano, 'Documenti figurativi per la storia delle campagne nei secoli XI–XVI', in *Studi sul paesaggio* (Turin: Einaudi, 1978), pp. 3–91.
17 Jean-Louis Gaulin and François Menant, 'Crédit rural et endettement paysan dans l'Italie communale', in Maurice Berthe (ed.), *Endettement paysan et crédit rural dans l'Europe médiévale et moderne (Actes des XVIIe Journées internationales d'histoire de l'abbaye de Flaran, septembre 1995)* (Toulouse: Privat, 1998), pp. 35–68 (p. 65).
18 Andrea Zorzi, 'Siena nella trasformazione dell'Italia comunale. A proposito di *Fedeltà ghibellina, affari guelfi. Saggi e riletture intorno alla storia di Siena fra Duecento e Trecento*, a cura di G. Piccinni (Pisa, Pacini 2008)', *Bullettino senese di storia patria*, 115, 2008, pp. 266–305.
19 Roxann Prazniak, 'Siena on the Silk Roads: Ambrogio Lorenzetti and the Mongol Global Century, 1250–1350', *Journal of World History*, 21–2, 2010, pp. 177–217.
20 Michel Baridon, *Naissance et renaissance du paysage* (Arles: Actes Sud, 2006), p. 364.
21 Anne-Laure Imbert, 'Le Paysage comme fragment de nature, prémisse faussée de l'histoire du paysage. Une discussion à partir du cas siennois', *Revue de l'Art*, 173 (3), 2011, pp. 21–31.
22 Piero Camporesi, *Le belle contrade: nascita del paesaggio italiano* (Milan: Garzanti, 1992).
23 Philippe Descola, *Beyond Nature and Culture*, trans. Janet Lloyd (Chicago and London: University of Chicago Press, 2013).

24 Giovanni Boccaccio, *Decameron*, trans. John Payne, available online at http://www.gutenberg.org/files/23700/23700-h/23700-h.htm, p. 319.
25 Sandra Baragli, 'L'iconografia del cantiere come propaganda politica. Qualche considerazione', in Élisabeth Crouzet-Pavan (ed.), *Pouvoir et Édilité. Les grands chantiers dans l'Italie communale et seigneuriale* (Rome: École française de Rome, 2003), pp. 79–104 (pp. 86–90).
26 Anna Little, 'Du lieu à l'espace. Transformations de l'environnement pictural en Italie centrale (XIIIe–XVe siècle)', Ph.D. thesis, ed. Maurice Brock, Université François-Rabelais de Tours, 2010, pp. 161–4.
27 Brogi and Bianciardi, *Nella Siena ritrovata di Ambrogio Lorenzetti*.
28 Hubert Damisch, *The Origin of Perspective*, trans. John Goodman (Cambridge, MA: MIT Press, 1994), p. 171.
29 Daniel Arasse, *L'Annonciation italienne* (Paris: Hazan, 1999), p. 59.
30 Jean-Philippe Antoine, 'Mémoire, lieux et invention spatiale dans la peinture italienne des XIIIe et XIVe siècles', *Annales ESC*, 48 (6), 1993, pp. 1447–69 (pp. 1464ff).
31 Little, 'Du lieu à l'espace', p. 170.
32 Jean-Christophe Bailly, *La Phrase urbaine* (Paris: Seuil, 2013), p. 174.
33 Uta Feldges-Henning, 'The Pictorial Programme of the Sala della Pace: A New Interpretation', *Journal of the Warburg and Courtauld Institutes*, 35, 1972, pp. 145–62.
34 Jean-Claude Milner, *Pour une politique des êtres parlants. Court traité politique 2* (Lagrasse: Verdier, 2011).
35 John White, *The Birth and Rebirth of Pictorial Space*, 3rd edn (London and Boston, MA: Faber and Faber, 1987), p. 98.
36 Ibid., p. 93.
37 Ibid., p. 95.
38 Patrick Boucheron, 'Sauver le passé', preface to Walter Benjamin, *Sur le concept d'histoire* (Paris: Payot, 'Petite bibliothèque Payot', 2013), pp. 7–50. The Benjamin quotation can be found in Walter Benjamin, 'The Work of Art in the Age of Its Technological Reproducibility: Second Version', in *Selected Writings*, ed. Marcus Bullock and Michael W. Jennings, 4 vols (Cambridge, MA: and London: Belknap Press, 1996–2003), Vol. 3, *1935–1938*, pp. 19–55 (p. 40).
39 White, *Birth and Rebirth*, p. 95.
40 Chiara Frugoni, *Una lontana città. Sentimenti e immagini nel Medioevo* (Turin: Einaudi, 1983), p. 162; Jack M. Greenstein, 'The Vision of Peace: Meaning and Representation in Ambrogio Lorenzetti's *Sala della Pace* Cityscapes', *Art History*, 11, 1988, pp. 492–510 (p. 498); Roger P. Tarr, 'A Note on the Light in Ambrogio Lorenzetti's Peaceful City Fresco', *Art History*, 13, 1990, pp. 388–92.

Chapter 12 Well, now you can dance

1 Anne-Marie Lecocq, *Le Bouclier d'Achille. Un tableau qui bouge* (Paris: Gallimard, 2010).
2 Homer, *Iliad*, trans. A. T. Murray, revised William F. Wyatt, 2 vols (Cambridge, MA, and London: Harvard University Press, 1999), Vol. 2, Book 18, lines 490–5.
3 Jacob Burckhardt, *Italian Renaissance Painting According to Genres*, introduction by Maurizio Ghelardi; trans. David Britt and Caroline Beamish (Los Angeles: Getty Research Institute, 2005).
4 Marco Santucci, 'Immagini della città da Omero ad Ambrogio Lorenzetti', *Rivista di Filologia e Istruzione Classica*, 134, 2006, pp. 404–28.
5 Petrarch, *Familiares* XVIII, 2
6 Mariane Pade, 'Boccaccio, Leonzio, and the Transformation of the Homeric Myths', in Luisa Capodieci and Philip Ford (eds), *Homère à la Renaissance. Mythe et transfigurations* (Paris and Rome: Somogy, 'Collection d'histoire de l'art de l'Académie de France à Rome', 2011), pp. 27–40.
7 Mary D. Edwards, 'Ambrogio Lorenzetti and Classical Painting', *Florilegium*, 2, 1980, pp. 146–60.
8 Pierre Vidal-Naquet, *The Black Hunter: Forms of Thought and Forms of Society in the Greek World*, trans. Andrew Szegedy-Maszak (Baltimore, MD: Johns Hopkins University Press, 1986), p. 257.
9 Pierre Rosenstiehl, 'Déposé au centre, le butin n'appartient plus à personne. *Lectures*', in Maurice Olender and François Vitrani (eds), *Jean-Pierre Vernant dedans-dehors*, *Le Genre humain*, 53 (Paris: Seuil, 2013), pp. 145–9.
10 Max Seidel, 'Vanagloria. Studi sull'iconografi a degli affreschi di Ambrogio Lorenzetti nella "Sala della Pace"', in *Arte italiana del Medioevo e del Rinascimento*, Vol. 1, *Pittura* (Venice: Marsilio, 2003 [1997]), pp. 293–340 (p. 308).
11 Jane Bridgeman, 'Ambrogio Lorenzetti's Dancing "Maidens": A Case of Mistaken Identity', *Apollo*, 133, 1991, pp. 245–51.
12 Seidel, 'Vanagloria', pp. 297–9.
13 Maria A. Ceppari Ridolfi and Patrizia Turrini, *Il mulino della vanità. Lusso e ceremonie nella Siena medievale* (Siena: Il Leccio, 1993).
14 Georges Didi-Huberman, *The Surviving Image: Phantoms of Time and Time of Phantoms. Aby Warburg's History of Art*, trans. Harvey Mendelsohn (University Park: Pennsylvania State University Press, 2017 [2002]).
15 Jean Campbell, 'The City's New Clothes: Ambrogio Lorenzetti and the Poetics of Peace', *The Art Bulletin*, 83 (2), 2001, pp. 240–58 (pp. 247ff).
16 Jean Starobinski, *L'Encre de la mélancolie* (Paris: Seuil, 2012).
17 Philippe Buc, *The Dangers of Ritual: Between Early Medieval Texts*

and Social Scientific Theory (Princeton, NJ, and Chichester: Princeton University Press, 2001), pp. 65–6.

18 Quentin Skinner, *Visions of Politics*, Vol. 2, *Renaissance Virtues* (Cambridge: Cambridge University Press, 2002), pp. 111 and 113.

19 Andrea Zorzi, 'L'angoscia delle repubbliche. Il "timor" nell'Italia comunale degli anni trenta del Trecento', in Andrea Gamberini, Jean-Philippe Genet and Andrea Zorzi (eds), *Languages of Political Society. Western Europe, 14th–17th Centuries* (Rome: Viella, 2011), pp. 287–324.

20 Pierangelo Schiera, 'Il Buongoverno "melancolico" di Ambrogio Lorenzetti e la "costituzionale faziosità" della città', *Scienza e Politica*, 34, 2006, pp. 93–108.

21 Walter Benjamin, 'Theses on the Philosophy of History', in *Illuminations*, trans. Harry Zohn (New York: Schocken, 1968), pp. 253–64 (p. 258). See also Patrick Boucheron, 'Sauver le passé', preface to Walter Benjamin, *Sur le concept d'histoire* (Paris: Payot, 'Petite bibliothèque Payot', 2013), pp. 7–50.

22 Gabriella Piccinni, 'Il sistema senese del credito nella fase di smobilitazione dei suoi banchi internazionali. Politiche comunali, spesa pubblica, propaganda contro l'usura, 1332–1340', in *Fedeltà ghibellina, affari guelfi. Saggi e riletture intorno alla storia di Siena fra Duecento e Trecento* (Pisa: Pacini, 2008), Vol. 1, pp. 209–89 (pp. 281–6).

23 Gerrit Jasper Schenk, 'Enter the Emperor: Charles IV and Siena between Politics, Diplomacy, and Ritual (1355 and 1368)', *Renaissance Studies*, 20, 2006, pp. 161–79.

24 Victor Rutenburg, 'La Vie et la mort des *Ciompi* de Sienne', *Annales ESC*, 20–1, 1965, pp. 80–109 (p. 109).

25 Donato di Neri, 'Cronaca senese', in *Cronache senesi*, ed. Alessandro Lisini and Fabio Iacometti, *Rerum Italicarum Scriptores*, new edn, XV–6 (Bologna: N. Zanichelli, 1933–5), p. 577.

26 Amedeo De Vincentiis, 'Politica, memoria, oblio a Firenze nel XIV secolo. La tradizione documentaria della signoria del duca d'Atene', *Archivio Storico Italiano*, CLXI, 2003, pp. 209–48.

27 Donato di Neri, 'Cronaca senese', p. 578.

28 Catherine de Sienne, *Lettres aux laïcs, 1*, in *Les Lettres*, Vol. 3, ed. and trans. Marlène Raoila (Paris: Cerf, 2010), no. 358, p. 141.

29 Cesare Brandi, 'Chiarimenti su "Buon Governo" di Ambrogio Lorenzetti', *Bollettino d'Arte*, 40, 1955, pp. 119–23.

Appendix: Inscriptions in the vernacular: transcription, edition and translation

1 Transcription and edition after Furio Brugnolo, 'Le iscrizioni in volgare: testo e commento', in Enrico Castelnuovo (ed.), *Ambrogio Lorenzetti: il Buon Governo* (Milan: Electa, 1995), pp. 381–91 (p. 384), taking into account (for editing) the remarks of Rosa Maria Dessì, 'Il bene comune

nella comunicazione verbale e visiva. Indagini sugli affreschi del "Buon Governo", in *Il bene comune: forme di governo e gerarchie sociali nel basso medioevo. Atti del XLVIII Convegno storico internazionale, Todi, 9–12 ottobre 2011* (Spoleto: Centro italiano di studi sull'alto medioevo, 2012), pp. 89–130 (pp. 98–9). The author acknowledges the help of Romain Descendre with the translation.

Published sources

Agnolo di Tura del Grasso, 'Cronache senesi', ed. Alessandro Lisini and Fabio Iacometti, *Rerum Italicarum Scriptores*, XV–6, new edn (Bologna: N. Zanichelli, 1933–5).

Augustine, St, *The City of God*, trans. Henry Bettenson (London: Penguin, 1972).

Bernardino da Siena, *Le prediche volgari. La predicazione del 1425 in Siena*, ed. Ciro Cannarozzi (Florence: Libreria Editrice Fiorentina, 1940), 3 vols.

Bernardino da Siena, *Prediche volgari sul Campo di Siena 1427*, ed. Carlo Delcorno (Milan: Rusconi, 1989), 2 vols.

Boccaccio, Giovanni, *Decameron*, trans. John Payne, available online at http://www.gutenberg.org/files/23700/23700-h/23700-h.htm.

Catherine de Sienne, *Lettres aux laïcs, 1*, in *Les Lettres*, Vol. 3, ed. and trans. Marlène Raoila (Paris: Cerf, 2010)

Cicero, *Ethical Writings I (De Officiis* [etc.]), trans. Andrew P. Peabody (Boston: Little Brown, and Company, 1887), available online at http://oll.libertyfund.org/titles/cicero-on-moral-duties-de-officiis.

Compagni, Dino, *Dino Compagni's Chronicle of Florence*, trans. Daniel E. Boorstein (Philadelphia: University of Pennsylvania Press, 1986).

'Cronaca senese dei fatti riguardanti la città ed il suo territorio di autore anonimo del secolo XIV', in *Cronache senesi*, ed. Alessandro Lisini and Fabio Iacometti, *Rerum Italicarum Scriptores*, XV–6, new edn (Bologna: N. Zanichelli, 1933–5).

Dante, *The Divine Comedy*, trans. Robin Kirkpatrick, 3 vols (London: Penguin, 2006–7).

Donato di Neri, 'Cronaca senese', in *Cronache senesi*, ed. Alessandro Lisini and Fabio Iacometti, *Rerum Italicarum Scriptores*, new edn, XV–6 (Bologna: N. Zanichelli, 1933–5).

Ghiberti, Lorenzo, *I Commentarii*, ed. Lorenzo Bartoli (Florence: Giunti, 1998).

Giovanni da Viterbo, *Liber de regimine civitatum*, ed. Gaetano Salvemini, in

Biblioteca juridica medii aevi, Vol. 3 (Bologna: Biblioteca Juridica Medii Aevi, 1901), pp. 215–80.

Homer, *Iliad*, trans. A. T. Murray, revised William F. Wyatt, 2 vols (Cambridge, MA, and London: Harvard University Press, 1999).

Latini, Brunetto, *Trésor*, ed. Pietro G. Beltrami, Paolo Squillacioti, Plinio Torri and Sergio Vatteroni (Turin: Einaudi, 2007).

Marsilius of Padua, *The Defender of the Peace*, ed. and trans. Annabel Brett (Cambridge : Cambridge University Press, 2005). Milanesi, Gaetano, *Documenti per la storia dell'arte senese* (Siena: Torrini, 1854).

Mussato, Albertino, *Écérinide. Épîtres métriques sur la poésie. Songe*, ed. and trans. Jean-Frédéric Chevalier (Paris: Les Belles Lettres, 2000).

Orfino de Lodi, *De regimine et sapientia potestatis* in *Miscellanea di storia italiana*, Vol. VII, ed. Angelo Ceruti (Turin, 1869), pp. 33–94.

Vasari, Giorgio, *Lives of the Most Eminent Painters, Sculptors and Architects*, Vol. 1, *Cimabue to Agnolo Gaddi*, trans. Gaston du C. de Vere, available online at http://www.gutenberg.org/files/25326/25326.txt.

Villani, Giovanni, *Nuova Cronica*, ed. Giovanni Porta (Parma: Ugo Guanda Editore, 1991).

Bibliography

Agamben, Giorgio, *The Omnibus Homo Sacer*, trans. Daniel Heller-Roazen (Stanford, CA: Stanford University Press, 2017 [1995]).

Alexander, Jonathan J. G., 'Dancing in the Streets', *Journal of the Walters Art Gallery*, 54, 1996, pp. 147–62.

Amberger, Annelies, '*Ordo* und *Aequitas*, das Szepter und die Lupa: zur Justitia-personifikation an Nicola Pisanos Domkanzel in Siena', *Mitteilungen des Kunsthistorischen Institutes in Florenz*, 53 (1), 2009, pp. 1–34.

Angelini, Alessandro, 'I restauri di Pietro di Francesco agli affreschi di Ambrogio Lorenzetti nella "Sala della Pace"', *Prospettiva*, 31, 1982, pp. 78–82.

Anheim, Étienne, 'La Forge de Babylone. Pouvoir pontifical et culture de cour sous le règne de Clément VI (1342–1352)', Ph.D. thesis, École pratique des hautes études, 2004.

Anheim, Étienne, 'Expertise et construction de la valeur artistique (XIVe–XVe siècle)', *Revue de synthèse*, 132, 2011, pp. 13–31.

Antoine, Jean-Philippe, '*Ad perpetuam memoriam*. Les nouvelles fonctions de l'image peinte en Italie: 1250–1400', *Mélanges de l'École française de Rome. Moyen Âge*, 100 (2), 1988, pp. 541–615.

Antoine, Jean-Philippe, 'Mémoire, lieux et invention spatiale dans la peinture italienne des XIIIe et XIVe siècles', *Annales ESC*, 48 (6), 1993, pp. 1447–69.

Arasse, Daniel, 'L'Art et l'illustration du pouvoir', in *Culture et idéologie dans la genèse de l'État moderne. Actes de la table ronde organisée par le Centre national de la recherche scientifique et l'École française de Rome, Rome 15–17 octobre 1984* (Rome: École française de Rome, 1985), pp. 231–44.

Arasse, Daniel, *Le Détail. Pour une histoire rapprochée de la peinture* (Paris: Flammarion, 1992).

Arasse, Daniel, *L'Annonciation italienne* (Paris: Hazan, 1999).

Arasse, Daniel, *Histoires de peintures* (Paris: Denoël, 2004).

Artifoni, Enrico, 'I Podestà professionali e la fondazione retorica della politica comunale', *Quaderni storici*, 63, 1983, pp. 687–719.

Artifoni, Enrico, 'Sull'eloquenza politica nel Duecento italiano', *Quaderni Medievali*, 35, 1993, pp. 57–78.

Artifoni, Enrico, 'Retorica e organizzazione del linguaggio politico nel Duecento italiano', in Paolo Cammarosano (ed.), *Le forme della propaganda politica nel due e nel trecento* (Rome: École française de Rome, 1994), pp. 157–82.

Artifoni, Enrico, 'L'Éloquence politique dans les cités communales (XIIIe siècle)', in Isabelle Heullant-Donat (ed.), *Cultures italiennes (XIIe–XVe siècle)* (Paris: Cerf, 2000), pp. 269–96.

Ascheri, Mario, 'Legislazione, statuti e sovranità', in *Antica legislazione della Repubblica di Siena* (Siena: Il Leccio, 1993), pp. 1–40.

Ascheri, Mario, *Lo spazio storico di Siena* (Rome: Silvana, 2001).

Ascheri, Mario, 'La Siena del Buon Governo (1287–1355)', in Simonetta Adorni Braccesi and Mario Ascheri (eds), *Politica e cultura nelle repubbliche italiane dal Medioevo all'età moderna: Firenze, Genova, Lucca, Siena e Venezia, Atti del Convegno Siena 1997* (Rome: Istituto Storico Italiano per l'età moderna e contemporanea, 2001), pp. 87–107.

Ascheri, Mario, *Le città-stato. Le radici del municipalismo e del repubblicanesimo italiani* (Bologna: Il Mulino, 2006).

Ascheri, Mario and Rodolfo Funari, 'Il proemio dello Stato comunale del "Buon Governo" (1337–1339)', *Bollettino Senese di Storia Patria*, XCVI, 1989, pp. 350–64.

Ascheri, Mario and Cecilia Papi, *Il 'Costituto' del Comune di Siena in volgare (1309–1310). Un episodio di storia della giustizia?* (Siena: Aska, 2009).

Bachelard, Gaston, *The Poetics of Space*, trans. Richard Kearney (London: Penguin, 2014).

Bagnoli, Alessandro, *La Maestà di Simone Martini* (Milan: Silvana Editoriale, 1999).

Bailly, Jean-Christophe, *La Phrase urbaine* (Paris: Seuil, 2013).

Balestracci, Duccio Balestracci, 'L'acqua a Siena nel Medioevo', in Jean-Claude Maire Vigueur and Agostino Paravicini Bagliani (eds), *Ars et Ratio. Dalla torre di Babele al ponte di Rialto* (Palermo: Sellerio, 1990), pp. 19–31.

Balestracci, Duccio, 'From Development to Crisis: Changing Urban Structures in Siena between the Thirteenth and Fifteenth Century', in Thomas W. Bloomquist and Maureen Fennell Mazzoui (eds), *The 'Other Tuscany': Essays in the History of Lucca, Pisa and Siena during the Thirteenth, Fourteenth and Fifteenth Centuries* (Kalamazoo, MI: Medieval Institute Publications, 1994), pp. 199–213.

Balestracci, Duccio, *Cilastro che sapeva leggere. Alfabetizzazione e istruzione nelle campagne toscane alla fine del Medioevo (XIV–XVI secolo)* (Ospedaletto [Pisa]: Pacini Editore, 2004).

Balestracci, Duccio and Gabriella Piccini, *Siena nel Trecento, assetto urbano e struttura edilizia* (Siena: CLUSF, 1977).

Baragli, Sandra, 'L'iconografia del cantiere come propaganda politica. Qualche considerazione', in Élisabeth Crouzet-Pavan (ed.), *Pouvoir et Édilité. Les grands chantiers dans l'Italie communale et seigneuriale* (Rome: École française de Rome, 2003), pp. 79–104.

Baridon, Michel, *Naissance et renaissance du paysage* (Arles: Actes Sud, 2006).

Baron, Hans, *The Crisis of the Early Italian Renaissance* (Princeton, NJ: Princeton University Press, 1955).

Barthes, Roland 'The Reality Effect, in *The Rustle of Language*, trans. Richard Howard (Berkeley and Los Angeles: University of California Press, 1989), pp. 141–8.

Baschet, Jérôme, *Les Justices de l'au-delà. Les représentations de l'enfer en France et en Italie (XIIe–XVe siècle)* (Rome: École française de Rome, 1993).

Baxandall, Michael, 'Art, Society and the Bouguer Principle', *Representations*, 12, 1985, pp. 32–43.

Baxandall, Michael, *Giotto and the Orators: Humanist Observers of Painting in Italy and the Discovery of Pictorial Composition 1350–1450* (Oxford: Clarendon, 1971).

Bellosi, Luciano, '*Castrum pingatur in palatio*, 2: Duccio e Simone Martini pittori di castelli senesi al'esemplo come erano', *Prospettiva*, 28, 1982, pp. 41–65.

Bellosi, Luciano, *Duccio. La Maestà* (Paris: Gallimard, 1999 [1998]).

Belting, Hans, 'The New Role of Narrative in Public Painting of the Trecento: *Historia* and Allegory', *Studies in the History of Arts*, 16, 1985, pp. 151–68.

Belting, Hans, 'Das Bild als Text. Wandmalerei und Literatur im Zeitalter Dantes', in Hans Belting and Dieter Blume (eds), *Malerei und Stadtkultur in der Dantezeit: die Argumentation der Bilder* (Munich: Hirmer, 1989), pp. 23–8.

Belting, Hans, 'Langage et réalité dans la peinture monumentale publique en Italie au Trecento', in Xavier Barral i Altet (ed.), *Artistes, artisans et production artistique au Moyen Âge. Fabrication et consommation de l'œuvre. Actes du colloque de Rennes, 2–6 mai 1983*, Vol. 3 (Paris: Picard, 1990), pp. 491–509.

Belting, Hans, 'The Madonnas of Siena: The Image in Urban Life', in *Likeness and Presence: A History of the Image before the Era of Art*, trans. Edmund Jephcott (Chicago: University of Chicago Press, 1994 [1990]), pp. 377–408.

Belting, Hans, 'The Coat of Arms and the Portrait: Two Media and the Body', in *An Anthropology of Images: Picture, Medium, Body*, trans. Thomas Dunlap (Princeton, NJ: Princeton University Press, 2011 [2001]), pp. 62–83.

Belting, Hans, 'Media and Bodies: Dante's Shadows and Greenaway's TV', in *An Anthropology of Images: Picture, Medium, Body*, trans. Thomas Dunlap (Princeton, NJ: Princeton University Press, 2011 [2001]), pp. 128–43.

Ben-Aryeh Debby, Nirit, 'War and Peace: The Description of Ambrogio Lorenzetti's Frescoes in Saint Bernardino's 1425 Siena Sermons', *Renaissance Studies*, 15 (3), 2001, pp. 272–86.

Benjamin, Walter, 'Theses on the Philosophy of History', in Illuminations, trans. Harry Zohn (New York: Schocken, 1968), pp. 253–64.

Benjamin, Walter, 'The Work of Art in the Age of Its Technological Reproducibility: Second Version', in *Selected Writings*, ed. Marcus Bullock and Michael W. Jennings, 4 vols (Cambridge, MA, and London: Belknap Press, 1996–2003), Vol. 3. *1935–1938*, pp. 19–55.

Black, Anthony, 'Society and the Individual from the Middle Ages to Rousseau: Philosophy, Jurisprudence and Constitutional Theory', *History of Political Thought*, 1, 1980, pp. 145–66.

Blythe, James M., *Ideal Government and the Mixed Constitution in the Middle Ages* (Princeton, NJ: Princeton University Press, 1992).

Boisseul, Didier, *Le Thermalisme en Toscane à la fin du Moyen Âge. Les bains siennois de la fin du XIIIe siècle au début du XVIe siècle* (Rome: École française de Rome, 2002).

Bolzoni, Lina, '"Come tu vedi dipinto": la predica e le pitture cittadine', in *La rete delle immagini. Predicazione in volgare dalle origini a Bernardino da Siena* (Turin: Einaudi, 2002), pp. 67–190.

Bonne, Jean-Claude, *L'Art roman de face et de profil. Le tympan de Conques* (Paris: Le Sycomore, 1984).

Borges, Jorge Luis, 'The Aleph' (1949), in *The Aleph and Other Stories*, trans. Andrew Hurley (London: Penguin, 1998), pp. 118–33.

Boucheron, Patrick, 'De l'urbanisme communal à l'urbanisme seigneurial. Cités, territoires et édilité publique en Italie du Nord (XIIIe–XVe siècle)', in Élisabeth Crouzet-Pavan (ed.), *Pouvoir et Édilité. Les grands chantiers dans l'Italie communale et seigneuriale* (Rome: École française de Rome, 2003), pp. 41–77.

Boucheron, Patrick, 'Tout est monument. Le mausolée d'Azzone Visconti à San Gottardo in Corte de Milan (1342–1346)', in Dominique Barthélemy and Jean-Marie Martin (eds), *Liber largitorius: Études d'histoire médiévale offertes à Pierre Toubert par ses élèves* (Geneva: Droz, 2003), pp. 303–26.

Boucheron, Patrick, '"Tournez les yeux pour admirer, vous qui exercez le pouvoir, celle qui est peinte ici". La fresque dite du Bon Gouvernement d'Ambrogio Lorenzetti', *Annales HSS*, 6, 2005, pp. 1137–99.

Boucheron, Patrick, 'Paroles de paix et seigneurs de guerre en Italie dans le premier tiers du XIVe siècle: quelques problèmes iconographiques', in Sylvie Caucanas, Rémy Cazals and Nicolas Offenstadt (eds), *Paroles de paix en temps de guerre* (Toulouse: Privat, 2006), pp. 165–79.

Boucheron, Patrick, 'È possibile un investimento disinteressato? Alcuni considerazioni sul finanziamento delle cattedrali nelle città dell'Italia centro-settentrionale alla fine del Medio Evo', *Città e storia*, 4, 2009, pp. 1–16.

Boucheron, Patrick, 'Connotations, accentuations, signatures. Remarques conclusives', *Annali di Storia moderna e contemporanea*, 16, 2010 (*Atti del Convegno: Immagini, culti, liturgie: le connotazioni politiche del messaggio religioso*), pp. 473–81.

Boucheron, Patrick, 'Politisation et dépolitisation d'un lieu commun. Remarques sur la notion de "bien commun" dans les villes d'Italie centro-septentrionale entre commune et signoria', in Élodie Lecuppre-Desjardin (ed.), *'De Bono Communi'. Discours et pratique du Bien Commun dans les villes d'Europe occidentale (XIIIe–XVIe siècle)*, Urban History, 22 (Turnhout: Brepols, 2010), pp. 237–51.

Boucheron, Patrick, 'L'Implicite du signe architectural: notes sur la rhétorique politique de l'art de bâtir entre Moyen Âge et Renaissance', *Perspectives*, 2012, pp. 173–80.

Boucheron, Patrick, 'Sauver le passé', preface to Walter Benjamin, *Sur le concept d'histoire* (Paris: Payot, 'Petite bibliothèque Payot', 2013), pp. 7–50.

Boucheron, Patrick and Nicolas Offenstadt (eds), *L'Espace public au Moyen Âge. Débats autour de Jürgen Habermas* (Paris: PUF, 'Le nœud gordien', 2011).

Boulnois, Olivier, *Au-delà de l'image. Une archéologie du visuel au Moyen Âge, Ve–XVIe siècle* (Paris: Seuil, 2008).

Boureau, Alain, *La Religion de l'État. La construction de la République étatique dans le discours théologique de l'Occident médiéval (1250–1350)* (Paris: Belles Lettres, 2006).

Boureau, Alain, 'On ne doit pas parler la bouche pleine. Un épisode d'histoire politique non thomiste (Bourdieu, Foucault, Sennelart)', *L'Atelier du Centre de recherches historiques*, 1, 2008 (available online: http://acrh.revues.org/316).

Bowsky, William, 'The *Buon Governo* of Siena (1287–1355): A Medieval Italian Oligarchy', *Speculum*, 37, 1962, pp. 368–81.

Bowsky, William, *A Medieval Italian Commune: Sienna under the Nine, 1287–1355* (London, Berkeley and Los Angeles: University of California Press, 1981).

Brandi, Cesare, 'Chiarimenti su "Buon Governo" di Ambrogio Lorenzetti', *Bollettino d'Arte*, 40, 1955, pp. 119–23.

Brenot, Anne-Marie, *Sienne au XIVe siècle dans les fresques de Lorenzetti. La cité parfaite* (Paris: L'Harmattan, 1999).

Bridgeman, Jane, 'Ambrogio Lorenzetti's Dancing "Maidens": A Case of Mistaken Identity', *Apollo*, 133, 1991, pp. 245–51.

Brogi, Andrea and Francesca Bianciardi, *Nella Siena ritrovata di Ambrogio Lorenzetti* (Siena: NIE, 2005).

Brugnolo, Furio, 'Le iscrizioni in volgare: Testo e commento', in Enrico Castelnuovo (ed.), *Ambrogio Lorenzetti: il Buon Governo* (Milan: Electra, 1995), pp. 381–91.

Brugnolo, Furio, '"Voi che guardate . . ." Divagazioni sulla poesia per pittura del Trecento', in Claudio Ciociola (ed.), *'Visibile parlare'. Le scritture esposte nei volgari italiani dal Medioevo al Rinascimento* (Naples: ESI, 1997), pp. 305–39.

Buc, Philippe, *The Dangers of Ritual: Between Early Medieval Texts and Social Scientific Theory* (Princeton, NJ, and Chichester: Princeton University Press, 2001).

Burckhardt, Jacob, *Italian Renaissance Painting According to Genres*, introduction by Maurizio Ghelardi; trans. David Britt and Caroline Beamish (Los Angeles: Getty Research Institute, 2005).

Cammarosano, Paolo, 'Il comune di Siena dalla solidarietà imperiale al guelfismo: celebrazione e propaganda', in Paolo Cammarosano (ed.), *Le forme della propaganda politica nel due e nel trecento* (Rome: École française de Rome, 1994), pp. 455–67.

Cammarosano, Paolo, 'Élites sociales et institutions politiques des villes libres en Italie de la fin du XIIe au début du XIVe siècle', in *Les Élites urbaines au Moyen Âge. Actes du XXIVe Congrès de la SHMES (Rome, 1996)* (Paris and Rome: Publications de la Sorbonne and École française de Rome, 1997), pp. 193–200.

Cammarosano, Paolo, 'L'Éloquence laïque dans l'Italie communale (fin du XIIe–XIVe siècle)', *Bibliothèque de l'École des Chartes*, 158, 2000, pp. 431–42.

Campbell, Jean, 'The City's New Clothes: Ambrogio Lorenzetti and the Poetics of Peace', *The Art Bulletin*, 83 (2), 2001, pp. 240–58.

Camporesi, Piero, *Le belle contrade: nascita del paesaggio italiano* (Milan: Garzanti, 1992).

Cardinali, Philippe, *L'Invention de la ville moderne. Variations italiennes 1297–1580* (Paris: Éditions de la Différence, 2002).

Carli, Enzo, *I Lorenzetti* (Milan: Silvana Editoriale, 1960).

Carli, Enzo, 'Luoghi ed opere d'arte senesi nelle prediche di Bernardino del 1427', in *Bernardino predicatore nella Società del suo tempo (16° Convegno del Centro di studi sulla spiritualità medievale, Todi, 9–12 ottobre 1975)* (Todi: L'Accademia Tudertina, 1976), pp. 155–82.

Carli, Enzo, *La pittura senese del Trecento* (Milan: Electa, 1980).

Carli, Enzo, *La pittura senese* (Florence: Scala Group, 1982).

Carlotti, Mariella, *Il bene di tutti. Gli affreschi del Buon Governo di Ambrogio Lorenzetti nel Palazzo Pubblico di Siena* (Florence: SEF, 2010).

Carniani, Alessandra, *I Salimbeni quasi una signoria. Tentativi di affermazione politica nella Siena del 1300* (Siena: Protagon Editori Toscani, 1995).

Carter-Southard, Edna, *The Frescoes in Siena's Palazzo Pubblico, 1289–1539: Studies in Imagery and Relations to Other Communal Palaces in Tuscany* (London and New York: Garland Publishing, 1979).

Carter-Southard, Edna, 'Ambrogio Lorenzetti's Frescoes in the Sala della Pace: A Change of Name', *Mitteilungen des Kunsthistorischen Institutes in Florenz*, 24, 1980, pp. 361–5.

Casagrande, Carla and Silvana Vecchio, *I sette vizi capitali. Storia dei peccati nel Medievo* (Turin: Einaudi, 2000).

Cassagnes-Brouquet, Sophie, *Les Couleurs de la norme et de la déviance. Les fresques d'Ambrogio Lorenzetti au Palazzo Pubblico de Sienne* (Dijon: Publications de l'Université de Bourgogne, 1993).

Castelnuovo, Enrico, *Un pittore italiano alla corte di Avignone: Mattio Giovannietti e la pittura di Provennza nel secolo XIV* (Turin: Einaudi, 1991 [1962]).

Castelnuovo, Enrico (ed.), *Ambrogio Lorenzetti: il Buon Governo* (Milan: Electa, 1995).

Castelnuovo, Guido and Carole Mabboux, 'I letterari e l'epidemia del 1348', in Sergio Luzzatto and Gabriele Pedullà (eds), *Atlante delle letteratura italiana*, Vol. 1, *Dalle origini al Rinascimento*, ed. Amedeo De Vincentiis (Turin: Einaudi, 2010), pp. 221–3.

Ceppari Ridolfi, Maria A. and Patrizia Turrini, *Il mulino della vanità. Lusso e ceremonie nella Siena medievale* (Siena: Il Leccio, 1993).

Chartier, Roger, 'Pouvoirs et limites de la représentation. Marin, le discours et l'image', in *Au bord de la falaise. L'histoire entre certitudes et inquiétude* (Paris: Albin Michel, 1998), pp. 173–90.

Chittolini, Giorgio, '"Crisi" e "lunga durata" delle istituzioni comunali in alcuni dibatti recenti', in Luigi Lacchè, Carlotta Latini, Paolo Marchetti and Massimo Meccarelli (eds), *Penale, giustizia, potere. Metodi, ricerche, storiografie. Per ricordare Mario Sbriccoli* (Macerata: EUM, 2007), pp. 125–54.

Ciccaglioni, Giovanni, 'Dal comune alla signoria? Lo spazio politico di Pisa nella prima metà del XIV secolo', *Bollettino dell'Istituto Storico Italiano per il Medioevo*, 109, 2007, pp. 235–70.

Ciociola, Claudio (ed.), *'Visibile parlare'. Le scritture esposte nei volgari italiani dal Medioevo al Rinascimento* (Naples: ESI, 1997).

Coccia, Emanuele and Sylvain Piron, 'Poésie, sciences et politique. Une génération d'intellectuels italiens (1290–1330)', *Revue de Synthèse*, 129 (4), 2008, pp. 551–86.

Colli, Alberto (ed.), *Il cofano nuziale istoriato attribuito ad Ambrogio Lorenzetti* (Milan: Electa, 2000).

Colli, Alberto, *Ambrogio Lorenzetti. La vita del Trecento in Siena e nel contado senese nelle commitenze istoriate pubbliche e private. Guida al Buongoverno* (Siena, 2004).

Comba, Rinaldo (ed.), *Gli Angiò nell'Italia nordoccidentale (1259–1382)* (Milan: Unicopli, 2006).

Cordaro, Michele, 'Le vicende costruttive', in Cesare Brandi (ed.), *Palazzo Pubblico di Siena. Vicende costruttive e decorazione* (Milan: Pizzi-Monte dei Paschi di Siena, 1983), pp. 29–143.

Cosnet, Bertrand, 'Les Personnifications dans la peinture monumentale en Italie au XIVe siècle: la grisaille et ses vertus', in Marion Boudon-Machuel, Maurice Brock and Pascale Charron (eds), *Aux limites de la couleur. Monochromie et polychromie dans les arts (1300–1600)* (Turnhout: Brepols, 'Études renaissantes', 2011), pp. 125–32.

Crouzet-Pavan, Élisabeth, *Enfers et paradis. L'Italie de Dante et de Giotto* (Paris: Albin Michel, 2001).

Crouzet-Pavan, Élisabeth, '"Pour le bien commun . . ." À propos des politiques urbaines dans l'Italie communale', in Élisabeth Crouzet-Pavan (ed.), *Pouvoir et Édilité. Les grands chantiers dans l'Italie communale et seigneuriale* (Rome: École française de Rome, 2003), pp. 11–40.

Cunningham, Colin, 'For the Honour and Beauty of the City: The Design of Town Halls', in Diana Norman (ed.), *Siena, Florence and Padua: Art, Society and Religion, 1280–1400* (New Haven, CT, and London: Yale University Press, 1995), Vol. 2, pp. 29–54.

D'Amico, Juan Carlo, *Le Mythe impérial et l'allégorie de Rome. Entre Saint-Empire, Papauté et Commune* (Caen: Presses universitaires de Caen, Cahiers de Transalpina, 2009).

Damisch, Hubert, *The Origin of Perspective*, trans. John Goodman (Cambridge, MA: MIT Press, 1994).

de Baecque, Antoine, *Godard. Biographie* (Paris: Grasset, 2010).

Descola, Philippe, *Beyond Nature and Culture*, trans. Janet Lloyd (Chicago and London: University of Chicago Press, 2013).

Desportes, Marc, *Paysages en mouvement. Transports et perception de l'espace XVIIIe–XXe siècle* (Paris: Gallimard, 2005).

Dessì, Rosa Maria, 'La giustizia in alcune forme di comunicazione medievale. Intorno ai protesti di Giannozzo Manetti e alle prediche di Bernardino da Siena', in Ginetta Auzzas, Giovanni Baffetti and Carlo Delcorno (eds), *Letteratura in forma di sermone. I rapporti tra predicazione e letteratura nei secoli XIII–XVI* (Florence: Leo S. Olschki, 2003), pp. 201–32.

Dessì, Rosa Maria, 'Pratiche della parola di pace nella storia dell'Italia urbana', in *Pace e guerra nel basso medioevo. Atti del XL Convegno storico internazionale, Todi, 12–14 ottobre 2003* (Spoleto: Centro italiano di studi sull'alto medioevo, 2004), pp. 271–312.

Dessì, Rosa Maria, '*Diligite iustitiam vos qui iudicatis terram* (Sagesse, I, 1): sermons et discours sur la justice dans l'Italie urbaine (XIIe–XVe siècle)', *Rivista internazionale di diritto comune*, 18, 2007, pp. 197–230.

Dessì, Rosa Maria, 'L'invention du "Bon Gouvernement". Pour une histoire des anachronismes dans les fresques d'Ambrogio Lorenzetti (XIVe–XXe siècle)', *Bibliothèque de l'École des Chartes*, 165, 2007, pp. 129–80.

Dessì, Rosa Maria, 'Da Toso Pichi ad Aristotele: visioni risorgimentali del "Buon Governo" di Lorenzetti', *Rivista storica italiana*, 122 (3), 2010, pp. 1146–70.

Dessì, Rosa Maria, 'Il bene comune nella comunicazione verbale e visiva. Indagini sugli affreschi del "Buon Governo"', in *Il bene comune: forme di governo e gerarchie sociali nel basso medioevo. Atti del XLVIII Convegno storico internazionale, Todi, 9–12 ottobre 2011* (Spoleto: Centro italiano di studi sull'alto medioevo, 2012), pp. 89–130.

De Vincentiis, Amedeo, 'Politica, memoria, oblio a Firenze nel XIV secolo. La tradizione documentaria della signoria del duca d'Atene', *Archivio Storico Italiano*, CLXI, 2003, pp. 209–48.

Didi-Huberman, Georges, 'Before the Image, Before Time: The Sovereignty of Anachronism', in Claire Farago and Robert Zwijnenberg (eds), *Compelling Visuality: The Work of Art in and Out of History* (Minneapolis: University of Minnesota Press, 2003), pp. 31–44.

Didi-Huberman, Georges, *The Surviving Image: Phantoms of Time and Time of Phantoms: Aby Warburg's History of Art*, trans. Harvey Mendelsohn (University Park: Pennsylvania State University Press, 2017 [2002])

Dohrn-van Rossum, Gerhard, *History of the Hour: Clocks and Modern Temporal Orders*, trans. Thomas Dunlap (Chicago and London: University of Chicago Press, 1996).

Donato, Maria Monica, 'Testi, contesti, immagini politiche nel tardo Medioevo: esempi toscani. In margine a una discussione sul *Buon Governo*', *Annali dell'Istituto storico italo-germanico in Trento*, 19, 1993, pp. 305–55.

Donato, Maria Monica, '"Cose morali, e anche appartenenti secondo e' luoghi": per lo studio della pittura politica nel tardo medioevo toscano', in Paolo Cammarosano (ed.), *Le forme della propaganda politica nel due e nel trecento* (Rome: École française de Rome, 1994), pp. 491–517.

Donato, Maria Monica, 'La "bellissima inventiva": immagini e idee nella Sala della Pace', in Enrico Castelnuovo (ed.), *Ambrogio Lorenzetti: il Buon Governo* (Milan: Electa, 1995), pp. 23–41.

Donato, Maria Monica, 'Immagini e iscrizioni nell'arte "politica" fra Tre e Quattrocento', in Claudio Ciociola (ed.), *'Visibile parlare'. Le scritture esposte nei volgari italiani dal Medioevo al Rinascimento* (Naples: ESI, 1997), pp. 341–96.

Donato, Maria Monica, 'Ancora sulle "Fonti" nel *Buon Governo* di Ambrogio Lorenzetti: dubbi, precisazioni, anticipazioni', in Simonetta Adorni Braccesi and Mario Ascheri (eds), *Politica e cultura nelle repubbliche italiane dal Medioevo all'età moderna: Firenze, Genova, Lucca, Siena e Venezia, Atti del Convegno Siena 1997* (Rome: Istituto Storico Italiano per l'età moderna e contemporanea, 2001), pp. 43–79.

Donato, Maria Monica, 'Il *princeps*, il giudice, il "sindacho" e la città. Novità su Ambrogio Lorenzetti nel Palazzo Pubblico di Siena', in Francesca Bocchi and Rosa Smurra (eds), *Imago urbis. L'immagine della città nella storia d'Italia. Atti del convegno internazionale (Bologna, 5–7 settembre 2001)* (Rome: Viella, 2003), pp. 389–416.

Donato, Maria Monica, '"Quando i contrari son posti da presso . . ." Breve itinerario intorno al Buon Governo, tra Siena e Firenze', in Giuseppe Pavanello (ed.), *Il Buono e il Cattivo Governo. Rappresentazioni nelle Arti dal Medioevo al Novecento* (Venice: Marsilio, 2004), pp. 21–43.

Donato, Maria Monica, 'Il pittore del Buon Governo: le opere "politiche" di Ambrogio in Palazzo Pubblico', in Chiara Frugoni (ed.), *Pietro e Ambrogio Lorenzetti* (Florence: Le Lettere, 2004), pp. 201–55.

Donato, Maria Monica, 'Dal "Comune rubato" di Giotto al "Comune sovrano" di Ambrogio Lorenzetti (con una proposta per la "canzone" del Buon Governo)', in Arturo Carlo Quintavalle (ed.), *Medioevo: immagine e racconti. Atti del convegno internazionale di studi (Parma, 2002)* (Milan: Electa, 2005), pp. 489–509.

Edwards, Mary D., 'Ambrogio Lorenzetti and Classical Painting', *Florilegium*, 2, 1980, pp. 146–60.

Favre, Monique, 'Petit texte sur petit tableau à grand espace: Duccio, *La Guérison de l'aveugle*', *Chroniques italiennes*, 13–14 (*Mélanges offerts à André Bouissy*), 1988 (available online: http://chroniquesitaliennes.univ-paris3.fr/numeros/13. html).

Feldges-Henning, Uta, 'The Pictorial Programme of the Sala della Pace: A New Interpretation', *Journal of the Warburg and Courtauld Institutes*, 35, 1972, pp. 145–62.

Feldges, Uta, *Landschaft als topographisches Porträt. Der Wiederbeginn der europäischen Landschaftsmalerei in Siena* (Berne: Benteli, 1980).

Fenech Kroke, Antonella, *Giorgio Vasari, la fabrique de l'allégorie. Culture et fonction de la personnification au Cinquecento* (Florence: Leo S. Olschki, 2011).

Fourcade, Dominique, 'en laisse', in *en laisse* (Paris: P.O.L., 2005), pp. 37–51.

Friedman, David, 'Palaces and the Street in Late Medieval and Renaissance Italy', in Jenny Whitehand and Peter Larkham (eds), *Urban Landscape: International Perspectives* (London and New York: Routledge, 1992), pp. 69–113.

Friedman, David, 'Talamone, 1306', in Marco Folin (ed.), *Rappresentare la città. Topografi e urbane nell'Italia di antico regime* (Reggio Emilia: Diabasis, 2010), pp. 57–76.

Frugoni, Chiara, 'Il governo dei Nove a Siena e il loro credo politico nell'affresco di Ambrogio Lorenzetti', *Quaderni medioevali*, 7, 1979, pp. 14–42, and 8, 1979, pp. 71–103.

Frugoni, Chiara, *Una lontana città. Sentimenti e immagini nel Medioevo* (Turin: Einaudi, 1983).

Frugoni, Chiara (ed.), *Pietro e Ambrogio Lorenzetti* (Florence: Le Lettere, 2004).

Frugoni, Chiara, *L'affare migliore di Enrico. Giotto e la cappella Scrovegni* (Turin: Einaudi, 2008).

Frugoni, Chiara and Odile Redon, 'Accusé Guido Riccio, défendez-vous!', *Médiévales*, 9, 1985, pp. 118–31.

Fubini, Riccardo, 'Renaissance Historian: The Career of Hans Baron', *Journal of Modern History*, 64, 1992, pp. 541–74.

Gabbrielli, Fabio, *Siena medievale. L'architettura civile* (Siena: Protagon Editori, 2010).

Gaulin, Jean-Louis and François Menant, 'Crédit rural et endettement paysan dans l'Italie communale', in Maurice Berthe (ed.), *Endettement paysan et crédit rural dans l'Europe médiévale et moderne (Actes des XVIIe*

Journées internationales d'histoire de l'abbaye de Flaran, septembre 1995) (Toulouse: Privat, 1998), pp. 35–68.

Genet, Jean-Philippe, 'Revisiter Assise: la lisibilité de l'image médiévale', in Corinne Péneau (ed.), *Itinéraires du savoir de l'Italie à la Scandinavie (Xe–XVIe siècle). Études offertes à Élisabeth Mornet* (Paris: Publications de la Sorbonne, 2009), pp. 391–419.

Gianola, Giovanna Maria, 'L'*Ecerinis* di Albertino Mussato tra Ezzelino e Cangrande', in Giorgio Gracco (ed.), *Nuovi studi ezzeliniani* (Rome : Istituto storico italiano per il Medio Evo, 1992), Vol. 2, pp. 536–74.

Gibbs, Robert, 'In Search of Ambrogio Lorenzetti's Allegory of Justice: Changes to the Frescoes in the Palazzo Pubblico', *Apollo*, 159 (447), 1999, pp. 11–16.

Gilbert, Creighton, 'The Fresco by Giotto in Milan', *Arte Lombarda*, 47–8, 1977, pp. 31–72.

Gilli, Patrick, *Au miroir de l'humanisme. Les représentations de la France dans la culture savante italienne à la fin du Moyen Âge* (Rome: École française de Rome, 1997).

Ginatempo, Maria and Lucia Sandri, *L'Italia delle città. Il popolamento urbano tra Medioevo e Rinascimento (secoli XIII–XVI)* (Florence: Le Lettere, 1990).

Ginzburg, Carlo. 'The Sword and the Lightbulb: A Reading of *Guernica*', in *Fear, Reverence, Terror: Five Essays in Political Iconography* (Calcutta: Seagull. 2017), pp. 165–242.

Giorgi, Andrea and Stefano Moscadelli, *Costruire una cattedrale. L'Opera di Santa Maria di Siena tra XIIe e XIVe secolo* (Munich: Deutscher Kunstverlag, 2005).

Greenstein, Jack M., 'The Vision of Peace: Meaning and Representation in Ambrogio Lorenzetti's *Sala della Pace* Cityscapes', *Art History*, 11, 1988, pp. 492–510.

Grévin, Benoît, *Rhétorique du pouvoir médiéval. Les Lettres de Pierre de la Vigne et la formation du langage politique européen (XIIIe–XVe siècle)* (Rome: École française de Rome, 2008).

Grévin, Benoît, *Le Parchemin des cieux. Essai sur le Moyen Âge du langage* (Paris: Seuil, 2012).

Guerreau, Alain, 'Chasse', in Jacques Le Goff and Jean-Claude Schmitt (eds), *Dictionnaire raisonné de l'Occident médiéval* (Paris: Fayard, 1999), pp. 166–78.

Guerrini, Roberto, '*Dulci pro libertate*. Taddeo di Bartolo: il ciclo di eroi antichi nel Palazzo Pubblico di Siena (1413–1414). Tradizione classica ed iconografi a politica', *Rivista storica italiana*, 112, 2000, pp. 510–68.

Heers, Jacques, 'Les Villes d'Italie centrale et l'urbanisme: origines et affirmation d'une politique (environ 1200–1350)', *Mélanges de l'École française de Rome, Moyen Âge*, 101 (1), 1989, pp. 67–93.

Holmes, George, 'The Emergence of an Urban Ideology at Florence', *Transactions of the Royal Historical Society*, 23, 1973, pp. 111–34.

Hubert, Étienne, 'La Construction de la ville. Sur l'urbanisation dans l'Italie médiévale', *Annales HSS*, 59 (1), 2004, pp. 109–39.

Imbert, Anne-Laure, 'Le Paysage comme fragment de nature, prémisse faussée de l'histoire du paysage. Une discussion à partir du cas siennois', *Revue de l'Art*, 173 (3), 2011, pp. 21–31.

Imbert, Anne-Laure, 'Un miroir pour la Commune: les peintures de bataille à Sienne entre Tre- et Quattrocento', in Philippe Morel (ed.), *Le Miroir et l'espace du prince dans l'art italien de la Renaissance* (Rennes and Tours: Presses universitaires de Rennes and Presses universitaires François-Rabelais, 2012), pp. 257–81.

Jacoff, Rachel, '"Diligite iustitiam": Loving Justice in Siena and Dante's *Paradiso*', *MLN*, 124–5, 2009, pp. 81–95.

Jenkins, Marianna, 'The Iconography of the Hall of the Consistory in the Palazzo Pubblico, Siena', *Art Bulletin*, LIV, 1972, pp. 430–51.

Kantorowicz, Ernst, 'An "Autobiography" of Guido Faba', *Medieval and Renaissance Studies*, 1, 1941–3, pp. 253–80.

Kantorowicz, Ernst, *The King's Two Bodies: A Study in Medieval Political Theology*, preface by William Chester Jordan; introduction by Conrad Leyser (Princeton, NJ: Princeton University Press, 2016 [1957]).

Kempers, Bram, *Painting, Power and Patronage: The Rise of the Professional Artist in the Italian Renaissance*, trans. Beverley Jackson (London: Allen Lane, 1992 [1987]).

Klapisch-Zuber, Christiane, *Retour à la cité. Les magnats de Florence, 1340–1440* (Paris: Éditions de l'EHESS, 2006).

Krautheimer, Richard, *Lorenzo Ghiberti* (Princeton, NJ: Princeton University Press, 1956, new edn 1982).

Kristeller, Paul Oscar, 'Humanism and Scholasticism in the Italian Renaissance', in Michael Mooney (ed.), *Renaissance Thought and Its Sources* (New York: Columbia University Press, 1979), pp. 85–105.

Kupfer, Marcia, 'The Lost Wheel Map of Ambrogio Lorenzetti', *Art Bulletin*, 78 (2), 1996, pp. 287–310.

La Roncière, Charles-Marie de, Philippe Contamine and Robert Delort, 'Le Paysage rural autour de Sienne et en Toscane', in *L'Europe au Moyen Âge*, Vol. 3, *Fin XIIIe siècle–fin XVe siècle* (Paris: Armand Colin, 1971), pp. 135–45.

Lecuppre-Desjardin, Élodie and Anne-Laure Van Bruaene (eds), *Emotions in the Heart of the City (14th–16th Century)* (Turnhout: Brepols, 'Studies in European Urban History', 5, 2005).

Lecocq, Anne-Marie, *Le Bouclier d'Achille. Un tableau qui bouge* (Paris: Gallimard, 2010).

Lefort, Claude, 'Machiavel et la *verità effetuale*', in *Écrire. À l'épreuve du politique* (Paris: Calmann-Lévy, 1992).

Leoncini, Alessandro, *Siena in fasce. Topografia e immagini della Sena vetus* (Monteriggioni: Il Leccio, 1998).

Little, Anna, 'Du lieu à l'espace. Transformations de l'environnement pictural en Italie centrale (XIIIe–XVe siècle)', Ph.D. thesis, ed. Maurice Brock, Université François-Rabelais de Tours, 2010.

Lopez, Roberto S., 'Économie et architecture médiévales. Ceci aurait-il tué cela?', *Annales ESC*, 7, 1952, pp. 433–8.

Loraux, Nicole, *The Divided City: On Memory and Forgetting in Ancient Athens*, trans. Corinne Pache with Jeff Fort (New York: Zone Books, 2002).

Lugarini, Renato, 'Il ghibellino: Provenzano Salvani tra mito e dimensione storica', in Gabriella Piccinni (ed.), *Fedeltà ghibellina, affari guelfi. Saggi e riletture intorno alla storia di Siena fra Duecento e Trecento* (Pisa: Pacini, 2008), Vol. 2, pp. 467–97.

Luzi, Mario, *Earthly and Heavenly Voyage of Simone Martini*, trans. Luigi Bonaffini (Los Angeles: Green Integer, 2003 [1994]).

Maginnis, Hayden, 'Chiarimenti documentari: Simone Martini, i Memmi e Ambrogio Lorenzetti', *Rivista d'arte*, 51, 1989, pp. 3–23.

Maginnis, Hayden, *The World of the Early Sienese Painter* (University Park: Pennsylvania State University Press, 2001).

Mainoni, Patrizia (ed.), *Politiche finanziarie e fiscali nell'Italia settentrionale (secoli XIII–XV)* (Milan: Unicopli, 2001).

Maire Vigueur, Jean-Claude, 'Échec au Podestàt. L'expulsion de Comacio Galluzzi Podestàt de Todi (17 juillet 1268)', *Bollettino della deputazione di storia patria per l'Umbria*, 92, 1995, pp. 5–41.

Maire Vigueur, Jean-Claude, *Cavaliers et Citoyens. Guerre, conflits et société dans l'Italie communale, XIIe–XIIIe siècles* (Paris: Éditions de l'EHESS, 2003).

Mane, Perrine, 'Les travaux et les jours', in Jacques Dalarun (ed.), *Le Moyen Âge en lumière. Manuscrits enluminés des bibliothèques de France* (Paris: Fayard, 2002), pp. 139–71.

Marin, Louis, *On Representation*, trans. Catherine Porter (Stanford, CA: Stanford University Press, 2001 [1994]).

Martindale, Andrew, 'The Problem of "Guidoriccio"', *The Burlington Magazine*, 128, 1986, pp. 259–73.

Meiss, Millard, *Painting in Florence and Siena after the Black Death: The Arts, Religion and Society in the Mid-Fourteenth Century* (New York: Harper & Row, 1964).

Menziger, Sara, *Giuristi e politica nei comuni di popolo. Siena, Perugia e Bologna, tre governi a confront* (Rome: Viella, 2006).

Meoni, Maria Luisa, *Utopia and Reality in Ambrogio Lorenzetti's Good Government: Formal Example in the Representation of Human Activity. An Anthropological Analysis* (Florence: Edizioni IFI, 2005).

Michon, Pierre. *The Eleven*, trans. Elizabeth Deshays and Jody Gladding (Brooklyn, NY: Archipelago Books, 2013).

Milani, Giuliano, *L'esclusione dal comune. Conflitti e bandi politici a Bologna e in altre città italiane tra XII e XIV secolo* (Rome: ISIME, 2003).

Milani, Giuliano, 'Prima del Buongoverno. Motivi politici e ideologia popolare nelle pitture del Broletto di Brescia', *Studi medievali*, 49 (1), 2008, pp. 19–85.

Milani, Giuliano, 'Avidité et trahison du bien commun. Une peinture infamante du XIIIe siècle', *Annales HSS*, 66 (3), 2011, pp. 705–39.

Milner, Jean-Claude, *Pour une politique des êtres parlants. Court traité politique 2* (Lagrasse: Verdier, 2011).

Milner, Jean-Claude, *Malaise dans la peinture. À propos de La Mort de Marat* (Paris: Ophrys/INHA, 2012).

Mineo, E. Igor, 'Liberté et communauté en Italie (milieu XIIIe–début XVe siècle)', in Claudia Moatti and Michèle Riot-Sarcey (eds), *La République dans tous ses états. Pour une histoire intellectuelle de la république en Europe* (Paris: Payot, 2009), pp. 215–50.

Moeglin, Jean-Marie, 'Henri VII et l'honneur de la majesté impériale: les redditions de Crémone et de Brescia (1311)', in Dominique Boutet and Jacques Verger (eds), *Penser le pouvoir au Moyen Âge. Études offertes à Françoise Autrand* (Paris: Presses de l'ENS, 2000), pp. 211–45.

Molho, Anthony, 'Hans Baron's Crisis', in David S. Peterson and Daniel E. Bornstein (eds), *Florence and Beyond. Culture, Society and Politics in Renaissance Italy: Essays in Honour of John M. Najemy* (Toronto: Center for Reformation and Renaissance Studies, 2008), pp. 61–90.

Morel, Barbara, 'Justice et bien commun. Étude comparée de la fresque du bon gouvernement d'Ambrogio Lorenzetti et d'un manuscrit juridique bolonais', *Mélanges de l'École française de Rome, Moyen Âge*, 113 (1), 2001, pp. 685–97.

Mundy, John Hine, 'In Praise of Italy: The Italian Republics', *Speculum*, 64, 1989, pp. 815–34.

Nardi, Paolo, *L'insegnamento superiore a Siena nei secoli XI-XIV. Tentativi e realizzazioni dalle origini alla fondazione dello Studio generale* (Milan: Giuffrè, 1996).

Nederman, Cary J., 'The Meaning of "Aristotelianism" in Medieval Moral and Political Thought', *Journal of the History of Ideas*, 57, 1996, pp. 563–85.

Neri, Laura, 'Culture et politique à Sienne au début du XIVe siècle: le Statut en langue vulgaire de 1309–1310', *Médiévales*, 22–3, 1992, pp. 207–21.

Nevola, Fabrizio, 'Revival or Renewal: Defining Civic Identity in Fifteenth-Century Siena', in Marc Boone and Peter Stabel (eds), *Shaping Urban Identity in Late Medieval Europe* (Louvain: Garant, 2000), pp. 109–35.

Nevola, Fabrizio, *Siena: Constructing the Renaissance City* (New Haven, CT, and London: Yale University Press, 2007).

Norman, Diana (ed.), '"Love Justice, You Who Judge the Earth": The Paintings of the Sala dei Nove in the Palazzo Pubblico, Siena', in *Siena, Florence and Padua: Art, Society and Religion, 1280–1400*, 2 vols. (New Haven, CT, and London: Yale University Press, 1995), Vol. 1, pp. 145–67.

Norman, Diana, 'Pisa, Siena and the Maremma: A Neglected Aspect of Ambrogio Lorenzetti's Paintings in the Sala dei Nove', *Renaissance Studies*, 11 (4), 1997, pp. 310–42.

Norman, Diana, *Painting in Late Medieval and Renaissance Siena (1260–1555)* (New Haven, CT, and London: Yale University Press, 2003).

Orofino, Giulia, 'Decorazione e miniatura del libro comunale: Siena e Pisa', in *Atti della Società ligure di storia patria*, 103, 1989 (*Civiltà Comunale: libro, scrittura, documento*), pp. 463–91.

Pade, Mariane, 'Boccaccio, Leonzio, and the Transformation of the Homeric Myths', in Luisa Capodieci and Philip Ford (eds), *Homère à la Renaissance. Mythe et transfigurations* (Paris and Rome: Somogy, 'Collection d'histoire de l'art de l'Académie de France à Rome', 2011), pp. 27–40.

Panofsky, Erwin, *Perspective as Symbolic Form*, trans. Christopher S. Wood (New York: Zone Books, 1991).

Pelham, Georgina, 'Reconstructing the Programme of the Tomb of Guido Tarlati, Bishop and Lord of Arezzo', in Joanna Cannon and Beth Williamson (eds), *Art, Politics, and Civic Religion in Central Italy, 1261–1352* (Aldershot: Ashgate, 2000), pp. 71–115.

Piccinni, Gabriella, 'La campagna e le città (secoli XII–XIV)', in Alfio Cortonesi, Gianfranco Pasquali and Gabriella Piccinni, *Uomini e campagna nell'Italia medievale* (Rome and Bari: Laterza, 2002), pp. 123–89.

Piccinni, Gabriella, 'Il sistema senese del credito nella fase di smobilitazione dei suoi banchi internazionali. Politiche comunali, spesa pubblica, propaganda contro l'usura, 1332–1340', in *Fedeltà ghibellina, affari guelfi. Saggi e riletture intorno alla storia di Siena fra Duecento e Trecento* (Pisa: Pacini, 2008), Vol. 1, pp. 209–89.

Pinto, Giuliano, '"Honor" and "Profit": Landed Property and Trade in Medieval Siena', in Trevor Dean and Chris Wickham (eds), *City and Countryside in Late Medieval and Renaissance Italy: Essays Presented to Philip Jones* (London: Continuum, 1990), pp. 81–92.

Poeschke, Joachim, *Italian Frescoes: The Age of Giotto, 1280–1400* (New York: Abbeville Press, 2005).

Polzer, Joseph, 'Ambrogio Lorenzetti's War and Peace Murals Revisited: Contribution to the Meaning of the Good Government Allegory', *Artibus et historiae*, 45, 2002, pp. 63–105.

Pontalis, J.-B., *Le Dormeur éveillé* (Paris: Gallimard, 2004).

Popp, Dietmar, 'Lupa senese: zur Inszenierung einer mythischen Vergangenheit in Siena (1260–1560)', *Marburger Jahrbuch für Kunstwissenschaft*, 24, 1997, pp. 41–58.

Prazniak, Roxann, 'Siena on the Silk Roads: Ambrogio Lorenzetti and the Mongol Global Century, 1250–1350', *Journal of World History*, 21–2, 2010, pp. 177–217.

Quaglioni, Diego, *Politica e diritto nel Trecento italiano. Il 'De Tyranno' di Bartolo da Sassoferrato (1314–1357)* (Florence: Leo S. Olschki, 1983).

Quaglioni, Diego, 'Politica e diritto al tempo di Federico II. L'"Oculus pastoralis" (1222) e la "sapienza civile"', in *Federico II e le nuove culture (Atti del XXXI Convegno storico internazionale, Todi, 9–12 ottobre 1994)* (Spoleto: Centro italiano di studi sull'alto medioevo, 1995), pp. 3–26.

Raveggi, Sergio, 'Appunti sulle forme di propaganda nel conflitto tra magnati e popolani', in Paolo Cammarosano (ed.), *Le forme della propaganda politica nel due e nel Trecento* (Rome: École française de Rome, 1994), pp. 469–89.

Raveggi, Sergio, 'Sienna nell'Italia dei guelfi e dei ghibellini', in Gabriella Piccinni (ed.), *Fedeltà ghibellina, affari guelfi. Saggi e riletture intorno alla storia di Siena fra Duecento e Trecento* (Pisa: Pacini, 2008), Vol. 1, pp. 29–61.

Redon, Odile, *Uomini e comunità del contado senese del Duecento* (Siena: Accademia degli Intronati, 1982).

Redon, Odile, *L'Espace d'une cité. Sienne et le pays siennois (XIIIe–XIVe siècles)* (Rome: École française de Rome, 1994).

Redon, Odile (ed.), *Les Langues de l'Italie médiévale* (Turnhout: Brepols, 2002).

Riess, Jonathan, 'Uno studio iconografico della decorazione ad affresco del 1297 nel Palazzo dei Priori a Perugia', *Bollettino d'Arte*, 66, 1981, pp. 43–58.

Riess, Jonathan, 'Justice and Common Good in Giotto's Arena Chapel Frescoes', *Arte cristiana*, LXXII, 1984, pp. 69–80.

Riklin, Aloïs, *Ambrogio Lorenzettis politische Summe* (Berne: Stämpfli Verlag AG, 1996).

Rizzi, Alessandra, 'Le Jeu dans les villes de l'Italie médiévale', *Histoire urbaine*, 1, 2000, pp. 47–64.

Romano, Dennis, 'A Depiction of Male Same-Sex Seduction in Ambrogio Lorenzetti's *Effects of Bad Government* Fresco', *Journal of the History of Sexuality*, 21 (1), 2012, pp. 1–15.

Romano, Giovanni, 'Documenti figurativi per la storia delle campagne nei secoli XI–XVI', in *Studi sul paesaggio* (Turin: Einaudi, 1978), pp. 3–91.

Ronen, Avraham, 'Due paesaggi nella Pinacoteca di Siena già attribuiti ad Ambrogio Lorenzetti', *Mitteilungen des Kunsthistorischen Institutes in Florenz*, 50 (3), 2006, pp. 367–400.

Rosenstiehl, Pierre, 'Déposé au centre, le butin n'appartient plus à personne. *Lectures*', in Maurice Olender and François Vitrani (eds), *Jean-Pierre Vernant dedans-dehors*, *Le Genre humain*, 53 (Paris: Seuil, 2013), pp. 145–9.

Rouchon Mouilleron, Véronique, 'Miracle et charité: autour d'une image du *Livre du biadaiolo* (Florence: Bibliothèque Laurentienne, ms Tempi 3)', *Revue Mabillon*, 180, 2008, pp. 157–89.

Rowley, George, *Ambrogio Lorenzetti* (Princeton, NJ.: Princeton University Press, 1958).

Rubinstein, Nicolai, 'Political Ideas in Sienese Art: The Frescoes by Ambrogio Lorenzetti and Taddeo di Bartolo in the Palazzo Pubblico', *Journal of the Warburg and Courtauld Institutes*, 21, 1958, pp. 179–207.

Rubinstein, Nicolai, 'Le allegorie di Ambrogio Lorenzetti nella Sala della Pace e il pensiero politico del suo tempo', *Rivista storica italiana*, 109, 1997, pp. 781–802.

Russo, Daniel, 'Le Nom de l'artiste, entre appartenance au groupe et écriture personnelle', in Dominique Iogna-Prat et Brigitte Bedos-Rezak (eds), *L'Individu au Moyen Âge. Individuation et individualisation avant la modernité* (Paris: Aubier, 2005), pp. 235–46.

Rutenburg, Victor, 'La Vie et la mort des *Ciompi* de Sienne', *Annales ESC*, 20–1, 1965, pp. 80–109.

Santucci, Marco, 'Immagini della città da Omero ad Ambrogio Lorenzetti', *Rivista di Filologia e Istruzione Classica*, 134, 2006, pp. 404–28.

Saxl, Fritz, 'I figli dei planeti', in Salvatore Settis (ed.), *La fede negli astri. Dall'antichità al Rinascimento* (Turin: Einaudi, 1985), pp. 274–9.

Sbriccoli, Mario, 'La Triade, le bandeau, le genou. Droit et procès pénal dans les allégories de la Justice du Moyen Âge à l'âge moderne', *Crime, Histoire et Sociétés*, 9 (1), 2005 (available online: http://chs.revues.org/382).

Sbriccoli, Mario, 'Justice négociée, justice hégémonique. L'émergence du pénal public dans les villes italiennes des XIIIe et XIVe siècles', in Jacques Chiffoleau, Claude Gauvard and Andrea Zorzi (eds), *Pratiques sociales et politiques judiciaires dans les villes de l'Occident à la fin du Moyen Âge* (Rome: École française de Rome, 2007), pp. 389–421.

Schenk, Gerrit Jasper, 'Enter the Emperor: Charles IV and Siena between Politics, Diplomacy, and Ritual (1355 and 1368)', *Renaissance Studies*, 20, 2006, pp. 161–79.

Schiera, Pierangelo, 'Il Buongoverno "melancolico" di Ambrogio Lorenzetti e la "costituzionale faziosità" della città', *Scienza e Politica*, 34, 2006, pp. 93–108.

Schild, Wolfgang, 'Gerechtigkeitsbilder', in Wolfgang Pleister and Wolfgang Schild (eds), *Recht und Gerechtigkeit im Spiegel der europäischen Kunst* (Cologne: DuMont Buchverlag, 1988), pp. 86–171.

Scrivano, Riccardo, 'Bindo di Cione del Frate', *Dizionario biografico degli Italiani*, Vol. 10 (Rome: Fondazzione Treccani, 1968), pp. 495–6.

Seidel, Max, '"Castrum pingatur in palatio", 1. Ricerche storiche e iconografiche sui castelli dipinti nel Palazzo Pubblico di Siena', *Prospettiva*, 28, 1982, pp. 17–41.

Seidel, Max, *Dolce vita. Ambrogio Lorenzettis Porträt des Sienneser Staates*, Basel, 'Vorträge der Aeneas-Silvius-Stiftung an der Universität Basel', 33, 1999.

Seidel, Max, 'Vanagloria. Studi sull'iconografi a degli affreschi di Ambrogio Lorenzetti nella "Sala della Pace"', in *Arte italiana del Medioevo e del Rinascimento*, Vol. 1, *Pittura* (Venice: Marsilio, 2003 [1997]), pp. 293–340.

Sennelart, Michel, *Les Arts de gouverner. Du regimen médiéval au concept de gouvernement* (Paris: Seuil, 1995).

Sère, Bénédicte, *Penser l'amitié au Moyen Âge. Études historiques des commentaires sur les livres VIII et IX de l'Éthique à Nicomaque (XIIIe–XVe siècle)* (Turnhout: Brepols, 2007).

Skinner, Quentin, 'Motives, Intentions and Interpretations of Texts', *New*

Literary History, 3, 1972, pp. 393–408 [reprinted as 'Motives, Intentions and Interpretation', in *Visions of Politics*, Vol. I, *Regarding Method* (Cambridge: Cambridge University Press, 2002), pp. 90–102].

Skinner, Quentin, *The Foundations of Modern Political Thought*, Vol. 1, *The Renaissance* (Cambridge: Cambridge University Press, 1978).

Skinner, Quentin, 'Ambrogio Lorenzetti: The Artist as Political Philosopher', *Proceedings of the British Academy*, 122, 1986, pp. 1–56.

Skinner, Quentin, 'Machiavelli's *Discorsi* and the Prehumanist Origins of Republican Ideas', in Gisela Bock, Quentin Skinner and Maurizio Viroli (eds), *Machiavelli and Republicanism* (Cambridge: Cambridge University Press, 1990), pp. 121–41.

Skinner, Quentin, 'Ambrogio Lorenzetti's "Buon Governo" Frescoes: Two Old Questions, Two New Answers', *Journal of the Warburg and Courtauld Institutes*, 72, 1999, pp. 1–28.

Skinner, Quentin, 'Ambrogio Lorenzetti e la teoria dell'autogoverno repubblicano', in Simonetta Adorni Braccesi and Mario Ascheri (eds), *Politica e cultura nelle repubbliche italiane dal Medioevo all'età moderna: Firenze, Genova, Lucca, Siena e Venezia, Atti del Convegno Siena 1997* (Rome: Istituto Storico Italiano per l'età moderna e contemporanea, 2001), pp. 21–42.

Skinner, Quentin, *Visions of Politics*, Vol. 2, *Renaissance Virtues* (Cambridge: Cambridge University Press, 2002).

Skinner, Quentin, *La Vérité et l'historien* (Paris: Éditions de l'EHESS, 2012 [2010]).

Sonnay, Jean-François, 'Paix et bon gouvernement: à propos d'un monument funéraire du *Trecento*', *Arte medievale*, IV (2), 1990, pp. 189–91.

Starn, Randolph, *Ambrogio Lorenzetti. Le palais communal, Sienne* (Paris: Hazan, 1995 [1994]).

Starn, Randolph and Loren Partridge, *Arts of Power: Three Halls of State in Italy, 1300–1600* (Berkeley, Los Angeles and Oxford: University of California Press, 1992).

Starobinski, Jean, *L'Encre de la mélancolie* (Paris: Seuil, 2012).

Szabó, Thomas, 'Le rete stradale del contado di Siena. Legislazione statutaria e amministrazione comunale del Duecento', *Mélanges de l'École française de Rome. Moyen Âge*, 87 (1), 1975, pp. 141–86.

Tabacco, Giovanni, *The Struggle for Power in Medieval Italy: Structures of Political Rule*, trans. Rosalind Brown Jensen (Cambridge: Cambridge University Press, 1989 [1974]).

Tanzini, Lorenzo, 'Emergenza, eccezione, deroga: tecniche e retoriche del potere nei comuni toscani del XIV secolo', in Massimo Vallerani (ed.), *Tecniche di potere nel tardo medioevo. Regimi comunali e signorie in Italia* (Rome: Viella, 2010), pp. 149–81.

Tarr, Roger P., 'A Note on the Light in Ambrogio Lorenzetti's Peaceful City Fresco', *Art History*, 13, 1990, pp. 388–92.

Théry, Julien, 'Faide nobiliaire et justice inquisitoire de la papauté à Sienne au temps des Neuf: les *recollectiones* d'une enquête de Benoît XII contre l'évêque Donosdeo de' Malavolti (ASV, Collectoriae 61A et 404A)', in Susanne Lepsius and Thomas Wetzstein (eds), *Als die Welt in die Akten kam. Prozeßschriftgut im europäischen Mittelalter* (Frankfurt: Klostermann, 'Rechtsprechung', 2008), pp. 275–345.

Tomei, Alessandro (ed.), *Le biccherne di Siena: arte e finanza all'alba dell'economia moderna* (Rome: Retablo, 2002).

Turner, Anthony, '"The Accomplishment of Many Years": Three Notes towards a History of the Sand-Glass', *Annals of Science*, 39, 1982, pp. 161–72.

Varanini, Gian Maria, 'Propaganda dei regimi signorili. Le esperienze venete del trecento', in Paolo Cammarosano (ed.), *Le forme della propaganda politica nel due e nel trecento* (Rome: École française de Rome, 1994), pp. 311–34.

Varanini, Gian Maria, 'Aristocrazie e poteri nell'Italia centro-settentrionale dalla crisi comunale alle guerre d'Italia', in Renato Bordone, Gian Maria Varanini and Guido Castelnuovo, *Le aristocrazie dai signori rurali al patriziato* (Rome and Bari: Laterza, 2004), pp. 121–93.

Vauchez, André, 'La Commune de Sienne, les Ordres Mendiants et le culte des saints. Histoire et enseignements d'une crise (novembre 1328–avril 1329)', *Mélanges de l'École française de Rome. Moyen Âge*, 89 (2), 1977, pp. 757–67.

Vidal-Naquet, Pierre, *The Black Hunter: Forms of Thought and Forms of Society in the Greek World*, trans. Andrew Szegedy-Maszak (Baltimore, MD: Johns Hopkins University Press, 1986).

Villard, Renaud: *Du bien commun au mal nécessaire. Tyrannies, assassinats politiques et souveraineté en Italie, vers 1470–vers 1600* (Rome: École française de Rome, 2008).

von Moos, Peter, 'La retorica nel Medioevo', in *Lo spazio letterario del Medioevo*, Vol. 1, *Medioevo latino, la produzione del testo* (Rome: Salerno, 1993), pp. 231–71.

Vuilleumier-Laurens, Florence, 'Allégories en affrontement: une version sérielle de la *stoa poikilè*', in Colette Nativel (ed.), *Le Noyau et l'écorce. Les arts de l'allégorie, XVe–XVIIe siècles* (Paris and Rome: Somogy, 'Collection d'histoire de l'art de l'Académie de France à Rome', 2009), pp. 233–51.

Wainwright, Valerie, 'The Will of Ambrogio Lorenzetti', *The Burlington Magazine*, 117, 1975, pp. 543–4.

Wesselow, Thomas de, 'The "Guidoriccio" Fresco: A New Attribution', *Apollo*, 159, 2004, pp. 3–12.

Wesselow, Thomas de, 'The Form and Imagery of the *New Fresco* in Siena's Palazzo Pubblico', *Artibus et Historiae*, 59, 2009, pp. 195–217.

White, John, *Duccio: Tuscan Art and the Medieval Workshop* (London: 1979).

White, John, *The Birth and Rebirth of Pictorial Space*, 3rd edn (London and Boston, MA: Faber & Faber, 1987).

White, Lynn, Jr, 'The Iconography of Temperantia and the Virtuousness of Technology', in Theodore K. Rabb and Jerrold Seigels (eds), *Action and Conviction in Early Modern Europe: Essays in Memory of E. H. Harbinson* (Princeton, NJ: Princeton University Press, 1969), pp. 197–219.

Wirth, Jean, *L'Image à la fin du Moyen Âge* (Paris: Cerf, 2011).

Witt, Ronald, *In the Footsteps of the Ancients: The Origins of Humanism from Lovato to Bruni* (Leiden: Brill, 2003).

Witt, Ronald, *The Two Latin Cultures and the Foundation of Renaissance Humanism in Medieval Italy* (Cambridge: Cambridge University Press, 2007).

Zorzi, Andrea, 'La justice pénale dans les États italiens (communes et principautés territoriales) du XIIIe au XVIe siècle', in Xavier Rousseaux and René Lévy (eds), *Le Pénal dans tous ses états. Justice, États et sociétés en Europe (XIIe–XXe siècles)* (Brussels: Publications des facultés universitaires Saint-Louis, 1997), pp. 47–63.

Zorzi, Andrea, 'Siena nella trasformazione dell'Italia comunale. A proposito di *Fedeltà ghibellina, affari guelfi. Saggi e riletture intorno alla storia di Siena fra Duecento e Trecento*, a cura di G. Piccinni (Pisa, Pacini 2008)', *Bullettino senese di storia patria*, 115, 2008, pp. 266–305.

Zorzi, Andrea, *Le signorie citadine in Italia (secoli XIII–XV)* (Milan: Mondadori, 2010).

Zorzi, Andrea, 'L'angoscia delle repubbliche. Il "timor" nell'Italia comunale degli anni trenta del Trecento', in Andrea Gamberini, Jean-Philippe Genet and Andrea Zorzi (eds), *Languages of Political Society: Western Europe, 14th–17th Centuries* (Rome: Viella, 2011), pp. 287–324.

Zorzi, Andrea, 'Un segno della "mutazione signorile": l'arroccamento urbano', in Patrick Boucheron and Jean-Philippe Genet (eds), *Marquer la ville. Signes, empreintes et traces du pouvoir dans les espaces urbains (XIIIe–XVIIe siècle)* (Paris and Rome: Publications de la Sorbonne and École française de Rome, 2013), pp. 23–40.

Picture credits

Illustrated section

1, 2, 5, 6 and 9: © Electa / Leemage
3 and 4: © De Agostini / Leemage
7 and 14–18: © Raffael / Leemage
8 and 12: © Ricciarini / Leemage
10 and 13: © Fine Art / Leemage
11: © MP / Leemage

Appendices

The square of the *campo*: map legends after Diana Norman (ed.), *Siena, Florence and Padua: Art, Society and Religion, 1280–1400*, 2 vols (New Haven, CT, and London: Yale University Press, 1995).

Arrangement of the rooms: map legends after Joachim Poeschke, *Italian Frescoes: The Age of Giotto, 1280–1400* (New York: Abbeville Press, 2005).

The fresco of the Sala della Pace: drawings after Randolph Starn, *Ambrogio Lorenzetti. Le palais communal, Sienne* (Paris: Hazan, 1995 [1994]).

Index

Note: page numbers in italics refer to illustrations